"As a financial journalist, I've been recommending Larry Swedroe's books for years because they are filled with invaluable advice that can make any reader a more successful investor. I will now be adding *The Only Guide to Alternative Investments You'll Ever Need* to my favored reading list."

— LYNN O'SHAUGHNESSY
Financial journalist and author, *The College Solution*

"Larry Swedroe and Jared Kizer have written a different sort of investment book, and one that has been sorely needed: a comprehensive guide to the theory, peer-reviewed literature, and practical nitty-gritty of actually deploying portfolio assets. It is a gold mine for even the most experienced of practitioners, and a vital lifeline for small investors. This volume is destined to become the most marked and Post-it–noted tome on the average investment shelf."

— WILLIAM BERNSTEIN
Author of *The Intelligent Asset Allocator* and *The Four Pillars of Investing*

"What's missing in your library? Larry's new *Alternative Investments*! You've already got tons of books on stocks, bonds, and funds. *The Only Guide to Alternative Investments You'll Ever Need* is all about the future of investing, the new stuff that'll give you an edge in the twenty-first century. An absolute must-read!"

— PAUL B. FARRELL, JD, PhD
Columnist, *DowJones-MarketWatch*
Author of *The Millionaire Code*, *The Winning Portfolio*, and *The Lazy Person's Guide to Investing*

"Swedroe and Kizer provide a thorough analysis of the pros and cons of each alternative investment. They recommend 'good' alternatives to add to a diversified portfolio of high-grade bonds and stocks. Perhaps more important, they warn investors about the dangers of truly 'bad' and 'ugly' alternatives."

— DR. WILLIAM REICHENSTEIN, CFA
Pat and Thomas R. Powers Chair in Investment Management
Hankamer School of Business
Baylor University

"Swedroe and Kizer have sorted through the clutter and confusion of alternative investments to provide the authoritative voice on these much hyped and frequently misunderstood financial products. Kudos to them for sharing their wisdom in a manner that can be easily understood by all."

—BILL SCHULTHEIS
Author, *The Coffeehouse Investor*

"What a great service this book is to the investing community! As investors reach out for higher returns, many will venture into the higher-risk category known as alternative investments. For those who are so tempted, this book provides an invaluable guide."

—EDWARD R. WOLFE, PHD
Professor of Finance and Director of the Financial Planning Program
Western Kentucky University

The Only Guide to Alternative Investments You'll Ever Need

Other titles from BLOOMBERG PRESS

Bonds: The Unbeaten Path to Secure Investment Growth
by Hildy Richelson and Stan Richelson

Hedge Fund of Funds Investing: An Investor's Guide
by Joseph G. Nicholas

Investing in Hedge Funds: Revised and Updated Edition
by Joseph G. Nicholas

Investing in REITs: Real Estate Investment Trusts (Third Edition)
by Ralph L. Block

The Trader's Guide to Key Economic Indicators
Updated and Expanded Edition
by Richard Yamarone

PIPEs: A Guide to Private Investment in Public Equity
Revised and Updated Edition
edited by Stephen Dresner with E. Kurt Kim

Books from *The Economist*

Guide to Economic Indicators: Making Sense of Economics
Sixth Edition

Guide to Hedge Funds:
What They Are, What They Do, Their Risks, Their Advantages
by Philip Coggan

Guide to Investment Strategy:
How to Understand Markets, Risk, Rewards, and Behaviour
by Peter Stanyer

A complete list of our titles is available at
www.bloomberg.com/books

The Only Guide to Alternative Investments You'll Ever Need

The Good, the Flawed, the Bad, and the Ugly

Larry E. Swedroe

Jared Kizer

Bloomberg Press
New York

BLOOMBERG, BLOOMBERG ANYWHERE, BLOOMBERG.COM, BLOOMBERG MARKET ESSENTIALS, *Bloomberg Markets*, BLOOMBERG NEWS, BLOOMBERG PRESS, BLOOMBERG PROFESSIONAL, BLOOMBERG RADIO, BLOOMBERG TELEVISION, and BLOOMBERG TRADEBOOK are trademarks and service marks of Bloomberg Finance L.P. ("BFLP"), a Delaware limited partnership, or its subsidiaries. The BLOOMBERG PROFESSIONAL service (the "BPS") is owned and distributed locally by BFLP and its subsidiaries in all jurisdictions other than Argentina, Bermuda, China, India, Japan, and Korea (the "BLP Countries"). BFLP is a wholly-owned subsidiary of Bloomberg L.P. ("BLP"). BLP provides BFLP with all global marketing and operational support and service for these products and distributes the BPS either directly or through a non-BFLP subsidiary in the BLP Countries. All rights reserved.

This publication contains the author's opinions and is designed to provide accurate and authoritative information. It is sold with the understanding that the author, publisher, and Bloomberg L.P. are not engaged in rendering legal, accounting, investment-planning, or other professional advice. The reader should seek the services of a qualified professional for such advice; the author, publisher, and Bloomberg L.P. cannot be held responsible for any loss incurred as a result of specific investments or planning decisions made by the reader.

First edition published 2008

1 3 5 7 9 10 8 6 4 2

Library of Congress Cataloging-in-Publication Data

Swedroe, Larry E.
    The only guide to alternative investments you'll ever need : the good, the flawed, the bad, and the ugly / Larry E. Swedroe, Jared Kizer.
        p. cm.
    Includes bibliographical references and index.
    Summary: "Investors are actively seeking investment options other than equities, bonds, and cash that will provide diversification and improved returns. The book offers an overview of a wide range of alternative investments, explaining what each is and how it works. The author shares his opinions on which to seriously consider and which to avoid at all costs"—Provided by publisher.
    ISBN 978-1-57660-310-9 (alk. paper)
    1. Portfolio management. 2. Asset allocation. 3. Investment analysis. 4. Investments.
I. Kizer, Jared. II. Title.

    HG4529.5.S936 2008
    332.63—dc22

                                                                                    2008032685

This book is dedicated to the memory of Rubin Hersch.
He was a sweet, kind, and sensitive man
who enriched the lives of all those he touched.

Contents

PART 4 The Ugly

List of Tables

Acknowledgments

No book is ever the work of one person, or, as in this case, two people. This book is no exception. We would like to thank the principals at Buckingham Asset Management and BAM Advisor Services for their support and encouragement: Susan Shackelford-Davis, Paul Forman, Steve Funk, Bob Gellman, Ed Goldberg, Joe Hempen, Ken Katzif, Mont Levy, Steve Lourie, Vladimir Masek, Bert Schweizer III, and Stuart Zimmerman.

We also thank Steve Nothum for his help with the data. Laura Latragna and David Ressner both made major editorial contributions. We also thank RC Balaban for his tireless efforts at fact checking. Any errors are certainly our own.

We also thank Sam Fleischman, our agent, for all of his efforts.

We would be remiss if we did not thank Stephen Isaacs, editorial director of Bloomberg Press, for his faith in the book and for his ongoing support. We also thank our development editors, Janet Coleman and, especially, Erica Levy Klein, for their assistance. They both made invaluable contributions.

Larry adds the following: I would like to especially thank the love of my life, my wife, Mona, for her tremendous support and understanding for the lost weekends and many nights that I sat at the computer well into the early morning hours. She has always provided whatever support was needed, and then some. Walking through life with her has truly been a gracious experience.

Jared adds the following: Like Larry, I would first like to thank my wife Lezlie for her support during our seven wonderful years of marriage. Without her support, I would certainly not be where I am today. I would also like to thank all the fellow practitioners (including Larry) and academicians who have taken time out of their busy schedules to answer my questions on investment theory and personal finance. Without them, I would never have become as well versed in both subjects as I am today.

Introduction

THE SEARCH FOR better performing assets usually leads investors to explore the broad category of *alternative investments*, which is a term generally used to describe investments outside of the familiar categories of equities; Treasury bonds; other high-quality, investment-grade debt; and bank instruments such as certificates of deposit. Greater numbers of people embark on this quest during periods when the performances of more familiar investments are lackluster. The 2000–2002 bear market in equities, for example, inspired many investors to investigate alternative investments. Similarly, the 2003 collapse of short-term interest rates to 1 percent and the 2005 drop in Treasury bond rates to below 4.2 percent led investors to look for higher-yielding fixed-income investments. And now, the huge federal budget and trade deficits and the impending crises in Social Security and Medicaid have sent investors searching for investments that will protect them from the risks of a falling U.S. dollar.

A TRAVEL GUIDE TO ALTERNATIVE INVESTMENTS

This book takes you on a "scenic tour" of the world of alternative investments. And like a good travel agent, it will provide you with recommendations on which tours to consider taking and which "tour operators" to hire or to avoid at all cost.

When Larry was growing up, his parents always took the kids on vacations. While there was always a main destination, some of his fondest memories were of the scenic "side tours" his dad would take the kids on, often just to explore some new road or small town. Abandoning their well-conceived plan, the family headed off on an adventure. Sometimes, the detour would completely change their plans. Sometimes they arrived late or not at all at their original destination—with hungry kids and a very angry mom.

Scenic tours can be a fun way to explore the world, but straying from a well-conceived investment plan to have adventures with interesting investments is likely to be dangerous to your financial health. As Gregory Baer and Gary Gensler, authors of *The Great Mutual Fund Trap*, point out, "If you're having fun investing, then there's a good chance that you're not properly diversified, you're trading too much, and you're taking too much risk."[1]

Taking detours in the investment world can cause investors to reach their goals later than planned, or perhaps, not at all. As experienced investment professionals know, the surest way to create a small fortune is to start out with a large one, and then make "interesting" and "exciting" investments. Having the discipline to stay on course is essential when it comes to implementing an investment strategy.

Experienced travelers know that the best way to ensure having a good vacation is to spend time learning as much as possible about a potential trip. They invest in travel guides to learn about the most beautiful sites, the best restaurants, and the experiences that should not be missed. They also learn which places are safe and which are too risky. Similarly, sophisticated investors know that they should never make an investment without a full investigation of the risks and potential benefits. And if they cannot fully understand the risks, they should not invest. Taking unnecessary risks can destroy a vacation—and a portfolio.

Some guided tours enhance a vacation; others are best avoided, because they are more likely to advance the tour operators' objectives than the travelers'. Like some investments, some tour packages come with high fees and hidden costs, like those "all-inclusive" trips that end up costing more than advertised.

Some investment products are so complex in design that it is very difficult, if not impossible, for the average investor to fully understand the risks entailed and the costs incurred. Make no mistake about it, the complexity is intentional. After all, if the investor fully understood the product, it is likely that he or she would never purchase it. That is why many of such products are truly "tourist traps"—designed to be sold, but never bought.

MODERN PORTFOLIO THEORY

In this book you will learn one of the tenets of modern portfolio theory (MPT): You should not consider the risk of an asset in isolation. Rather, you should evaluate its risk in terms of its diversification benefit—how its addition to a portfolio affects the risk level of the entire portfolio. This is because an investment that seems risky when viewed in isolation may actually reduce the overall risk of a portfolio. Some alternative investments have a negative correlation with stocks and bonds. This means they tend to produce above-average returns when they are needed most—when equities and bonds are producing below-average returns. On the other hand, some alternative investments don't mix well with equities because their risks tend to show up at the same time as the risks of equities.

In this book, we present data to support what we say about correlations and returns. Our goal in presenting the evidence is to provide you with the knowledge necessary to make your own judgment about whether these tours are worth taking.

THE GOOD, THE FLAWED, THE BAD, AND THE UGLY

There is an old saying among general managers of sports teams: "Sometimes the best trades are the ones you don't make." One of the main objectives of this book is to prevent you from making bad trades.

Thus, the book separates alternative investments into four categories—the good, the flawed, the bad, and the ugly. In some cases, even if some flaws exist, the preponderance of the evidence led us to place some of the investments in the good category. They are our Oscar nominees for supporting roles. In other cases, the flaws are significant enough that the investment might not be appropriate for all investors. Those investments were placed in the flawed category. Sufficient information has been provided for you to decide if the flaws are minor blemishes that you can overlook, or if they are large enough to make the asset class one you should avoid. The bad and the ugly speak for themselves—they are candidates for the Razzies, and salute the worst that Wall Street has to offer.

We evaluated each investment based on the following criteria:
- Expected returns
- Volatility (standard deviation)
- Distribution of returns
  This is important because most investors care about more than just volatility. They also care about whether the distribution of returns is normal (shaped like a bell

curve). Specifically, they care about whether the returns exhibit negative skewness and excess kurtosis (see the Glossary)—because when one or both are present, there is the potential for large losses.

■ How the alternative asset mixes with the other assets (stocks and bonds) in the portfolio
Some assets mix well (for example, commodities and Treasury inflation-protected securities [TIPS]) because they tend to produce above-average returns when they are needed most. Others don't mix as well (for example, hedge funds and high-yield bonds) because their risks tend to show up at the same time other portfolio assets are producing below-average returns.

■ Fees

■ Trading and other operating expenses
Strategies don't have costs, but implementing them does. Often, implementation expenses can exceed the disclosed fees (such as the operating expense ratio of the mutual fund or other type of investment vehicle).

■ Liquidity
Some investments (for example, venture capital investments/funds and hedge funds) entail significant lock-up periods.

■ Location
The academic research clearly shows that investors who hold both equities and bonds, and who have both taxable and tax-advantaged accounts, are better off holding equities in taxable accounts and bonds in tax-advantaged accounts. This has negative implications for hybrid securities, such as investments that exhibit both equity and bond risks (for example, high-yield bonds).

■ Tax efficiency

■ Ability to eliminate or significantly reduce unsystematic risk—risk for which investors do not receive compensation because it can be diversified away (for example, the risk of investing in one stock versus all the stocks in the same asset class)

- Ability to control the asset allocation decision
  Some assets, such as convertible bonds, have a shifting mix of equity and fixed-income allocations.
- Whether there are alternatives that achieve the same objective in a more efficient—less expensive and/or more tax efficient—manner

In 1998, the first edition of Larry's first book, *The Only Guide to a Winning Investment Strategy You'll Ever Need*, was published. That *Only Guide*, which was revised and updated in 2005, focused mainly on the world of equity investing. In 2006, Larry and coauthor Joseph Hempen published *The Only Guide to a Winning Bond Strategy You'll Ever Need*.

This guide to alternative investments completes the trilogy. We hope you enjoy the descriptions of the tours that Wall Street has created. Our fondest wish is that the book helps you to select only the tours that will provide you with the greatest chance of achieving your financial goals, and that will enable you to take the more important kind of tour—that cruise to Alaska or summer in Tuscany.

Please note that this book includes an extensive glossary for those terms with which you may be unfamiliar.

PART 1

The Good

Real Estate 1

"LET EVERY MAN divide his money into three parts, and invest a third in land, a third in business, and a third let him keep in reserve," advises the Jewish *Talmud*, which is dated somewhere between 1200 BC and 500 AD.

The quotation, one of the earliest descriptions of diversification we've found, shows not only that early civilization understood the need for diversification, but also that ownership of real estate was considered an important part of the process. Thus, it should come as no surprise that when investors begin to think about alternative investments, they usually turn first to real estate.

Excluding personal residences, the commercial real estate market consists of both private equity and public equity. Privately owned real estate—which includes ownership of property such as condominiums, commercial real estate, and undeveloped land—accounts for more than 90 percent of the real estate market. Public equity accounts for only about 9 percent of the total value of the real estate market. As a result, publicly traded real estate's share of the total U.S. equity market actually understates how U.S. investors allocate their capital.[1] For example, real estate accounts for less than 3 percent of the Russell 3000 Index. Individuals seeking to allocate their capital in a manner similar to how capital is allocated by all U.S. investors must, therefore, dedicate a separate allocation to real estate.

From the days of the Talmud until the early 1970s, the only way to invest in real estate was to actually go into the business—in other words, become a landlord. For the individual investor, private equity ownership of real estate could be (and continues to be) time intensive and expensive. It could also be difficult for an individual investor to diversify a private equity real estate portfolio by both geography and type of property.

Today's investors, however, have alternatives. They have easy access to publicly owned real estate equity through two vehicles: real estate investment trusts (REITs) and real estate operating companies (REOCs). REITs and REOCs are essentially closed-end mutual funds that hold real estate. (Closed-end funds have a fixed number of shares, trade on a public exchange just like stocks, and may deviate in price from their net asset value [NAV].) Investors also have the option of purchasing shares of open-end mutual funds or exchange-traded funds (ETFs) that own diversified portfolios of individual REITs or REOCs.

The public markets for equity REITs provide investors with the most efficient (that is, low-cost) way to achieve broad diversification across both geography and property type (for example, offices, warehouses, industrial buildings, multifamily residences, or hotels). Public REITs also have the advantage of greater liquidity than private ownership with none of the issues surrounding becoming a landlord (see "So You Want to Be a Landlord" later in this chapter).

Note: It is important to differentiate equity REITs from mortgage REITs. We would not recommend investing in mortgage REITs. Mortgage REITs hold mortgages or mortgage-backed securities. They are not equity investments. This discussion focuses only on equity REITs. (For more information about mortgage REITs, see Chapter 9 in *The Only Guide to a Winning Bond Strategy You'll Ever Need*, by Larry Swedroe and Joseph Hempen.)

As stated earlier, individual investors can gain exposure to this asset class without becoming landlords. Having established this, our next task is to help investors think through whether investing in real estate will help them achieve their goals.

The investor must consider eight issues:
1. How does real estate's risk and return compare to that of other asset classes?
2. How will including real estate in a portfolio affect the overall risk and return of the whole portfolio?

3. What are the most advantageous types of accounts for holding a real estate investment?
4. What should the investor look for when considering a specific investment vehicle?
5. What are the pros and cons of investing in international real estate?
6. What are the relevant tax issues?
7. Does owning a personal residence constitute diversification into real estate?
8. What are the advantages and disadvantages of private equity ownership?

The rest of this chapter considers each of these issues in turn.

HISTORICAL RETURNS AND RISK: U.S. REAL ESTATE, U.S. EQUITIES, AND INTERNATIONAL EQUITIES

The first step in deciding whether to invest in real estate is to look at the risk and returns of the asset class as compared to other, more familiar investments. **TABLE 1.1** compares the returns and risk of U.S. REITs, U.S. stocks, and international stocks during the period 1978–2007 in terms of returns, standard deviations (variability of returns), and Sharpe ratios. The Sharpe ratio is a measure of return *relative* to risk. The higher the Sharpe ratio, the more efficient the asset class or portfolio is at delivering returns relative to risk. (See the Glossary for definition and for the method for calculating the ratio.)

Table 1.1 Investment Efficiency, U.S. Stocks, International Stocks, and REITs, 1978–2007

	Annualized Return (%)	Standard Deviation (%)	Sharpe Ratio
U.S. stocks (CRSP 1–10 Index)*	12.9	15.3	0.52
International stocks (MSCI EAFE Index)	12.6	21.3	0.40
Dow Jones Wilshire REIT Index	13.9	17.5	0.53

*CRSP: Center for Research in Security Prices at the University of Chicago. Deciles 1–10 represent the entire market.

Over this thirty-year time period, U.S. REITs earned higher returns than both U.S. and international stocks. As indicated by the Sharpe ratio, U.S. REITs delivered the highest return per "unit" of risk.

Therefore, strictly in terms of risk and returns, U.S. REITs merit serious consideration. But how will an investment in this class affect the risk and return of the overall portfolio?

THE DIVERSIFICATION BENEFITS OF REITs

When considering an asset class for inclusion in a portfolio, it is not sufficient to examine its risk and return in isolation as we did in the previous section. Instead, investors need to consider the diversification benefit of the investment: how its inclusion will affect the risk and return of the overall portfolio. The benefit of diversification is greatest when the correlations of returns among all the investments in the portfolio are low. Ideally, when one investment "zigs," another "zags." **TABLE 1.2** shows the correlations of annual returns of various equity asset classes for the same 1978–2007 period.

The last entry in the table makes the diversification benefit of U.S. REITs clear. REIT returns had the lowest correlation with the total U.S. stock market of the major equity asset classes, making REITs the most effective diversifier. In other words, due to its low correlation with the various aforementioned equity asset classes, real estate was the best "tool" for dampening the volatility of a U.S. equity portfolio. It is even more effective than international equities.

Table 1.2 Correlation of Annual Returns

	U.S. Stocks (Total Market)
U.S. small-cap stocks (CRSP 6–10 Index)	0.84
U.S. large-cap value stocks*	0.78
U.S. small-cap value stocks*	0.53
International stocks (MSCI EAFE Index)	0.52
Dow Jones Wilshire REIT Index	**0.28**

*The Fama-French benchmark portfolios represent asset classes that are distinct, according to academic definitions, within the U.S. equity universe.

Anecdotal evidence supports this conclusion. During the following periods, REIT indexes outperformed the S&P 500 Index.

- In 1977, the S&P 500 fell more than 7 percent. That same year, the Don Keim Equity REIT Index rose 18 percent. (Today's most frequently cited REIT index, the Wilshire, was not introduced until 1978.)
- In 1981, the S&P 500 fell by about 5 percent, while the Dow Jones Wilshire REIT Index rose almost 18 percent.
- In 1984 and 1992, when the S&P 500 rose about 6 percent and 8 percent, respectively, the Dow Jones Wilshire REIT Index returned about 22 percent and 15 percent, respectively.
- From 2000 through 2002, when the S&P 500 fell almost 15 percent each year, the Dow Jones Wilshire REIT Index actually rose more than 15 percent each year.

There were also periods when the S&P 500 outperformed REITs:

- In 1987, when the S&P 500 rose just over 5 percent, the Dow Jones Wilshire REIT Index fell by almost 7 percent.
- In 1990, the S&P 500 fell just over 3 percent, while the Dow Jones Wilshire REIT Index fell more than 23 percent.
- From 1998 through 1999, the Dow Jones Wilshire REIT Index fell by just over 10 percent each year, while the S&P 500 rose almost 25 percent per year.
- In 2007, while the S&P 500 returned 5.5 percent, the Wilshire REIT Index fell by 17.6 percent.

Investors who hold equities will also typically hold bonds. The reason for this is that fixed-income securities and stocks have a low correlation.

Interestingly, the correlation of REITs to fixed-income assets is usually even lower than the correlation of stocks to bonds. For example, from 1978 through 2007, the correlation of annual returns of REITs to the Lehman Brothers Treasury Bond Index (1–30 years) was −0.03. The correlations of U.S. equities (CRSP 1–10 Index) to REITs was 0.28 and to the Lehman Treasury Bond Index was 0.18.

Thus, REITs appear to be at least as effective as equities at diversifying the risks of bonds. This is why we say that REITs are excellent diversifiers of overall portfolio risk.

There are logical explanations for the differences in performance of REITs and other equity asset classes. First, the long-term nature of many leases results in rents being more stable than corporate earnings. Second, real estate investment returns are driven primarily by those fairly stable net rental flows, not by the capital gains (or losses) that are the dominant component of equity returns. Third, since landlords are not generally trying to bring new technologies, new products, or new services to the market, they face a lower level of business risk than the typical business. Fourth, the dividend component has constituted more than 60 percent of the total return on equity REITs, helping to stabilize returns.[2] The bottom line is that REITs face fundamentally different business risks than do equities in general.

We have shown how and why REITs diversify equity and fixed-income risks. Next, we take a closer look at the diversification benefits of REITs by comparing four sample stock portfolios.

BENEFITS OF DIVERSIFICATION: SAMPLE PORTFOLIOS

For all the reasons stated above, we expect that equity portfolios that include REITs will have higher risk-adjusted returns than portfolios without REITs. To test this hypothesis, we compared the returns of four sample portfolios during the years 1978–2007. TABLE 1.3 lists the results. Two portfolios (1 and 2) include domestic-only equities; two include international equities (3 and 4). Portfolio 2 differs from Portfolio 1 only in its 10 percent allocation of REITs. Portfolio 4 differs

Table 1.3 Diversification Benefits of REITs, 1978–2007

	Portfolio 1 100% U.S. Stocks (%)	Portfolio 2 90% U.S. Stocks/10% REITs (%)	Portfolio 3 70% U.S. Stocks/30% International Stocks (%)	Portfolio 4 60% U.S. Stocks/30% International Stocks/10% REITs (%)
Annualized return	12.9	13.2	13.1	13.3
Standard deviation	15.3	14.4	15.1	14.2

from Portfolio 3 in the same way. The indexes used in Table 1.1 represent the performance of each asset class: the total market for U.S. equities, the MSCI EAFE Index for international stocks, and the Dow Jones Wilshire REIT Index for U.S. REITs.

Table 1.3 shows that the addition of a 10 percent allocation to U.S. REITs improved the efficiency of a domestic equity portfolio. Portfolio 2 produced a 0.3 percent higher return and 0.9 percent less volatility than Portfolio 1. Adding a REIT allocation to a portfolio including international as well as domestic stocks improved the efficiency of that portfolio as well. Portfolio 4 produced a 0.2 percent higher return and 0.9 percent less volatility than Portfolio 3.

These examples illustrate why diversification has been called the only free lunch in investing—resulting in potentially higher returns with less risk.

We now turn to another important consideration, the asset location decision.

ASSET LOCATION AND REAL ESTATE

Different from asset *allocation*, asset *location* is the process of determining the most advantageous type of account in which investments should be held. This decision is driven by tax considerations.

It is important to note that dividends from REITs are not considered qualified dividends and are therefore taxed at ordinary income rates. (Qualified dividends are currently taxed at the same low rate as long-term capital gains.) The result is that if one chooses to own REITs, they should be the first investments placed in tax-deferred or tax-exempt accounts, even prior to fixed-income investments—since investors can own municipal bonds in taxable accounts.

Once investors have decided where to locate their investment, they can turn their attention to selecting a specific investment vehicle.

RECOMMENDED INVESTMENT VEHICLES

Equity REIT mutual funds are the vehicle of choice for this asset class, specifically funds that are low-cost and passively managed. We recommend these for two reasons. First, there is no academic evidence to suggest that actively managed real estate funds will, on average, outperform funds with a passive strategy. Second, there is no academic evidence that the past performance of actively managed REIT funds (or any type of actively managed fund) is a good predictor of future performance.

The following example makes this point: For the ten-year period ending January 2008, our preferred choice, the Dimensional Fund Advisors (DFA) Real Estate Securities Portfolio, produced an annualized return of 10.98 percent. It outperformed the average actively managed fund that survived the full ten-year period by 0.53 percent per year. And only twelve (39 percent) of the thirty-one actively managed funds beat the DFA fund. It is also worth noting that while only five of the actively managed funds outperformed the DFA fund by more than 1 percent per year, twelve underperformed by more than 1 percent per year. And it is likely that the superior performance of the DFA fund is understated because the fund data has what is called *survivorship bias*—or a bias that skews performance data when actively managed funds that perform poorly are closed or merged out of existence.

Over ten-year periods, survivorship bias can be substantial. For example, in 1986 Lipper reported that 568 stock funds delivered an average 1986 return of 13.4 percent. By 1997, Lipper put the average 1986 return at 14.7 percent.[3] The reason for the 1.3 percent improvement is that 134 (24 percent) of the original 568 funds disappeared (their returns vanished from the data).

As of this writing we can recommend two specific funds: the Vanguard REIT Index Fund and the DFA Real Estate Securities Portfolio.

The Vanguard REIT Index Fund seeks to track the Morgan Stanley REIT Index. As of January 2008 the fund held one hundred securities, and the Investor Shares version of the fund had an expense ratio of just 0.21 percent. The Admiral Shares version had an expense ratio of only 0.14 percent. Admiral Shares is a lower-cost version available to investors who have at least $100,000 invested in a single holding in a Vanguard fund that offers Admiral Shares or has owned a single holding in a Vanguard fund for at least ten years that now has a balance of $50,000 or more, and the investor is registered for online access.

Investors working through an approved registered investment advisor firm can consider using DFA's Real Estate Securities Fund to gain exposure to REITs. As of February 2008 this fund had an expense ratio of 0.33 percent and held 110 securities. Unlike Vanguard's fund, this one does not track a specific index. Instead, it seeks to purchase all eligible REIT securities on a market-capitalization-weighted basis. Despite the somewhat higher expense ratio, for the period June 1996—the inception date for Vanguard's fund was May 13, 1996—through December 2007, the DFA fund outperformed the Admiral Shares version of Vanguard's fund by 0.44 percent per year (13.38 percent versus 12.94 percent). While there are some minor differences, the two funds are very similar in construction. It is likely, therefore, that the difference in returns is mostly attributable to DFA's patient trading strategy, which is a subject beyond the scope of this book.

In addition to these two funds, there are also ETFs—including the Vanguard REIT ETF, with an expense ratio of 0.12 percent—that allow investors to access this asset class in a low-cost, passive manner.

So far, our discussion has focused on the U.S. REIT market. In the next section we discuss the pros and cons of investing in international REITs.

INTERNATIONAL REAL ESTATE

Until the mid-1990s, the market for publicly traded REITs was limited to the United States, Australia, and the Netherlands. Things have changed. By the end of 2006, the total market for global REITs and other publicly traded equity real estate was approaching $1 trillion.[4] As of early 2008, about 20 developed countries had adopted REITs or REIT-like structures. At this size, international real estate has become an investable asset class for individuals and has attractive diversification benefits for U.S. investors.

Because REITs are relatively new structures in most of the world, the data is relatively sparse. However, the evidence we do have suggests that international real estate markets exhibit low correlation to both the U.S. and international stock markets. They also exhibit low correlation to each other, making tangible the expression "all real estate is local." The following is a brief summary of the monthly correlations.[5]

■ For the fifteen-year period ending March 2007, the correlation of Australian REITs to the public equity market in Australia was 0.76. In the Netherlands the correlation of the national REIT market to the national equity market was 0.52. The correlation of international REITs to international equities was 0.6, and the correlation of U.S. REITs to U.S. equities was just 0.34.

■ By limiting the data to the ten-year period ending in March 2007, we add two more countries. The correlations of REITs in Australia, the Netherlands, Belgium, and Canada to their local equity markets ranged from 0.49 to 0.77. The correlation of international REITs to international equities was just 0.62, and the correlation of U.S. REITs to U.S. equities was just 0.34.

■ When we limit the data to the five-year period ending March 2007, our universe expands to six countries, adding Japan and New Zealand. Correlations of REITs to their local equity markets ranged from 0.33 to 0.68. The correlation of international REITs to international equities was 0.59, and the correlation of U.S. REITs to U.S. equities was just 0.43.

The low correlations of REITs to their local markets, international equities, and U.S. equities suggest that the addition of this asset class to a portfolio should provide significant diversification benefits.

The data also suggests that international REITs have provided equity-like returns while exhibiting equity-like risks:

■ For the fifteen-year period ending March 2007, REITs in Australia and the Netherlands returned 14.2 and 12.3 percent, respectively. The standard deviations were 14.6 percent and 13.9 percent, respectively. By comparison, the S&P 500 returned 10.9 percent and exhibited a standard deviation of 13.5. The Dow Jones Wilshire REIT Index returned 15.5 percent, and its standard deviation was 13.6 percent.

■ For the ten-year period ending March 2007, returns on REITs in Australia, the Netherlands, Belgium, and Canada ranged from 13.8 percent to 16.8 percent and exhibited standard deviations ranging from 12.9 percent to 17.0 percent. The S&P 500 returned 8.2 percent, and its standard deviation was 15.2 percent. The Dow Jones Wilshire REIT Index returned 15.6 percent, and its standard deviation was 14.6 percent.

■ For the five-year period ending March 2007, returns on REITs in Australia, the Netherlands, Belgium, Canada, Japan, and New Zealand ranged from 27.3 percent to 35.2 percent, and standard deviations ranged from 10.4 to 15.6 percent. The S&P 500 returned 6.3 percent, and its standard deviation was 12.3 percent. The Dow Jones Wilshire REIT Index returned 22.7 percent, and its standard deviation was 15.2 percent.

While the historical returns relative to the risks look attractive, especially in light of the relatively low correlations, there are a few concerns with international real estate funds. The first is that most have high expenses, which is typical of actively managed funds. This reduces the diversification benefit since the investor is not capturing a significant portion of the market return. Very few—four as of this writing—are lower-cost, passive vehicles. Three are ETFs; one is a mutual fund.

The three ETFs are:

■ WisdomTree's dividend-weighted fund, the International Real Estate Fund (DRW), with an expense ratio of 0.58 percent

■ The State Street Global Advisors SPDR DJ (Dow Jones) Wilshire International Real Estate ETF (RWX), with an expense ratio of 0.60 percent

■ The iShares S&P World ex-U.S. Property Index Fund (WPS), with an expense ratio of 0.48 percent

The mutual fund is:

■ The DFA International Real Estate Securities Portfolio, with an expense ratio of 0.48 percent

DRW, RWX, AND WPS

The three ETFs have some significant differences. We will first discuss DRW and RWX, because they were introduced before WPS, which came to market in August 2007. Compared to RWX, which has 149 holdings, DRW offers broader diversification with 176 holdings as of January 31, 2008. Another difference between the two is in the dividend yield. As mentioned, DRW is a dividend-weighted fund. Thus, we should expect it to have a higher yield than RWX. As of March 5, 2008, DRW had a yield of 5.2 percent versus the 4.5 percent yield of RWX. However, the price-to-book ratios of the ETFs, another value indicator, were identical at 1.1.

Another difference between the two funds relates to country weights. While both are fairly well diversified by country, DRW is significantly weighted toward Australia (32 percent), Hong Kong (29 percent), and Singapore (10 percent). RWX has its highest weightings in Australia (22 percent), Japan (20 percent), and the United Kingdom (18 percent).

WPS, as of January 31, 2008, had 223 holdings. A significant portion of its assets are allocated to Hong Kong (21 percent), Japan (20 percent), and the United Kingdom (11 percent). As of March 6, 2008, the dividend yield was 5.4 percent, and price-to-book ratio was 1.13.

DFA INTERNATIONAL REAL ESTATE SECURITIES PORTFOLIO

The DFA International Real Estate Securities Portfolio is also a passively managed fund. As of March 2008, the fund's expense ratio was 0.48 percent. As of January 31, 2008, the fund had 157 holdings from the following countries: Australia, Belgium, Canada, China, France, Hong Kong, Japan, the Netherlands, New Zealand, Singapore, South Africa, and the United Kingdom. Though the fund is managed on a market-cap-weighted basis, DFA imposes a ceiling of 30 percent on any one country and a 5 percent ceiling on any single holding. As of January 31, 2008, the regional holdings were Asia Pacific (37 percent), the United Kingdom (23 percent), Japan (18 percent), and Europe (16 percent). The dividend yield was 5.17 percent, and the price-to-book ratio was 0.98.

TAX CONSIDERATIONS

Investors considering investing in international REITs should consider three issues related to tax efficiency.

First, REITs are not tax-efficient investment vehicles because most of the income they provide is considered either ordinary income or nonqualified dividends. In addition, unlike with other equities where much of the gains are deferred, REITs provide much of their return in the form of current income. As discussed earlier, the way to manage this problem is to locate REIT investments in a tax-advantaged account.

Second, some international REITs are treated as passive foreign investment companies (PFICs) for U.S. income tax purposes, which creates a problem because PFICs must mark-to-market their portfolios on an annual basis. Thus, what would otherwise be unrealized gains is converted into income that must be recognized for U.S. tax purposes. In other words, under the mark-to-market rules, a mutual fund holding PFICs must include, as income, any excess of the fair market value of a PFIC as of the close of the taxable year. In addition, any such income is treated as ordinary income. Thus, the tax inefficiency created by this situation means that individual investors who are not in the lowest tax bracket should not hold international REITs in anything but a tax-advantaged account.

Third, withholding taxes are assessed whether the asset is held in a taxable or a tax-deferred account. For taxable accounts, the investor may be able to claim a foreign tax credit for at least a portion of the taxes withheld. Unfortunately, the tax credit has no value for assets held in a tax-advantaged account. For tax-deferred accounts such as a traditional individual retirement account (IRA) or a 401(k) plan, and for nontaxable accounts such as a Roth IRA or a tax-exempt, nonprofit institutional account, as of early 2008 the impact is about 9 percent of the dividend yield (though that depends on withholding rates, the country allocation in the fund, and whether the United States has tax treaties with those countries). For example, if a fund had a dividend yield of 3 percent, the loss of the foreign tax credit would cost investors 0.27 percent. Thus, when investors are considering investing in an international REIT fund, they should add the cost of the loss of the foreign tax credit to the fund's operating expense ratio.

THE WRAP-UP ON INTERNATIONAL REITS

International REITs are an attractive asset class from a risk/reward perspective and from a diversification perspective. However, the investor must also consider asset location concerns and tax-efficiency concerns. The bottom line is that there is really no perfect location in which to hold international REITs. A taxable account would be an inefficient location for all but those investors in the lowest tax bracket. Holding international REITs in a tax-advantaged account also creates a tax inefficiency, though a much smaller one, due to the loss of the foreign tax credit. Faced with this situation, the investor should weigh the benefits of the incremental diversification versus the total costs of investing in the asset class. For those that value the significant diversification benefits, the benefits could exceed the costs.

One final note. Currently, DFA estimates that the global REIT market has an approximate weighting of 60 percent U.S. and 40 percent international. This provides investors with at least a starting point when they are deciding how much to allocate to domestic real estate and how much to allocate to international.

YOUR HOME AND THE ASSET ALLOCATION DECISION

Homeowners need to consider how to treat their residence in terms of their balance sheet and the asset allocation process.

A home is clearly real estate. However, it is a single, highly concentrated asset with its own unique risk characteristics. This creates several problems in terms of asset allocation.

Although there are many types of real estate, such as hotels, industrial buildings, and multifamily residences, a home is undiversified by type. Owning a home gives exposure to just the residential component of the larger asset class of real estate. Further, owning a single-family home omits exposure to multifamily residences. And a home is undiversified geographically. Home prices might be rising in one part of the country and falling in another.

Another problem is that home prices may be more related to exposure to an industry than to real estate in general. For example, in the 1980s, home prices in Texas and other oil-producing regions collapsed when oil prices collapsed. This kind of situation creates another problem if the homeowner's employment prospects are highly correlated with the value of the residence. This is true where a single company or industry is a dominant employer in a town or region. The problem of the lack of diversification would be further compounded if the homeowner's investment portfolio were concentrated in equities with exposure to the same industry to which the home was exposed. This is often true of executives who own stock or options, or both, in their companies. It is also true of employees who invest in their employers' stock through retirement plans.

Here's an example: Before the technology industry settled there, Seattle used to be considered a one-company (Boeing) town. Accordingly, the following situation might have been a typical one. A senior executive at Boeing owns an expensive home in Seattle. She has a large percentage of her financial assets invested in Boeing stock. She contributes to Boeing's retirement plan, purchasing more Boeing stock. She also has stock options. She thought she had some diversification of assets because her home was considered real estate exposure—supposedly unrelated to her employment and financial asset risks.

On several occasions, recessions in the airline industry adversely affected Boeing. The company's stock, reflecting those troubles, fell sharply. Strike one for our investor.

Boeing reacted to a recession by dismissing employees, including our investor. Strike two.

Seattle home prices collapsed because so many people were unemployed. Strike three for our unlucky investor.

All of this investor's investment risks were highly correlated. Those who owned homes in Rochester, New York, when Eastman Kodak and Xerox were dominant employers, understood this problem well.

The bottom line is that a primary residence is no more representative of the real estate asset class than Boeing is representative of the equity asset class. The correlation of any one stock to the overall stock market might turn out to be very low. The market as a whole might be up, but a single stock might be down. Similarly, real estate as a whole might be up, but the price of a specific home might be down. Therefore, it is best not to consider a home as exposure to real estate.

In many parts of the country, land is by far a more important component of home prices than the cost of construction. Therefore, the only real protection a home provides is against inflation in construction costs. And that may not be much protection at all.

The last problem that needs to be addressed concerns rebalancing. Rebalancing a portfolio of financial assets to maintain a desired asset allocation is a simple, low-cost, and tax-efficient process. This is certainly not the case with a nonfinancial asset such as a home.

Wrap-Up on the Home as an Investment

A home is an asset that has value. It should appear on the balance sheet, but it should not be treated as a financial asset. Therefore, it should not be part of either a real estate allocation or an overall asset allocation plan.

So You Want To Be a Landlord

A person who wants a gourmet meal can go into the kitchen and prepare one or go out to a fine restaurant and order from the menu. Each has its pleasures. Real estate investors have the same kind of decision to make. They can invest in a diversified REIT fund, or they can become landlords and manage properties themselves.

One of the alternative investments individuals ask about most frequently is investing in individual real estate properties. Typically, the individual is considering the purchase of a local property— usually a rental apartment building, sometimes an office building or a warehouse.

We do not recommend this type of investment for many reasons, all based on the principles of prudent investing. The first and most important reason is that an investor who purchases a single piece of property is taking what economists call *uncompensated risk* (see the

Glossary). By owning just one investment, or a small group of similar investments, within an asset class—be it a property or a stock—an investor is putting all his or her investment eggs in one basket.

Risk that cannot be diversified away, like the risk of owning real estate (or stocks) in general, is called *compensated risk*. Effective diversification results in the elimination, or at least reduction, of uncompensated risk.

By purchasing a single property, an investor is undiversified not only geographically, but also by property type. As discussed earlier, there are many different types of properties—such as apartments, hotels, and malls—within the asset class of real estate. The most effective way to diversify this type of risk is to own a passively managed real estate fund that owns all types of properties and is also broadly diversified in terms of geography.

A second consideration is that an investment in a broadly diversified real estate fund is a highly liquid investment. Not only can investors access their funds on a daily basis, they can also regularly rebalance their portfolios, thereby maintaining asset allocations regardless of market movements.

Neither of these is possible with an investment in a single property.

At a minimum, very significant transaction costs would be incurred upon sale. In addition, should the market be weak when an investor wanted to sell, there would be a significant risk that it might be difficult to sell the property in a timely manner without taking a substantial markdown. And there is really no way to effectively rebalance the portfolio in an efficient manner.

A third consideration is that property owners who are also landlords face all the headaches of property ownership: deadbeat tenants, late-night plumbing problems, potential lawsuits (where liability is not limited to the size of the investment), and other assorted surprises. This is not a trivial issue. The costs of the time spent renting out and managing the property should be factored into the expected net return. Of course, an investor can hire a property manager to deal with many of the issues. That increases costs and reduces returns. Plus, it does not eliminate the headaches; it only reduces them.

The fourth factor is psychological. As previously mentioned, the most common situation is one in which someone is considering buying a local property. The question that needs to be asked is this: Why is this particular property the best investment as opposed to similar properties in other geographic locations? It seems to be a very common error for individuals to believe that something is a safer investment if they are familiar with it. For example, residents of Georgia have owned a disproportionate share of Coca-Cola (whose headquarters are in Atlanta). This is true despite the fact that it clearly is not any safer an investment for residents of Georgia than it is for residents of any other state.

The fifth factor is related to another psychological problem called *recency*. Recency is the tendency to give too much weight to recent experience, while ignoring the lessons of long-term historical evidence. Investors subject to recency make the mistake of extrapolating the most recent past into the future, almost as if it is ordained that the recent trend will continue.

How does this apply to real estate? Real estate was a very hot asset class from 2000 through 2006. The Dow Jones Wilshire REIT Index returned 31, 12, 4, 36, 33, 14, and 36 percent, respectively, in those years, producing an annualized return of just over 23 percent. These kinds of returns cause investors to think that real estate investing is not risky. Yet not that long ago (in the 1980s) there were many areas in the United States where property values collapsed and owners were mailing in their keys to their mortgage lender because they had negative equity in their properties. In 1990, real estate prices in Japan began a long and steady decline after several decades of spectacular returns. It took more than a decade before the first signs appeared indicating that prices had finally stopped falling. And 2007 provided a domestic reminder that real estate investing is risky. For example, Vanguard's REIT Index Fund lost 16.5 percent that year.

A sixth factor relates to a significant difference between the stock market and the market for real estate. The equity market is highly efficient and highly liquid. Such markets prevent professional investors from exploiting less sophisticated investors because the price quoted is the one most likely to be the correct price. This is not as true in the private real estate market.

Finally, it is important to consider the cost of one of our most precious resources: time. Directly owning real estate requires a great commitment of the investor's time, including negotiating and closing transactions. Unless directly owning real estate is the investor's primary business or personal passion, he or she is probably better off letting the capital markets work on his or her behalf in the form of a low-cost real estate fund.

WRAP-UP ON DIRECT OWNERSHIP

The bottom line: prudent investing means taking only compensated risk. Therefore, investors who are not real estate professionals should gain exposure to the asset class through low-cost mutual funds because this is the most efficient way to achieve broad diversification. Broad diversification is the safest way to minimize the risk inherent in all investments.

SUMMARY

The evidence from academic studies demonstrates that equity REITs, both domestic and international, offer an attractive risk/return trade-off and provide meaningful diversification benefits to portfolios. Thus, investors with the ability to hold equity REITs in a tax-advantaged account should consider them as a *core* holding, not as an alternative asset.

The reasons that equity real estate should be considered a core asset can be summarized as follows:

- REITs reduce the overall risk of the portfolio by adding an asset class whose response to events is different from that of other asset classes.
- REITs have expected returns well above the risk-free rate.
- As real assets, REITs provide a reasonably good long-term hedge against unexpected inflation.
- Adding an allocation to REITs allows investors to create a portfolio that is more reflective of the overall investment universe.

Investors seeking to add real estate to their portfolios should consider an allocation of between 5 and 15 percent of the *equity* portion of the portfolio. As discussed earlier in this chapter, limiting one's choices to passively managed funds is also recommended. This allows individual investors to gain broadly diversified exposure to the asset class of real estate without the major expenditure of capital—or any of the headaches of being a landlord—that private ownership requires.

Inflation-Protected Securities   *2*

INFLATION-PROTECTED SECURITIES are also known as *real* return bonds because they provide a guaranteed real (inflation-adjusted) return. Nominal return bonds are not adjusted for inflation. (To determine the real return of a nominal return bond, subtract the rate of inflation experienced over the relevant time period from the nominal return.)

Real return bonds offered by the U.S. Treasury convey benefits that will interest most investors:

- They insulate investors from the risks of unexpected inflation.
- They are generally less volatile than nominal return bonds of similar maturity.
- They have lower correlations to equities than nominal return bonds, making them more effective diversifiers of equity risk.
- They have no credit risk.

The U.S. government issues two types of real return bonds: Treasury inflation-protected securities (TIPS) and inflation-linked savings bonds (I bonds). TIPS are sold at auction and receive a fixed real rate of return. The principal is adjusted for inflation before the fixed-interest payment is calculated. Like TIPS, I bonds provide a fixed real rate of return and an inflation-protection component. However, there are significant differences between these securities, which we will elaborate on in this chapter.

Unlike many of the investments covered in this book, TIPS and I bonds can be purchased directly at little to no cost. Buying individual TIPS gives investors the ability to control the maturity of their holdings, a considerable advantage (for more about this, see the section "A Shifting Maturity Strategy"). TIPS can also be accessed through mutual funds. However, the only real benefit a mutual fund provides is convenience, including the reinvestment of interest. As of this writing, we can recommend three funds to those who value the convenience: The Vanguard Inflation-Protected Securities Fund (VIPSX), the iShares Lehman TIPS Bond Fund (TIP), and the Dimensional Fund Advisors (DFA) Inflation-Protected Securities Portfolio. All three have an expense ratio of 0.20 percent. They all have a similar average maturity of nine to ten years.

REAL OR NOMINAL RETURN BONDS: WHICH ARE RISKIER?

There is no one answer to this important question.

For some investors, real return bonds are riskier. Consider a defined benefit pension plan, the future obligations of which are fixed in nominal dollars. For such a plan, the riskless instrument is a zero-coupon Treasury bond that matches the maturity of the known fixed obligation. Owning inflation-indexed bonds would create the risk of failing to have sufficient assets to meet obligations. The risk shows up if future inflation is less than expected.

The future liabilities of most individuals and endowments are real liabilities: the costs of goods and services that rise with inflation. For such individuals, nominal bonds become the risky asset. The risk shows up if future inflation is greater than expected.

Investors should consider their own personal situations and how their assets, including intellectual capital and earning power, relate to their liabilities, including future expenditures. Remember that while investors are working, it is likely that their wages will at least keep pace with inflation. However, once retired, an investor's sensitivity to the risk of unexpected inflation increases. This is especially true for retirees whose pensions are not indexed to inflation. Investors with more exposure to the risk of unexpected inflation should consider increasing their allocation to real return bonds.

Duration is a good measure of risk to use when comparing the risks of different nominal return bonds. However, it is not a good measure to use when comparing the risks of a nominal return bond with that of a real return bond.

To explain why, we begin with a definition: *Duration* can be defined as an estimate of the percentage change in the price of a bond given a 1 percent change in the yield on that bond. The greater the duration, the greater the sensitivity of that bond's price to changes in interest rates—the higher the duration, the greater the volatility, or risk.

All else being equal, lower yields produce longer durations. Real return bonds have lower yields than nominal return bonds. This is because the yield of a real return bond represents only the real return: The inflation adjustment is made to the principal. The yield on nominal bonds represents the real rate plus the expected rate of inflation and an inflation risk premium.

Thus, real return bonds have longer duration than nominal return bonds—making them appear to be riskier. However, the duration of a real return bond reflects only the price sensitivity to real rates, not inflation. Thus, we are comparing apples to oranges.

In fact, as mentioned earlier, while the duration of real return bonds is longer than that of comparable-maturity nominal return bonds, they are actually less volatile.

Fortunately, there are other ways for investors to assess whether TIPS will help them meet their goals. The next four sections help the investor understand:

■   How TIPS adjust for inflation
■   How TIPS correlate to inflation and other asset classes
■   What risks TIPS are exposed to
■   The pros and cons of investing in TIPS

TIPS: DOING THE MATH

A TIPS is a bond sold at auction that receives a fixed stated real rate of return but also increases its principal according to the changes in inflation, as measured by the non–seasonally adjusted U.S. Consumer Price Index for All Urban Consumers (CPI-U), City Average,

All Items, published by the Bureau of Labor Statistics. Its fixed-interest payment is calculated based on the value of the principal plus inflation, which is eventually repaid at maturity.

For example, if a $1,000 TIPS had a stated real interest rate of 4 percent and the CPI-U rose 2 percent during the year, the math would work as follows: First, the adjustment to principal is calculated. Thus, the principal would rise from $1,000 to $1,020, an increase of 2 percent. Second, the interest payment would be calculated from the new principal. With a real rate of 4 percent, based on principal of $1,020, the amount of interest would be $40.80. This increase gives an investor protection against inflation by providing a guaranteed *real* return over a predetermined investment horizon. Interest is paid (the real rate) and accrued (the inflation adjustment) semiannually. At maturity, the bondholder receives the greater of the inflation-adjusted value or par.

CORRELATIONS WITH EQUITIES AND INFLATION

Correlations are most significant when they are based on many years of data.

Although the U.S. Treasury has only been issuing inflation-protected securities since 1997, other countries have been doing so since 1945, which gives us a substantial amount of data.

Ironically, according to author Robert J. Shiller, "The world's first known inflation-indexed bonds were issued by the Commonwealth of Massachusetts in 1780 during the Revolutionary War. The bonds were invented to deal with severe wartime inflation and with the angry discontent among soldiers in the U.S. Army with the decline in purchasing power of their pay. Although the bonds were successful, the concept of indexed bonds was abandoned after the immediate extreme inflationary environment passed, and largely forgotten until the twentieth century."[1]

Finland reintroduced inflation-protected securities to the market in 1945. In 1955, Israel and Iceland did the same. Brazil, Chile, and Colombia came next in the 1960s followed by Argentina in the 1970s. Shortly thereafter the United Kingdom became the first major developed market to introduce them. By the end of the century, more than twenty countries were issuing inflation-linked bonds.[2] Thus, while the U.S. market for TIPS is relatively new, we do have data on the performance and risks of such bonds for longer periods.

The historical evidence is that equities have a negative correlation with inflation. (Inflation has a negative impact on equity returns.) Because the returns on TIPS should be positively correlated with inflation—the higher the inflation, the higher the return—TIPS should have a negative correlation with equities. And that has been the case. For the ten-year period 1998–2007, the quarterly and annual correlations of TIPS with inflation were positive at 0.02 and 0.20, respectively. The quarterly and annual correlations between the S&P 500 Index and inflation were negative at –0.27 and –0.19, respectively. The quarterly and annual correlations of TIPS with the S&P 500 were –0.53 and –0.68, respectively. And the evidence suggests that the positive correlation of TIPS with inflation increases with the length of the investment horizon.[3] (Although not the case for TIPS with short maturities, longer-maturity TIPS may have large enough price volatility due to real rate changes that, *over short horizons*, they may not exhibit a positive correlation with inflation.) With nominal return bonds, the longer the remaining term, the higher the correlation of returns with equities.

The positive correlation of TIPS with inflation and their negative correlation with equities help reduce the overall risk of the portfolio. This is an advantage over intermediate- to longer-term nominal bonds. It is important to note, however, that if real interest rates, as opposed to changes in inflation, are driving changes in the rate of nominal bonds, TIPS and nominal bonds will have high positive correlation.

Inflation, Price, and Interest Rate Risk

Inflation Risk

As stated earlier, rising inflation has a negative impact on both stocks and nominal return bonds. It can also have a positive impact on TIPS prices, because when investors expect inflation to increase, the likely result is an increase in investor demand for inflation protection. Thus, the real yield on TIPS may fall. The 2004 study, "Asset Allocation with Inflation-Protected Bonds," by S.P. Kothari and Jay Shanken, found that such a relationship does exist. The authors found that changes in inflation-indexed bond *yields* are negatively correlated with inflation (a correlation of –0.27).[4]

PRICE RISK

Investors should note that longer-term TIPS, like most fixed-income instruments with a long maturity, are subject to price risk. For example, if an investor purchased TIPS with a long maturity when they had a 3 percent real interest rate, and the current real rate had risen to 4 percent, the principal value of TIPS would have fallen. The following is a good example:

In April 1999, the 30-year TIPS (maturity 2029) was trading at par (100) and yielding 3.9 percent. By January 2000 the real yield had risen to 4.4 percent. This caused the price of the 2029 TIPS to fall from 100 to 92. Of course, the reverse is true. Using the same example, by March 2000 the real yield on the 2029 TIPS had fallen back to almost 4 percent, and the price of the TIPS had risen to about 97.

INTEREST RATE RISK

An important difference between TIPS and nominal return bonds is that we should expect that TIPS with the same maturity as Treasury bonds will have less interest rate risk because *real* interest rates are less volatile than *nominal* interest rates. Again, this is a positive characteristic of TIPS. Also, note that because TIPS have been around since 1997, investors can buy individual TIPS in the secondary market to meet specific maturity requirements. Investors who purchase TIPS through mutual funds or exchange-traded funds (ETFs), although benefiting from the convenience of mutual funds, lose the ability to control the maturity risk of TIPS (and because there is no credit risk with TIPS, no credit diversification is needed—a benefit that mutual funds can otherwise provide).

TIPS: PROS AND CONS

PROS

■ TIPS offer almost complete protection against unexpected inflation. They are the best pure inflation hedge available.

They don't offer complete protection because TIPS are still subject to price risk (the real rate can change), and—because the inflation adjustment is subject to taxation, in taxable accounts—*after-tax* real returns could turn negative if inflation is high enough for taxable accounts. (For example, if the real rate is 2 percent, the inflation adjustment is 10 percent, and the tax rate is 25 percent, then the pretax nominal return will be 12 percent and the after-tax nominal return will be 9 percent. With 10 percent inflation, a 9 percent nominal return becomes a real return of –1 percent.) However, TIPS still provide the best pure hedge against inflation. Therefore, they should be preferred by investors, such as retirees, who have above-average exposure to the risks of inflation.

■ TIPS should outperform conventional Treasuries when realized inflation is greater than the expected inflation plus the risk premium. Note that we should expect the return of TIPS to be slightly less than the expected return of conventional U.S. Treasury securities of the same maturity. The difference is caused by the premium received by investors in nominal bonds for bearing the risk of unexpected inflation. For example, the yield on a Treasury bond with ten years left to maturity might be 5 percent, and the real yield on a TIPS with the same remaining term to maturity might be 3 percent. The difference between 5 percent and 3 percent reflects *both* the market's expectation of inflation for the period and a risk premium. While we currently have no way of separating the two (we can only estimate it), the inflation expectation might be 1.6 percent and the risk premium might be 0.4 percent (or the inflation expectation might be 1.95 percent and the risk premium might be 0.05 percent). The total of the 3 percent real yield on TIPS, plus the 1.6 percent expected inflation, plus the 0.4 percent inflation risk premium equals the 5 percent yield on the nominal bond.

■ TIPS are great equity and fixed-income diversification instruments. They have negative correlation with equities and relatively low correlation with most types of fixed-income investments.

■ TIPS entail no credit risk.

■ TIPS provide a guaranteed long-term real rate of return while diversifying the risk of equities in much the same way that short-term, high-quality fixed-income investments do.

■ TIPS have lower expected volatility than conventional Treasury bonds of the same maturity due to lower sensitivity to nominal interest rate movements.

■ TIPS have lower volatility than other investments that hedge unexpected inflation (for example, commodities and real estate investment trusts).

■ As is the case with all Treasury instruments, TIPS are exempt from state and local taxes.

■ In terms of real returns, TIPS are subject to far less volatility than either stocks or nominal bonds. A study found that conventional bonds exhibit five times the volatility (standard deviation of 11.5 percent) of inflation-indexed bonds (standard deviation of 2.3 percent), and stocks exhibit seven times the volatility (standard deviation of 15.8 percent).[5]

■ *TIPS have provided their highest returns when equities have produced poor returns.* For example, from 1970 through 1997, whenever inflation exceeded 8 percent, the average real return of stocks was a negative 5.7 percent.[6] As another example, in 2000, 2001, and 2002, the S&P 500 returned –9.1 percent, –11.9 percent, and –22.1 percent, respectively. For the same years TIPS (as measured by the Lehman Brothers U.S. Treasury TIPS Index) returned 13.2 percent, 7.9 percent, and 16.6 percent, respectively.

Cons

■ The value of TIPS could fluctuate significantly over short intervals. However, investors who plan to hold them to maturity should not be affected by short-term price volatility.

■ As stated above, the expected return of TIPS should be less than the expected return of conventional Treasuries of the same maturity.

- TIPS would be expected to underperform conventional bonds when realized inflation is less than expected inflation.
- TIPS would not perform as well as conventional intermediate- or long-term bonds during periods of deflation.
- Unless an investor is not subject to income taxes, TIPS are not a perfect hedge against inflation because the inflation adjustment to principal is taxed.
- The deferral until maturity of the payment for the inflation adjustment may have negative cash flow implications for taxable investors, especially for those already in retirement. This is one reason why TIPS, in general, should be held in tax-advantaged accounts.

ALLOCATING BETWEEN REAL AND NOMINAL RETURN FIXED-INCOME ASSETS

The investor who is interested in participating in the benefits offered by inflation-adjusted bonds must decide how much, if any, to allocate to real return bonds and how much to nominal return bonds. There are three issues to consider:

First, TIPS should have, at least in theory, a lower expected return than similar-maturity nominal return coupon bonds. Therefore, investors have to decide if the hedge against inflation is worth the price paid in terms of lower returns.

Second, as described previously, TIPS provide a hedge against inflation. Similar, though not identical, protection against the risk of inflation can be obtained by purchasing short-term (instead of long-term) fixed-income investments. A short maturity results in yields adjusting upward due to rising inflation with only a short lag—and the shorter the maturity, the less the inflation risk. Unfortunately, short-term instruments do not provide a perfect hedge against inflation. In fact, 1-month Treasury bills provided negative pretax real returns in all but three of the nineteen years between 1933 and 1951. They also provided negative real returns in six of the seven years from 1974 through 1980 and in all four of the years from 2002 to 2005—though they provided positive real returns in every year from 1959 through 1972 and from 1981 through 2001. Note also that there is another significant difference between longer-term TIPS and short-term fixed-income instruments. Longer-term TIPS have more price risk (are more volatile), because they are exposed to changes in real interest rates.

An investor who has a high aversion to the risk of inflation faces the following decision: He may not want to consider longer-term nominal bonds because of inflation risk. (He may also not be comfortable with the higher correlation of equities to longer-term bonds.) This investor is trying to decide if he should purchase either a TIPS fund (average maturity of about ten years) or, say, a 1-year Treasury instrument. (Investors who purchase individual TIPS in the secondary market can buy any maturity, from very short-term to twenty years or longer.) From a risk perspective, one major difference between the two is that TIPS provide a guaranteed real return (until maturity), while the 1-year Treasury instrument provides a floating real rate of return. In other words, short-term investments with long horizons entail reinvestment risk because the funds must be reinvested upon maturity at which point interest rates may have fallen. Since there is no evidence that investors can forecast which strategy will provide the higher return over the full period, in general, one good strategy is to diversify the risk of changing real rates of return. This is accomplished by purchasing some TIPS and some 1-year instruments. However, investors who face negative consequences from a fall in real rates might prefer a TIPS fund of longer-term individual TIPS.

The third issue to consider is the effect TIPS may have on the overall portfolio. As mentioned previously, the expected returns of TIPS should, in theory, be lower than those of nominal bonds. However, from an overall portfolio perspective, the lower expected return might be offset by the slightly negative correlation with equities. Short-term (up to about one year), investment-grade fixed-income instruments have virtually no correlation with equities, and longer-term bonds have positive correlation (the longer the maturity and the lower the credit quality, the higher the correlation). The lower correlation of TIPS will have a greater impact on reducing the volatility of the overall portfolio than would an allocation to nominal return short-term bonds. The result is a positive impact on the compound return of the portfolio. The net result of the somewhat lower return and the diversification benefit is likely to be small.

The investor's decision on the allocation of nominal bonds and real return bonds should become part of the investment policy statement. For example, an investor might set a target allocation of 50 percent nominal bonds and 50 percent real return bonds. She might also allocate a minimum of 45 percent and a maximum of 55 percent for each asset class. Then, she would rebalance as necessary, checking perhaps quarterly, semiannually, or at least annually.

Disciplined rebalancing has the benefit of enforcing a buy low/ sell high strategy. For example, if we experience a period when inflation is lower than expected, nominal bonds will outperform real return bonds. This would lead to an increase in the allocation to nominal bonds. To restore the allocation to the desired target level, the investor would need to sell some nominal bonds (relatively high) and buy some TIPS (relatively low). The investor would go through the opposite process after periods of unexpectedly high inflation.

A Shifting Allocation Approach

While a fixed-allocation strategy is a good one, investors should at least consider an alternative strategy. The alternative strategy shifts allocations between nominal and real bonds, depending on the current real yield on TIPS. Note that as of this writing the Treasury currently issues 5-year, 10-year, and 20-year TIPS. It previously issued 30-year TIPS, but that maturity was discontinued in 2002. In the following example, we will focus on 10-year TIPS:

We begin by examining the historical real return on longer-term bonds. For the period 1926–2007, longer-term Treasury bonds provided a real return of 2.4 percent. While we cannot know exactly how much of a risk premium the market is willing to pay to hedge the inflation risk inherent in longer-term bonds, we might guess that it would be something on the order of 0.4 percent. This is within range of the estimated inflation risk premium found by some studies.[7] Note that the price investors are willing to pay for inflation protection will logically depend on the volatility of inflation. Thus, investors in Brazil, with a long history of periods of extremely high inflation, would likely be willing to pay a steeper premium than would U.S. or Swiss investors. Even in the United States we should not expect this premium to remain constant. For example, we would have expected the premium to be higher during the 1970s, when inflation was rising and volatile, than in the early years of the twenty-first century when inflation was not only low, but also stable. In fact, it appears that in 2007, if we consider the consensus forecast for inflation, there was very little, if any, inflation risk premium.

When considering TIPS, each investor should determine for herself how much of a risk premium against unexpected inflation she is willing to pay. The size of that premium should be based on how exposed she is to the risks of unexpected inflation. We need just a little more information before we can develop a strategy.

Logically, there should be some relationship between the real growth of the economy and the real rate on bonds. With this assumption, we can develop a disciplined strategy to determine how much an investor should allocate to TIPS and how much to nominal return bonds.

The long-term real growth rate of the U.S. economy has been about 3.5 percent. We should expect to see that the average long-term real return on bonds has been below that to have provided a risk premium. In fact, as we have seen, it has been well below that figure: Long-term Treasuries have provided a real return of 2.4 percent. On the other end of the spectrum, unless we were to experience another Great Depression, it is unlikely that real interest rates will fall below zero for any extended period. We should also expect that when the U.S. economy experiences periods of stronger than average economic growth, the real rate would rise somewhat above its long-term average. Over the long term, we believe that it is likely that for *most* time periods the real yield on TIPS will range between 1 percent and 4 percent. (It is important to note that we are not suggesting that real yields cannot be expected to move beyond that range. However, we would not expect them to *stay outside* the range for long periods.)

Having established what we believe is the likely range (1 percent to 4 percent) for most periods, we can consider how this impacts the risk of owning TIPS at various real yields. Because there is an expectation of a likely range to exist over most periods, when real yields are at the lower end of the range, the price risk of

TIPS is probably greater than when yields are at the higher end of the range. The reason is that TIPS prices move in inverse relationship to their real yield. Also, buying at the low end may result in investors locking in a relatively low real return while buying at the higher end of the range, which allows them to lock in the relatively high yield.

DEVELOPING A STRATEGY

We are now ready to develop a strategy to help decide on allocations between TIPS and nominal return fixed-income instruments. Before providing a specific formula, however, note that there is no *right* answer here. The right answer will be determined by each investor's own need, willingness, and ability to take the risk that unexpected inflation will have a negative impact on his portfolio and lifestyle.

However, it is important for investors to develop a *disciplined* strategy so that they are not reacting to the noise of the market and the emotions that noise can cause. With that in mind, **TABLE 2.1** is offered as a suggested strategy, one which should be tailored to specific situations, to determine the allocation to TIPS versus nominal return bonds.

We provided ranges because each investor has different risk concerns. For example, those more concerned about the risk of inflation might consider the higher end of the suggested allocation to be more appropriate. In addition, they should also be willing to reduce the required yields in the left-hand column.

Table 2.1 Decision Table for Allocation of Short-Term Fixed-Income and of 10-Year TIPS or a TIPS Fund

Real Yield on TIPS	Allocation to TIPS
>3%	75%–100%
>2.5% and <3%	50%–75%
>2% and <2.5%	25%–50%
>1.5% and <2%	0%–25%
<1.5%	0%

IMPLEMENTATION

The preceding table should be used in the following manner: If the real yield on 10-year TIPS were 2.6 percent, an investor would allocate between 50 and 75 percent of his fixed-income assets to TIPS, and 25 to 50 percent to nominal return instruments. A specific number should be chosen up front and made part of the investment policy statement.

To prevent unnecessary trading costs caused by movements slightly above and then below the targets, the targeted rates should be treated as buy ranges—they should be used to make purchase decisions for new investments. A hold range of perhaps 0.25 percent should be created for sell purposes. For example, let's assume that the real rate on TIPS fell from 2.6 percent to 2.4 percent. What should an investor do with his current portfolio? Nothing—unless the rate fell to 2.25 percent (2.5 minus 0.25). However, if new cash were available for investment, it could be used to move the allocation toward, or even to, 50 percent (the targeted allocation when the real rate is 2.4 percent). Note that even if there were no trading costs, as might be the case with mutual funds, it would be unwise to alter positions with every small move in rates above and below the targeted levels.

As with the fixed-allocation approach, a shifting-allocation approach has the benefit of creating a buy low/sell high strategy. When the real rate on TIPS is historically high, investors are buying TIPS when prices are low. And they are selling TIPS when the real rate is historically low and prices are high.

Note that the preceding table does not imply that when the real yield is low TIPS are overvalued or that when the real yield is high they are undervalued. The market is highly efficient, meaning that the current price (yield) is the best estimate of the correct price. Thus, the table is not meant to convey that if an investor uses it, he will receive above-market returns by exploiting mispricing and thus outperform a buy-and-hold investor. The table is provided only as a risk-management tool. The underlying philosophy is that because of a natural limited expected range for the yield on TIPS, when yields are low, the price risk is greater on the downside than the upside, and vice versa. That says nothing about the likelihood of an event occurring.

To clarify, if the real yield on TIPS is currently 1.5 percent (near the lower end of the expected range), that tells nothing about the likelihood of it rising or falling from that level. However, if the assumption is correct about the expected range for TIPS yields, and if the real yield fell, it is unlikely to fall by much. On the other hand, if real rates rise, they could rise by a much greater amount, and prices could fall significantly. The reverse situation would be true if current yields were high.

A SHIFTING MATURITY STRATEGY

For those who buy individual TIPS the same type of shifting allocation approach can be developed in regard to maturity. In this case, investors would shift from shorter-term TIPS to longer-term TIPS as real yields rose and vice versa. The idea is to not only increase the allocation to TIPS as real yields rise, but to also lock in the high real yield for a *longer* period of time. By shifting maturities, investors would also avoid locking in low real rates for a long time. For example, consider **TABLE 2.2**. It combines the two approaches: shifting allocation and shifting maturity.

Note that while the TIPS yield curve is generally fairly flat (yields are similar across maturities), sometimes the yields on different maturities will result in different maturity recommendations. For example, the real yield on 5-year TIPS might be 2.49 percent, and the real yield on 10-year TIPS might be 2.51 percent. Our suggestion is that if the differences in yields are minor (for example, a few basis points), invest in the shorter maturity. On the other hand, if the difference is significant (for example, 0.1 percent), consider

Table 2.2 Decision Table for the Allocation and Maturity of TIPS

Real Yield on TIPS	Allocation to TIPS	Maturity of TIPS
>3%	75%–100%	20 years or longer
>2.5% and <3%	50%–75%	15 years
>2% and <2.5%	25%–50%	10 years
>1.5% and <2%	0%–25%	2 years
<1.5%	0%	2 years or less

extending the maturity. Bloomberg provides information on current TIPS yields at bloomberg.com/markets/rates/index.html.

The investor can combine the two strategies: shifting allocation and shifting maturity. Doing so will cause the investor both to increase his allocation to TIPS when real rates rise and to increase the maturity of his TIPS holdings at the same time. Thus, he will be locking in higher real rates for a longer time on a larger percentage of his holdings. When real rates fall, he will be both lowering his allocation to TIPS and shortening their maturity. He will, of course, also be taking profits.

I Bonds

As stated at the beginning of the chapter, the U.S. Treasury issues one other inflation-protected security: the I bond. An I bond works like a TIPS in that it provides a fixed real rate of return and an inflation-protection component. However, there are significant differences. The fixed rate on an I bond is announced by the Treasury in May and November and applies to all I bonds issued during the subsequent six months. Like zero-coupon bonds, their total return (fixed rate plus inflation adjustment) accrues in value. I bonds increase in value on the first of each month and compound semiannually. They pay interest for up to thirty years. They can be purchased and redeemed at most financial institutions. The redemption value can never go below par. All income is deferred for tax purposes until funds are withdrawn from the account holding the bond. The tax-deferral feature makes an I bond a more attractive candidate than a TIPS for a taxable account. Note that while I bonds can only be held in taxable accounts, they are exempt from state and local taxes.

Because they qualify for the U.S. Education Savings Bond Program, I bonds may provide a significant benefit. This program allows interest to be partially or completely excluded from federal income tax when the bondholder pays qualified higher education expenses of an eligible institution or a state tuition plan in the same calendar year the bonds are redeemed. The tax exclusion is gradually phased out over a range of modified adjusted gross income levels, which change each year. Thus, investors should check with their tax adviser to see if they could benefit from this treatment.

The maximum amount of I bonds that an investor can purchase annually is $5,000 in paper and $5,000 in electronic I bonds. They can be bought in denominations of $50, $75, $100, $200, $500, $1,000, $5,000, and $10,000.

Series I bonds issued in January 2003 or earlier may be cashed any time six months after the date of purchase. Bonds issued in February 2003 or later can be cashed anytime twelve months after the date of purchase. When cashing the bonds, investors receive the original investment plus the earnings. However, a prepayment penalty of three months' interest is charged if the bonds are not held for a minimum of five years. Note that if real rates were to rise significantly, the three-month penalty might be a small price to pay to redeem old I bonds and reinvest the proceeds in the newer, higher yielding I bonds. This can prove to be a valuable benefit and is one reason that I bonds carry a lower yield than TIPS. Another reason is that they can be redeemed at par at any time, and thus have no price volatility.

SUMMARY

Inflation-protected securities have many positive features that make them valuable additions to portfolios. Not only do they provide a guaranteed real rate of return, insulating investors from the risks of unexpected inflation, they are also less volatile than nominal return bonds of similar maturity. For example, for the period 1998–2007, the Lehman U.S. Treasury Inflation Notes Index (average maturity of about 10 years) experienced the same 5.0 percent volatility as the Lehman Brothers Treasury Bond Index (1–30 years). As supporting evidence, inflation-indexed bonds in both the United Kingdom and Australia (both with longer live data series) have experienced similar differences in volatility.[8]

TIPS also have a lower correlation with equities. This makes inflation-protected securities more effective diversifiers of equity risk than nominal return bonds. In other words they reduce the volatility of equity portfolios more than do nominal return bonds.

For example, the previously mentioned 2004 study, "Asset Allocation with Inflation-Protected Bonds," found that the standard deviation of an equal-weighted portfolio of stocks and bonds is about

13 percent lower when indexed bonds are included in the portfolio than when conventional bonds are included. And the risk reduction more than doubles for more conservative portfolios.[9] Thus, an investor who includes inflation-protected bonds can hold a higher allocation to equities—without increasing overall portfolio volatility—than can the investor who only holds nominal bonds. The result is a higher expected return from the overall portfolio.

The preference for inflation-protected securities is so strong that the study concluded that if there is no inflation risk premium, the optimal allocation of these securities in a portfolio is 80 percent. Even with an inflation risk premium of 0.5 percent, the optimal allocation is still 60 percent.

A similar study, published in 2006, "Diversification Benefits of Treasury Inflation Protected Securities: An Empirical Puzzle," by Abdullah Mamun and Nuttawat Visaltanachoti, examined both the U.S. and the U.K. markets—the latter as an out-of-sample test—and concluded that inflation-protected securities provide diversification benefits that enhance portfolio efficiency (that is, they offer a greater ratio of return to risk). According to the study, "These findings hold in different economic and inflationary environments, and they confirm the prediction of economic theory that indexed bonds are important for investors who are vulnerable to inflation."[10]

And finally, Philipp Illeditsch, author of the 2007 study "Idiosyncratic Inflation Risk and Inflation-Protected Bonds," concluded that because of the hedging benefits of TIPS, investors should hold, for the fixed-income portion of their portfolios, a 100 percent position in TIPS and a zero position in nominal bonds.[11]

Investors have found the risk-reduction benefits of inflation-indexed bonds so appealing that by 1999, in both the United Kingdom and Canada, roughly 50 percent of pension fund fixed-income holdings were allocated to real return bonds.[12]

The bottom line is that investors should consider devoting at least some significant portion of their fixed-income allocation to inflation-protected securities. In other words, this is one tour you probably don't want to miss.

Commodities   3

COMMODITIES, WHICH FALL within the broad category of hard assets, are an interesting class from a portfolio perspective. Since 1970, they have provided relatively high returns, exhibited negative correlations with equities and bonds, and acted as a hedge against event risk. As stated earlier, the attribute of negative correlation makes an asset class an excellent diversifier of risk. Thus, commodities appear to be worthy of consideration for inclusion in a globally diversified portfolio.

We base the analysis in this chapter on evidence accumulated since 1970 on the S&P GSCI—perhaps the most commonly cited commodities index. (The other major commodity index, the Dow Jones-AIG Commodity Index [DJ-AIGCI], has price history beginning in 1991 and went live in 1999. We will discuss that index later in the chapter.) The S&P GSCI represents a broad cross section of principal raw and semifinished goods used by producers and consumers; it contains commodities from all sectors: energy, industrial, precious metals, livestock, and agricultural products. The S&P GSCI is world-production weighted, and the quantity of each commodity in the index is determined by the average quantity produced in the past five years. As of February 2008, the weightings for the S&P GSCI were as follows:

- **Energy:** 71.4 percent, of which natural gas was about 7 percent and the balance was oil-related commodities
- **Industrial metals:** 8.1 percent, of which aluminum and copper were about 3 percent and the remainder consisted of lead, nickel, and zinc

■ **Precious metals:** 2.2 percent, of which gold was about 2 percent and silver was the remainder

■ **Agriculture:** 15.1 percent, of which wheat was about 5 percent, corn and soybeans were about 3 percent, and cotton, sugar, coffee, and cocoa—each making up 1.2 percent or less—were the remainder

■ **Livestock:** 3.2 percent, of which cattle was about 2.2 percent and hogs were about 1 percent

Just as the weightings of an equity index change as individual stock prices change, so do the proportions of the S&P GSCI change with changes in individual commodity prices.

The heavy weighting of energy-related commodities in the S&P GSCI contributes to the historically negative correlation of the index with both stocks and bonds. The United States has experienced more than one unexpected upward shock to energy prices. The upward shocks lead to unexpected increases in inflation (a negative for both stocks and bonds) and also act as a tax on consumers, depressing economic activity (another negative for stocks).

TABLE 3.1, which compares returns and the standard deviation (an indicator of volatility) of the S&P GSCI to stocks and bonds from 1973 through 2007, demonstrates that the S&P GSCI provided equity-like returns with equity-like volatility. Thus, it is a risky asset class (at least when viewed in isolation).

Many investors decline to participate when they realize that the asset class is volatile, which is unfortunate because commodities can reward the patient and disciplined investor. But the investor needs

Table 3.1   Returns and Volatility: Commodities, Stocks, and Bonds, 1973–2007

	Annualized Return (%)	Annual Standard Deviation (%)
S&P GSCI	10.9	24.5
S&P 500 Index	11.0	17.2
MSCI EAFE Index	11.1	21.6
Lehman Brothers Treasury Bond Index (1–30 years)	8.2	6.5

to possess both traits, because such a risky asset class can provide very poor returns for a very long time. For example, for the ten-year period ending 1999, the *real* return of the S&P GSCI Total Return Index (S&P GSCI-TR) was just 0.9 percent. This compares to a *real* return of 14.8 percent for the S&P 500. For the twenty-year period ending 1999, the comparable *real* returns were 3.1 and 13.3 percent, respectively. And finally, for the period 2000–2007 the S&P GSCI provided a real return of 10.4 percent, outperforming the S&P 500 by more than 11 percent a year, as the latter produced a real return of –1.2 percent.

Investors may fail to realize that commodities can convey substantial diversification benefits. Investors fall into this trap when they think about the risk of an asset class in isolation. To appreciate the diversification benefit of an asset class, it is necessary to examine how including it in a portfolio might affect total portfolio risk. We approach this problem the same way we did in earlier chapters: We look for negative correlations between commodities and other asset classes.

As the analysis in the next section will show, the S&P GSCI is negatively correlated with bonds and stocks and positively correlated with inflation. Because of these characteristics and the high volatility of the asset class, including an allocation to the S&P GSCI in a portfolio has historically improved a portfolio's risk-adjusted returns.[1]

CORRELATION WITH STOCKS, BONDS, AND INFLATION

Because commodities are a source of inflation, we expect commodity prices to be positively correlated with inflation. Because bonds (other than inflation-indexed bonds) provide nominal returns, they are negatively correlated with inflation. Thus, in periods of unexpectedly high inflation, nominal return bonds perform poorly. In addition, despite the conventional wisdom that equities provide a hedge against inflation, stocks have a slightly negative correlation with inflation, especially *unexpected* inflation. Thus, both stocks and bonds are negatively correlated with inflation. Therefore, commodities diversify some of the risks of owning both stocks and bonds. TABLE 3.2 shows the negative correlation of S&P GSCI with stocks and bonds.

Table 3.2 Major Asset Classes: Annual Correlation
with the S&P GSCI, 1973–2007

S&P 500 Index	−0.30
MSCI EAFE Index	−0.20
Lehman Brothers Treasury Bond Index (1–30 years)	−0.18

Table 3.3 Correlations of Commodities Futures Returns with Stocks, Bonds, and Inflation, July 1959–December 2004

Holding Period	Stocks	Bonds	Inflation
Monthly	0.05	−0.14*	0.01
Quarterly	−0.06	−0.27*	0.14
One year	−0.10	−0.30*	0.29*
Five years	−0.42*	−0.25*	0.45*

*Statistically significant at the 5 percent level
Note: Overlapping return data

The negative correlations with stocks and bonds tend to increase with the holding period—suggesting that the diversification benefits of commodity futures are larger over longer horizons. This can be seen in **TABLE 3.3**.[2]

The positive correlation of commodities futures with inflation also increases over time. Thus, commodities futures are a better inflation hedge than are equities.

There is another explanation for the low correlation of commodity returns and the returns of financial assets (stocks and bonds). The prices of financial assets are *anticipatory*—their value is derived from expectations regarding long-term cash flows. In fact, stock returns have been highest during periods of low output and low growth of output as investors anticipate an eventual turnaround. On the other hand, spot prices of commodities reflect current economic activity to a much greater degree. Thus, commodity prices tend to be low during periods of weak economic output. Consider the evidence in **TABLE 3.4** from a 2001 study by Goldman Sachs on business cycles and the returns of stocks and commodities.[3]

Table 3.4   S&P 500 and S&P GSCI: Returns Correlated with the Business Cycle

Description of the Business Cycle	S&P 500 (%)	S&P GSCI (%)
Low output/slow growth	18.5	−5.3
Low output/fast growth	12.1	11.2
High output/fast growth	7.2	29.4
High output/slow growth	−2.9	27.5

Table 3.5   Returns and Volatility of Stocks, Bonds, and the S&P GSCI, 1980–1989

	Annualized Return (%)	Annual Standard Deviation (%)
S&P GSCI	10.7	16.8
S&P 500 Index	17.6	12.7
MSCI EAFE Index	22.8	23.3
Lehman Brothers Treasury Bond Index (1–30 years)	12.2	7.8

The S&P GSCI returns are not just correlated with inflation; they are also correlated with changes in the rate of inflation. For example, during the 1980–1989 period (**TABLE 3.5**), inflation as measured by the Consumer Price Index (CPI) declined from 13.3 percent in 1979 to 4.6 percent in 1989 (hitting a low of just 1.1 percent in 1986).

During this period of declining inflation, the S&P GSCI underperformed not only stocks, but bonds as well. In addition, during this period, the volatility of the asset class was still quite high. However, we should not confuse strategy and outcome.

Gaining benefits in periods of unexpected high or rising inflation (or when both occur) means we should expect the reverse in periods of unexpected low or falling inflation. This is what diversification is all about. For the thirty-eight-year period 1970–2007, there were only two years (1981 and 2001) when the S&P GSCI-TR and either the S&P 500 or the MSCI EAFE Index produced negative returns. It is also worth noting that during the severe bear market of 1973–1974, the S&P GSCI-TR returned 75 percent in the first year and 40 percent in the second. This is a very important point given that most investors are risk averse. Thus, the average risk-averse investor should have a preference to hold assets that tend to perform well when other assets in their portfolio are performing poorly.

EVENT RISK

There is another reason to consider commodities: They provide a hedge against "event risk." Equities have significant exposure to event risk. Unexpected events like wars, disruption to oil supplies, political instability, or even a colder than normal winter or hotter than normal summer can drive up energy prices. Rising energy prices act like a tax on consumption and have a negative impact on the economy and stock prices.

Similarly, droughts, floods, and crop freezes can reduce the supply of agricultural products, and strikes and labor unrest can drive up the prices of precious and industrial metals.[4] These various events are uncorrelated with each other, providing an important diversification benefit if one has invested in a broad commodity index.

Most shocks to commodities are negatively correlated with financial assets because they tend to suddenly reduce supply. Supply shocks not only lead to inflation, which is negatively correlated with stocks, but also to higher costs of production inputs (putting pressure on profits). Because commodity shocks tend to accompany supply disruptions, commodities tend to provide positive returns at the same time financial markets are providing negative returns. Thus, the more investors are sensitive to event risks, the more they should consider holding commodities as a hedge against that type of risk. Therefore, while many investors think of commodities as "too risky," the more risk averse an investor, at least to event risk, the more they should consider including an allocation to commodities. And the more sensitive they are, the greater should be the allocation, within reason. For example, a 60 percent allocation to commodities would not be advisable for anyone.

A RISK-REDUCTION TOOL

The benefit of using commodities as a risk-reduction tool can be demonstrated by examining their returns during years when stocks or bonds or both experienced negative returns (see **TABLES 3.6** and **3.7**). During the period 1973–2007, there were two years when U.S. Treasury bonds had negative returns, producing an average loss of 3.0 percent. In both those years, commodities produced positive returns, averaging 23.1 percent. For the same period, the S&P 500 had eight years of negative returns, producing an average loss of 12.4 percent. In six of the eight years, commodities provided positive returns, with the average return for all eight years being 22.6 percent.

Here is one more bit of evidence that the diversification benefit of commodities works well when it is needed most. For the period July 1959–December 2004, during the 5 percent of months when

Table 3.6   Years of Negative Returns of Lehman Brothers Treasury Bond Index (1–30 years), 1973–2007

Year	Return of Lehman Brothers Treasury Bond Index (1–30 years) (%)	Return of GSCI Index (%)
1994	−3.4	5.3
1999	−2.5	40.9
Average Return	**−3.2**	**+23.1**

Table 3.7   Years of Negative Returns of the S&P 500, 1973–2007

Year	Return of the S&P 500 (%)	Return of the S&P GSCI Index (%)
1973	−14.7	75.0
1974	−26.5	39.5
1977	−7.2	10.4
1981	−4.9	−23.0
1990	−3.1	29.1
2000	−9.1	49.8
2001	−11.9	−31.9
2002	−22.1	32.1
Average Return	**−12.4**	**+22.6**

stocks had the worst returns, equities fell on average by 8.98 percent per month. During these periods, commodity futures returned 1.03 percent per month, which was *greater* than their *average* return of 0.89 percent per month. During the worst 1 percent of months for equities, the returns were a negative 13.87 percent per month, and a positive 2.36 percent per month for commodities futures.[5]

PORTFOLIO EFFICIENCY

To restate: Given the historical returns on commodities, their negative correlation with both stocks and bonds, and the fact that they have generally performed best just when their diversification benefits are needed most (in periods when stocks or bonds or both have negative returns), they should have intuitive appeal for inclusion in a portfolio. Does the intuition hold true?

Thomas Idzorek studied the evidence covering the period 1970–2004 and in his 2006 paper, "Strategic Asset Allocation and Commodities," states the following: "Under what can only be characterized as a very conservative commodity expected return estimate relative to historical commodity returns, we created forward-looking efficient frontiers with and without commodities included in the opportunity set. Using CAPM expected returns, the inclusion of commodities in the opportunity set improved the efficient frontier." He also states, "This suggests that allocations to commodities do not depend on continued high returns." Idzorek argues that it is the low correlation with traditional asset classes that drives the allocation to commodities futures.

Using three different methodologies Idzorek finds that the inclusion of commodities (with allocations running as high as 31 percent) improves forward-looking returns by from 0.35 percent to as much as 0.77 percent for each level of risk (the standard deviation of the portfolio). Using historical returns, he finds the inclusion of commodities improves returns by an average of 1.33 percent for each level of risk.

Idzorek concludes: "Given the inherent return of commodities, there seems to be little risk that commodities will dramatically underperform other assets on a risk-adjusted basis over any reasonably long period. If anything, the risk is that commodities will continue to produce equity-like returns, in which case the forward-looking strategic allocations to commodities are too low."[6]

GAINING EXPOSURE TO COMMODITIES

From a strategic standpoint, it appears that an allocation to commodities would be prudent.

Investors can gain exposure to commodities in three different ways. They can invest in individual commodities themselves. They can invest in the equities of commodity producers. And they can invest in collateralized commodity futures (CCFs) through the use of mutual funds and similar vehicles, including exchange-traded funds (ETFs), exchange-traded notes (ETNs), and commodity trading accounts. Since investing in CCFs has produced returns that are far superior to those of direct investments in commodities, we can set aside that alternative for now. We hope the evidence below clearly demonstrates that CCFs are superior to investing in the equities of commodity-related producers. Those who are not convinced should read the section titled "The Argument Against Investing in Commodity Producers." We present the evidence demonstrating that CCFs are superior to investing in the equities of commodity-related producers. (Note that the more specific category of precious metals equities is covered in Chapter 11.)

While CCFs can be used to invest passively or actively, we will use the term to refer to a passive, unleveraged, long only, fully collateralized futures position in a broad-based commodity futures index, usually either the S&P GSCI or the DJ-AIGCI. The collateral, representing the full value of the futures position, is typically invested in very high-quality instruments. Later in this chapter, the section titled "CTAs" discusses how commodity trading advisers (CTAs) use active strategies.

Unlike a passive equity portfolio, a passive futures portfolio requires regular transactions for the simple reason that futures contracts expire. Thus, contracts must be continually "rolled over" to the next maturity. Because futures contracts require collateral, typically in the form of U.S. Treasury bills, the return on an investment in commodities is not simply the change in price of the futures contract. Specifically, the total return (TR) on the CCF position is equal to the spot return plus two additional components: the interest from the financial collateral plus the futures' "roll yield."

Spot return: Represents the basic up-and-down movements in the price of the underlying commodities. The spot return of the S&P GSCI-TR is the production-weighted spot return of the underlying commodity futures.

Roll return: Represents the cost or benefit of rolling the futures positions forward each month. Whether this is positive or negative for an individual commodity depends on whether the price for the new contract is lower (backwardation) or higher (contango) than the old, expiring contract. The primary purpose of commodity futures markets is to provide an efficient and effective mechanism for managing the price risk of the producers and consumers of commodities. Buying or selling futures contracts establishes a current price level for commodities items that are to be delivered later, thus eliminating price risk.

The following is an example of how the roll can have a positive impact on the total return of CCFs. Let's assume the current spot rate for crude oil is $75.00 and the one-month forward rate is $74.50. If the spot rate remains unchanged over the month, the forward contract will produce a gain of $0.50. If this were repeated over the course of a year, the roll would produce a positive return of 8 percent. On the other hand, if the one-month forward price were $75.50, the roll return would be similarly negative.

Collateral return: This represents the interest earned on a collateral position equal to 100 percent of the dollar face value of the underlying futures contracts. The GSCI-TR imputes a three-month Treasury bill return to this collateral position.

MUTUAL FUNDS: QRAAX AND PCRIX

As of this writing, there are only two mutual funds available to the general public that focus on this asset class. (Later in the chapter, we discuss how to use ETFs and ETNs as alternatives to mutual funds.) The Oppenheimer Commodity Strategy Total Return Fund (QRAAX) attempts to mimic (not replicate) the S&P GSCI. The PIMCO Commodity Real Return Strategy Fund (PCRIX) replicates the DJ-AIGCI in terms of its exposure to commodities futures. However, instead of 3-month Treasury bills, the fund mainly uses TIPS as the collateral. The use of TIPS as collateral provides the important added benefit of providing a hedge against *unexpected* inflation.

There is an important difference between the S&P GSCI and the DJ-AIG indexes. The S&P GSCI is a production-weighted index. As a result, it is heavily weighted to oil and natural gas. This heavy weighting toward energy, as explained earlier, provides important diversification benefits. The DJ-AIGCI is a broad-based index of future contracts on twenty physical commodities. However, no group of related commodities (such as energy, precious metals, livestock, or grain) can make up more than 33 percent of the index, and no single commodity can constitute more than 15 percent or less than 2 percent of the index. The weightings are based on liquidity (two-thirds) and production (one-third). These constraints lead to broader diversification than exists with the S&P GSCI. The following are the weightings for the DJ-AIGCI for 2008: oil-related, 21 percent; grains, 20 percent; industrial metals, 20 percent; natural gas, 12 percent; livestock, 7 percent; soft commodities (coffee, cotton, and sugar), 9 percent; and precious metals (gold and silver), 10 percent. Note that two energy-related commodities (oil and natural gas) total 33 percent, the maximum allowed.

The DJ-AIGCI and the S&P GSCI produce similar correlations to stocks and bonds. For the period 1991–2007, the correlations of the annual returns of the DJ-AIGCI with the S&P 500 and the Lehman Brothers Treasury Bond Index (1–30 years) were –0.224 and –0.227, respectively. The negative correlations provide evidence that the DJ-AIGCI is a good diversifier of the risks of stocks and bonds. In addition, for the period 1991–2007, the DJ-AIGCI, relative to the S&P GSCI, provided higher returns (7.9 percent versus 6.8 percent) with less volatility (16.6 percent versus 25.6). Another benefit of the DJ-AIGCI relative to the S&P GSCI is that the DJ-AIGCI creates the potential for a larger "diversification return" (rebalancing bonus) within the index due to its construction methodology (non-market-capitalization weighting) and both the high volatility of the individual commodities and the low correlations between them.

The diversification return is the difference between the compound return of the portfolio and the weighted average compound return of the portfolio's components. The components that make up the DJ-AIGCI are highly volatile and have returns that are virtually uncorrelated. Regularly rebalancing such a portfolio leads to a greater reduction in the standard deviation and a lessening of the destructive effect of volatility on compound returns (the higher the variability of returns, the greater the difference between average returns and compound returns).

The diversification return for commodities futures is a large one. A 2006 paper, "The Tactical and Strategic Value of Commodity Futures," by Claude B. Erb and Campbell R. Harvey concludes that rebalancing an equal-weighted portfolio of commodities provides a diversification benefit that results in increasing annualized returns by as much as 4.5 percent.[7]

There is another important point we need to make. Despite the apparent benefits of the DJ-AIGCI over the S&P GSCI (higher annualized return, lower standard deviation, and a more negative correlation with the S&P 500), this does not mean that the S&P GSCI is not as effective as the DJ-AIGCI as a building block for the portfolio. Consider the following results, shown in TABLE 3.8, covering the period from 1991 through 2007.

Table 3.8   Sample Portfolios: DJ-AIGCI and S&P GSCI, 1991–2007

Portfolio Allocation	Annualized Return (%)	Annual Standard Deviation (%)
100% DJ-AIGCI	7.91	16.63
100% S&P GSCI	6.80	25.62
100% S&P 500	11.41	17.00
95% S&P 500 and 5% S&P GSCI	11.42	15.94
95% S&P 500 and 5% DJ-AIGCI	11.39	15.98

Note two important observations. First, while both the DJ-AIGCI and the S&P GSCI underperformed the S&P 500 by large amounts, the addition of a 5 percent allocation to either resulted in a more efficient portfolio. Second, despite the DJ-AIGCI's seeming advantages, the portfolio including the DJ-AIGCI produced a virtually identical return and volatility as did the portfolio that included the S&P GSCI. The reason is that when adding a small allocation of an asset with negative correlation to a portfolio, high volatility can be a good thing.

COMMODITY-RELATED ETFS

For all practical purposes, ETFs act like open-ended, no-load mutual funds. Like mutual funds, they can be created to represent virtually any index, asset class, or sector. A number of ETFs have been introduced that allow investors to gain exposure to commodities. New indexes are being created so sponsors can try to create some differentiation, thus avoiding commoditization of their products. Both Barclays Bank PLC and Deutsche Bank have created commodity-based ETFs.

Barclays Global Investors has an ETF based on the S&P GSCI that has an expense ratio of 0.75 percent and uses Treasury bills as collateral. For those investors more interested in gaining exposure to the S&P GSCI, the Barclays Bank ETF would be the clear choice over the Oppenheimer fund.

The newer Deutsche Bank ETF is structured more like the DJ-AIGCI in that it is more diversified. It also has a 0.75 percent expense ratio and uses Treasury bills as collateral.

Note that ETFs have some disadvantages over mutual funds that should also be considered:

- **Trading costs.** Because ETFs trade like stocks, bid-offer spreads are incurred when buying and selling them. Because mutual funds trade at their net asset value (NAV), there are no bid-offer spreads. However, there may be minor transactions costs involved if the fund is not purchased directly from the fund sponsor.
- **Brokerage commissions.** When an investor purchases a no-load mutual fund directly from the fund sponsor, no fees

are incurred. Once again, since ETFs are like stocks, brokerage commissions are always incurred. This becomes important when investing on a frequent basis or in very small amounts or both, such as in dollar-cost-averaging programs and retirement and profit-sharing plans.

COMMODITY-RELATED ETNs

Barclays Bank recently introduced two ETNs, called iPath ETNs—one, GSP, tracks the performance of the S&P GSCI-TR and the other, DJP, tracks the performance of the DJ-AIGCI Total Return Index (DJ-AIGCITR). The ETNs are 30-year senior, unsecured, unsubordinated debt securities of Barclays Bank. Both ETNs trade on the New York Stock Exchange (NYSE) in the same manner as individual stocks. Like ETFs they involve trading costs (bid-offer spreads and commissions) that mutual funds do not. The ETNs carry the same 0.75 percent expense ratio as the Barclays Bank ETFs and use Treasury bills as collateral. There are no other costs besides the expense ratio. As was the case with ETFs, our preference is DJP, the ETN that tracks the more diversified index, the DJ-AIGCI.

There is one major advantage of the ETNs over ETFs and mutual funds, at least for taxable accounts. While there is no case law, Barclays Bank expects the entire return to be unrealized capital gain. To the extent that this continues, the ETNs could (and, in fact, should) be held in taxable accounts. Thus, for the first time, taxable investors can gain exposure to commodities in a tax-efficient manner. However, the federal tax consequences of an investment in ETNs are uncertain. It is possible that the IRS could begin treating ETNs differently (for example, treating them like bonds). Thus, it is important to consult a tax adviser before investing in these vehicles.

Being able to hold ETNs in taxable accounts provides another advantage. As we have discussed, commodities are highly volatile. The more volatile the asset class, the more valuable is the option to harvest losses. Thus, ETNs allow investors to hold commodities in a manner that allows for efficient capital gains treatment, and they provide the potential for harvesting losses for tax purposes.

Unfortunately, there is another negative feature. The iPath ETN securities are unsecured debt of Barclays Bank, which is currently rated AA by Standard & Poor's and Aa1 by Moody's Investors Service. An investment in these products does involve credit risk. If Barclays Bank were to be downgraded or put on a credit watch, for example, the performance and liquidity of these products would be negatively affected in all likelihood.

CTAs

Investors can gain exposure to an actively managed commodities portfolio through CTAs. A CTA is an individual or trading organization, registered with the U.S. Commodity Futures Trading Commission and a member of the National Futures Association, that is granted the authority to make trading decisions on behalf of a customer in futures, options, and securities accounts established exclusively for that customer (the account is called a *managed account*). CTAs are similar to hedge funds (which are covered in Chapter 15) in the following ways:

- They manage unregulated pools of assets.
- They typically charge a high fixed fee as well as a percentage of profits, usually 20 percent.
- They typically have a high watermark that supposedly protects investors. (An incentive fee is paid only on the portion of the gains that exceed the historical peak of the fund's NAV.)

The light regulation of CTA funds results in limited information on the performance as well as riskiness of these funds. For example, a fund could provide high returns by using very high leverage, thus increasing risk in a highly volatile asset class. Several studies provide us with some insights into whether these vehicles are worthy of investor consideration. Let's look at the evidence.

- As of October 1996, there were 304 CTAs in operation. Since the end of 1986, 597 had been dissolved.[8] In less than ten years, almost twice as many funds had been terminated as there were in existence at the end of the period.

- Of the 323 CTAs in operation at the end of 1989, only ninety-five were left by the end of 1995—a failure rate of 71 percent in just seven years.[9]
- The 2000 study "Performance Characteristics of Hedge Funds and CTA Funds: Natural vs. Spurious Biases," by William Fung and David A. Hsieh, found that the probability of a commodity fund dropping out of the database was 19 percent per year, almost four times the 5 percent dropout rate for mutual funds. The study also found that for the period 1989–1997—once reported returns of existing funds were corrected for survivorship bias—realized returns were reduced by 3.6 percent a year.[10] This bias was two to three times as great as the survivorship bias typically found in mutual funds, and even worse than the survivorship bias found in hedge fund data.
- Funds that performed poorly tended to increase risks due to the incentive fee and the high watermark. This creates an unequal field in terms of incentives, what is known as *agency risk*, leading to the propensity for the manager to double down on bets, taking extreme risks when the CTA's incentive compensation is "out of the money." Therefore, characteristics that appear on the surface to be "investor-friendly" can, in fact, lead to increased risk. In addition, the high watermark increases the likelihood of a fund terminating its existence when it is out of the money in terms of incentive compensation.[11]

In summary, there is a significant body of evidence demonstrating that the only ones likely to create wealth from CTAs are the fund sponsors and the commission-driven salespeople or advisers who market them. As with many other interesting investments, the cachet of privately managed accounts often attracts investors. However, the evidence is that they are highly risky investments with poor risk/return characteristics. In addition, there is no logic or evidence to support the view that commodity markets are any less efficient than other capital markets, making active management a loser's game.

THE ARGUMENT AGAINST INVESTING IN COMMODITY PRODUCERS

Before concluding, we need to address the question of whether a portfolio of commodity-related stocks would provide the same benefits as direct exposure to commodities via CCFs. Unfortunately, such a portfolio does not provide pure exposure to the asset class.

What such a portfolio does provide is exposure to the management skills, business practices, and additional lines of business of the commodities producers as well as to the risks of equities in general. In fact a portfolio of commodity-related stocks has higher correlation with the stock market than it does with commodities.

A 2006 study, "Facts and Fantasies About Commodity Futures," by Gary Gorton and K. Geert Rouwenhorst, covering the period 1962–2003, found that the correlation between the returns on CCFs and the returns of commodity producers was just 0.40, while the correlation of commodity company stocks with the S&P 500 was 0.57. Contrast the 0.57 correlation of commodity-producing equities with the –0.28 correlation of CCFs with equities.[12]

While commodity-producing equities have relatively low correlation with equities, the correlation is still significantly positive. Thus, they behave more like other stocks than like commodities. Therefore, they are not as effective at hedging the risks of equities as are commodities themselves. Let's consider why this is the case.

First, ownership of the equities of commodity producers entails accepting all the risks of business ownership that may be unrelated to the price of the commodities themselves. These risks include agency risks (risks related to management of the company), environmental risks (for example, oil spills or asbestos lawsuits), the risks of expropriation of property (particularly foreign-owned assets), the risk of renegotiation of contracts with foreign governments, and even the risk of the imposition of a domestic "excess profits" tax. Investors, of course, should be rewarded for taking these risks. And they are through the equity risk premium.

Second, many commodity producers hedge their price risk by selling commodity futures. A 2006 study, "Firm Value and Hedging: Evidence from U.S. Oil and Gas Producers," by Yanbo Jin and Philippe Jorion, found that the average oil firm hedges 33 percent of its next year's production, and the average gas firm hedges 41 percent. Selling futures offsets the very hedge the investor is seeking. The market recognizes the hedging activity, and the result is that a 1 percent increase in oil prices results in only a 0.28 percent increase in the equities of oil producers, and a 1 percent increase in gas prices results in only a 0.41 percent increase in the equities of gas producers.[13]

THE EQUITIES OF OIL PRODUCERS

Further evidence that the equities of commodity producers do not make for good alternatives to CCFs comes from research on the stocks of four major oil companies and their correlations with both the market and crude oil itself (TABLE 3.9). Mark Anson, author of *Handbook of Alternative Investments*, examined the stock market betas of these four stocks as well as their crude oil betas for the period 1990–2000. (Beta measures the amount of market risk associated with a given security. A beta of more or less than one indicates that the stock has more or less risk than the overall market.) In the book, crude oil was defined as the price of crude oil traded in New York City.[14]

Note that the correlations of returns between the stocks of these four major oil producers and the overall market were extremely high and the correlations with the price of oil were extremely low. In addition, stocks' market betas were very high and their crude oil betas were very low. The evidence suggests that oil company stocks have high exposure to market risks and low exposure to oil price risks.

Table 3.9 Oil Stocks: Betas and Correlations with Equities and Oil Prices, 1990–2000

	Stock Market Beta	Stock Market Correlation	Crude Oil Beta	Crude Oil Correlation
ExxonMobil	0.839	0.99	0.089	0.045
Texaco	0.531	0.94	0.025	0.001
Chevron	0.698	0.97	−0.010	0.001
Royal Dutch Shell	0.819	0.97	0.080	0.045

IMPLEMENTATION

Many issues must be considered when implementing a strategy; these include tax efficiency, tracking error risk, and the pros and cons of the specific mutual funds under consideration.

Since all gains from an investment in CCFs result from interest income and the trading of futures contracts, the returns are produced in a tax-inefficient manner. Thus, this asset class was only appropriate for a tax-deferred or nontaxable account, such as a Roth IRA, until the introduction of ETNs. Another consideration is a psychological risk called *tracking error regret*. Adding commodities to a portfolio will virtually ensure that the portfolio's returns do not track those of the equity markets. However, this is not a problem unique to commodities, and it occurs with most asset classes. The negative correlation of commodities to equities increases the risk of tracking-error regret. Thus, only informed and disciplined investors should consider including commodities in their portfolio.

Both the Oppenheimer and the PIMCO funds have implementation problems, but the problems with the Oppenheimer fund are much more significant. First, the fund is expensive. The Class A shares of the fund have a high expense ratio: 1.23 percent. As if that were not bad enough, the fund also carries a 5.75 percent load. (A lower-cost institutional version is available through financial advisers. Its operating expense ratio is 0.65 percent.) As is the case with all mutual funds, the fund will incur transactions costs as it implements its futures trading strategy. Those trading costs are estimated to be about 0.06 percent. Second, the funds used as collateral for the futures contracts may be invested in instruments—such as mortgage-backed securities—that have both term and credit risk, rather than 3-month Treasury bills that are not exposed to either of those risks. Third, the fund is actively managed, allowing the manager discretion in terms of weighting exposure to the various commodities within the S&P GSCI. From inception in April 1997 through December 2006, the fund provided a compound annualized return of 3.4 percent, producing a total return of 38.6 percent. This is compared to annualized and total returns of 5.6 percent and

69.5 percent for the S&P GSCI. Active management and high costs destroyed value instead of adding it.

The PIMCO fund, which began operations in the summer of 2002, is a bit more investor friendly, with an expense ratio of 1.24 percent. Fortunately, a lower cost (0.74 percent) institutional version is available through investment advisers. Again, additional costs of about 0.06 percent to cover transactions costs should be assumed. Thus, the total cost of the fund is about 0.8 percent. As mentioned earlier, another positive feature of this fund is that it invests most of its collateral in TIPS. This provides a hedge against unexpected inflation. We believe this is a major advantage. However, like the Oppenheimer fund, the PIMCO fund does have the discretion to take on credit risk (for example, investing in junk bonds) and extension risk (for example, investing in mortgage-backed securities). The fund also has the ability to take on currency risk through investments in non-dollar-denominated assets. These should not be major issues, as PIMCO has historically been a conservative fund manager of fixed-income assets. (While the prospectus provides them the flexibility to drift from conservative assets, it is unlikely that the flexibility will be used to any great extent.)

SUMMARY

Philosopher Arthur Schopenhauer believed that "all great ideas go through three stages. In the first stage they are ridiculed. In the second stage, they are strongly opposed. And in the third stage they are considered to be self-evident." Until fairly recently commodities were viewed as too speculative to be considered an appropriate asset class for prudent investors. However, thanks to recent academic research, it is easy to understand the intuitive appeal of investing in commodities via a real return fund using an indexed-commodity approach, along with investing collateral in short-term or inflation-protected securities of the highest credit quality. The attractions are the negative correlation with both bonds and stocks and the inflation and event-risk hedges that neither stocks nor bonds offer. The more one is concerned about event risks that can have a negative impact on equities, the more consideration should be given to commodities. And the greater the risk of unexpected inflation to the financial health of an investor, the more PIMCO's Commodity Real Return Strategy Fund should be considered for inclusion in a portfolio. The reason, as we discussed, is that the fund's use of TIPS provides a hedge against unexpected inflation. As was noted, however, investors in commodities must be highly disciplined, patient, and willing and able to regularly rebalance their portfolio—increasing their investment in commodities after periods of relatively poor returns, when fear makes it hard for most investors to do so, and decreasing it after relatively good returns, when exuberance often takes over. Not only can the returns be very low for long periods, they can also be highly volatile. For example, the returns of the Oppenheimer fund (A shares) for the period 1998 through 2007 were –45, 37, 44, –31, 27, 23, 20, 26, –13, and 30 percent, respectively.

The bottom line is that CCFs have appeal for disciplined long-term investors seeking a hedge against the risks of stocks and bonds. And for those that use the PIMCO fund there is the added benefit of a hedge against unexpected inflation. The strongest appeal comes from the conclusion reached by Gary Gorton and K. Geert Rouwenhorst in their 2006 paper "Facts and Fantasies about Commodity Futures."

They said that commodity futures diversify the systematic risk of equity investing—the part that is not supposed to be diversifiable. They also concluded that the historical performance of collateralized investments in commodities suggests that commodities are an attractive asset class to diversify traditional portfolios of stocks and bonds.[15]

For tax-advantaged accounts (and taxable investors in the lowest tax bracket), the vehicle of choice is the PIMCO fund. For more highly taxed taxable accounts, investors should consider the iPath ETN that follows the DJ-AIGCI, and note the two cautions that they seek the counsel of their tax adviser and they do not ignore the credit risk of the issuer (Barclays).

International Equities 4

O NCE INVESTORS START to think beyond their own borders, one asset class they usually consider is the large-cap stocks of the developed markets.

Investing in international stocks, while providing expected returns similar to those of domestic stocks, provides the benefit of diversifying the economic and political risks of domestic investing. Thus, the gains from international diversification come from the relatively low correlation among international securities. This is especially important for those who are employed in the United States, as it is likely that their intellectual capital is highly correlated with domestic risks.

There have been long periods when U.S. stocks performed relatively poorly compared to international stocks. And, of course, the reverse has also been true. For example, for the period 1970 through 1986, the MSCI (Morgan Stanley Capital International) EAFE (Europe, Australasia, and the Far East) Index outperformed the S&P 500 Index 15.4 percent versus 10.6 percent a year. Over the next twenty years, from 1987 through 2006, the S&P 500 outperformed the MSCI EAFE Index 11.8 percent versus 8.4 percent a year. Over the entire period, the MSCI EAFE Index and the S&P 500 provided very similar returns, with the MSCI EAFE Index outperforming the S&P 500 by 11.6 percent versus 11.2 percent a year.

However, the MSCI EAFE Index exhibited greater volatility. Its annual standard deviation was 21.9 percent. This compares to the 16.8 percent standard deviation of the S&P 500. The average return of the two individual indexes was 11.4 percent, and the average standard deviation was 19.4 percent. A portfolio that allocated 50 percent to each index, and rebalanced annually, would have returned 11.7 percent (outperforming either index) and done so with a volatility of 17.2 percent—lower than the average standard deviation of the two indexes, and just slightly higher than the standard deviation of the S&P 500. This favorable outcome resulted from the relatively low correlation of the two indexes, at 0.59.

The logic of diversifying economic and political risks is why investors should consider allocating *at least* 30 percent, and as much as 50 percent, of their equity holdings to international equities. And the historical results provide evidence supporting the logic. The best way to access international large-cap stocks is to invest in an index fund that attempts to replicate the returns of the MSCI EAFE Index. Note that the MSCI EAFE Index is similar to the S&P 500 in that it consists of large-cap stocks.

International equities are not generally considered an alternative investment. Along with domestic stocks and bonds, they are one of the core asset classes. They have earned a place in this book because most investors limit their international holdings to large-cap stocks and therefore miss two important alternative investment opportunities: emerging market equities and international small-cap and value stocks.

EMERGING MARKET EQUITIES

The emerging markets comprise those nations whose economies are considered to be developing or emerging from underdevelopment, including all, or almost all, of the countries in Africa, Eastern Europe, Latin America, and the Middle East, and Russia and much of Asia, excluding Japan, Hong Kong, and Singapore.

Many travelers are hesitant to take a trip to an exotic location because of its unfamiliarity. Similarly, many investors shy away from investing in emerging markets because they are considered to be either highly risky investments or, even worse, pure speculations. The fact that the emerging markets are risky should not preclude investors from allocating some portion of their portfolio to them. Modern portfolio theory tells us that *sometimes* we can add risky assets to a portfolio and actually reduce the risk of the overall portfolio.

The reason is the diversification benefit. Another reason to consider investing in emerging markets is that because it is a risky asset class, an efficient market will appropriately price that risk. The result is higher expected returns. The historical evidence from a growing body of research shows that emerging market equities have high returns with high volatility. They also have low correlations with both domestic and international equities.

We begin our discussion on the role of emerging markets in portfolio construction by first reviewing the correlations and then by analyzing the effect of an allocation to emerging markets on several sample portfolios.

CORRELATIONS

While data is only available for a relatively short period, we do observe that emerging markets have experienced high volatility and low correlations with the U.S. and other developed markets. Thanks to Dimensional Fund Advisors (DFA), we have data for the period 1989 through 2007 (**TABLE 4.1**) on large-cap emerging market equities and on small-cap and value emerging market stocks. It allows us to see the effects of size and value in the emerging markets. Around the globe, in developed and emerging markets, both small-cap and value stocks have provided higher returns than large-cap and growth stocks because they are riskier, and investors demand higher returns as compensation for the greater risk.

Table 4.1   Comparative Performance: Emerging Markets, Emerging Market Small-Cap, and Emerging Market Value, 1989–2007

	Annualized Return (%)	Standard Deviation (%)	Sharpe Ratio	Correlation with S&P 500	Correlation with MSCI EAFE
Fama-French emerging markets*	15.9	32.3	0.48	.29	.69
Fama-French small-cap emerging markets*	16.9	35.9	0.49	.23	.64
Fama-French value emerging markets*	19.7	36.5	0.56	.22	.72

*The Fama-French benchmark portfolios represent distinct asset classes, which are based on academic definitions.

The following observations can be made from the data in the preceding table:

- Emerging markets are a high risk/high return asset class.
- The same size and value premiums (risk factors) that are present in the United States and international stocks are present in emerging market equities.
- The low correlation of emerging market equities to U.S. and other developed market equities makes them excellent diversifiers of portfolio risk.

SAMPLE PORTFOLIOS

The next step is to see what impact the addition of emerging market equities has on the overall risk and return of a *portfolio*. To capture an extra year of data, this time we will use the MSCI Emerging Markets Index instead of the Fama-French data (see **TABLE 4.2**). Our benchmark portfolio is 70 percent S&P 500 equities and 30 percent MSCI EAFE Index equities. We then shift one-third of the MSCI EAFE Index allocation to emerging markets, and then two-thirds, and then the full 30 percent. Finally, we will increase the emerging market allocation to 40 percent, reducing the allocation to the S&P 500 to 60 percent. We will examine the results in terms of the returns, the volatility, and the Sharpe ratio.

Table 4.2   Sample Portfolios, 1988–2007

Portfolio	Allocation	Annualized Return (%)	Standard Deviation (%)	Sharpe Ratio
A	70% S&P 500 and 30% MSCI EAFE	10.8	15.6	0.48
B	70% S&P 500, 20% MSCI EAFE, and 10% MSCI Emerging Markets	11.9	15.9	0.54
C	70% S&P 500, 10% MSCI EAFE, and 20% MSCI Emerging Markets	13.0	16.6	0.58
D	70% S&P 500 and 30% MSCI Emerging Markets	14.0	17.6	0.62
E	60% S&P 500 and 40% MSCI Emerging Markets	14.6	19.0	0.61

By shifting our allocation from international large-cap stocks to emerging market stocks, we increased portfolio returns. However, it is important to note that despite the low correlation of emerging market stocks to the other assets in the portfolio, the volatility of the portfolios did increase. This result was caused by the high volatility of emerging market equities outweighing the low correlations. The good news is that the risk-adjusted returns were higher, as the increase in returns was greater than the increase in volatility, which can be seen by looking at the Sharpe ratios. Note that there was no further benefit reflected in the Sharpe ratio once we reached the 30 percent allocation.

This is not to suggest that an investor consider allocating as much as 30 percent to emerging market equities (though, as was mentioned earlier in this chapter, we do recommend that investors consider at least a 30 percent allocation to the broader category of international equities). Investors care, or should care, about more things than just high expected returns and Sharpe ratios. The purpose of this exercise is to demonstrate that while emerging markets are risky, they have provided higher returns and have also improved the efficiency of portfolios. Thus, investors should at least consider allocating a portion of their equity holding to emerging market equities. Before deciding on what percentage should be allocated, investors should be fully aware of why investing in emerging markets is risky.

THE RISKS OF INVESTING IN EMERGING MARKETS

As we have seen, the historical evidence is that emerging markets are highly volatile. The high volatility alone scares off many investors. However, an asset class can be risky without exhibiting high historic volatility. For example, it just might be that the data are period specific, and the risk has just not shown up—at least not yet. In the case of emerging markets, there are many risk factors that make investing in them intuitively risky. In other words, we would know they were risky even if their volatility had not been high.

- A general lack of a strong regulatory body (similar to the Securities and Exchange Commission—SEC) to protect investor interests. According to Raghuram Rajan and Luigi

Zingales, in *Saving Capitalism from the Capitalists*, "Mandatory disclosure—one explanation goes—made the information that firms disclosed more credible. As investors became more informed, the volatility of securities was reduced. Over time, the reduction in price fluctuations benefited ordinary investors, enabling them to make better investment decisions and reducing the ability of informed but unscrupulous traders to take advantage of them."[1]

■ A general lack of consistent accounting standards that give investors confidence in the accuracy of data. "Study after study has shown that better accounting standards help make firms more transparent, making it easier for them to inspire confidence in investors," note Rajan and Zingales.[2] The lack of standards in many emerging market countries has led to greater opaqueness in the reporting of financial and other material information.

These first two issues are related to what is called *good corporate governance*. There are other factors that should also be considered:

■ Political risks—Emerging market countries are often characterized by governments that are less stable than those of developed countries. There may also be a lack of a tradition of democratic government, if a democracy exists at all. Political risks can even include the potential for the expropriation of property.

■ Lack of strong financial markets—Emerging markets often lack strong banking systems. Thus, these markets often face financial crises during which credit becomes very difficult, if not impossible, to obtain. This might explain why the value and the size premiums have been higher in emerging markets than they have been in developed markets. Small-cap and value companies not only have fewer choices in terms of raising capital, but because they generally have weaker credit (often not having assets that can be pledged as collateral), they are the first ones to be cut off from funding during a liquidity crisis. Therefore, investors demand a risk premium.

It is also worth noting that when the United States was an emerging market, it often faced banking and liquidity crises.

■ Currency risk—The currencies of emerging economies are often highly volatile, contributing to the high volatility of the asset class.

■ Default risk—Some emerging markets (for example, Argentina, Ecuador, and Russia) have at times defaulted on their sovereign debt. Defaults, or even the potential for default, can create substantial volatility in the capital markets.

■ Risk of capital controls being put in place, preventing the repatriation of capital—This happened as recently as 1997 during what came to be known as the Asian contagion. *Contagion* in financial markets refers to the idea that markets become highly correlated during crises. In the summer of 1997, the Asian financial crisis began with a shortage of foreign exchange that caused the value of currencies and equities throughout the region to drop. The first round was a precipitous drop in the value of the Thai baht, Malaysian ringgit, Philippine peso, and Indonesian rupiah. The crisis then spread with downward pressures hitting the Taiwan dollar, South Korean won, Brazilian real, Singaporean dollar, and Hong Kong dollar.

■ Lower levels of market liquidity leading to higher trading costs—In addition, other transaction-related fees—for example, custodial fees and taxes—are also likely to be greater. According to Joshua Feuerman, former manager of the SSgA (State Street Global Advisors) Emerging Markets Fund, a "round-trip" purchase and sale of a block of stock in a typical emerging market costs about 4.5 percent of the value of the stock. He called it "a disgustingly expensive asset class to trade in."[3] Lower levels of liquidity and greater trading costs create more risk, for which investors seek compensation via lower prices (and thus higher expected returns).

It is important to note that while some of these risks, such as political risk, can be diversified by owning a mutual fund that invests in many emerging market countries, not all the risk is diversifiable. Thus, as we have discussed, investors must be compensated for taking these nondiversifiable risks with higher expected returns. The markets have in fact delivered those higher returns, but only when investors have had the discipline to stay the course.

The following is a great illustration of the need for discipline when investing in emerging markets. For the period 1988–2007, the MSCI Emerging Markets Index outperformed the S&P 500 by 4.5 percent per year (16.3 percent versus 11.8 percent). For the period 1994 through 2002, the MSCI Emerging Markets Index produced a negative return of 4.6 percent a year. It also underperformed the S&P 500 by 13.9 percent a year during this period. This clearly demonstrates that investors must have the discipline to stay the course, enduring what can be long periods—in this case nine years—of significant underperformance.

The result of the high volatility and long periods of poor performance is that emerging markets are characterized not only by extreme volatility of prices, but also by extreme volatility of *enthusiasm for investing in them.* Perhaps the biggest risk to investors in emerging markets is the risk of not being there. Far too many investors get chased out of the asset class when times are bad. And there are always seemingly good arguments about why investing in emerging markets is a bad idea, and why investors never should have invested in them in the first place. Thus, only those with extreme discipline should even consider investing. To paraphrase Charles Ellis, author of the wonderful book *Investment Policy*, emerging market investors would do well to learn from deer hunters and fishermen who know the importance of "being there" and using patient persistence—so they are there when opportunity knocks.[4]

SMALL-CAP AND VALUE STOCKS

As discussed, both the logic and the historical evidence (though brief) show that emerging markets are risky and that they have delivered on the expectation of higher returns. Additionally, due to the types of risks discussed previously—especially those related to access

Table 4.3   Comparative P/E Ratios

Fund	P/E
DFA US Large Company Portfolio/DFA Emerging Markets Portfolio (Large)	16.5/16.4
DFA US Small Cap Portfolio/DFA Emerging Markets Small Cap Portfolio	19.0/14.4
DFA US Large Cap Value Portfolio/DFA Emerging Markets Value Portfolio	14.3/13.1

to capital—we should expect that the size and value premiums in the emerging markets would be greater than they have been in the developed countries—and this has been the case, at least for the period for which we have data. We can see some evidence of the greater degree to which emerging market equities are distressed (that is, priced lower for greater risk) by comparing the price-to-earnings (P/E) ratios of similar DFA funds (see **TABLE 4.3**). Data is as of January 1, 2007. Note that P/E ratios exclude negative earnings.

Note that in each case, the similar emerging market fund has a lower P/E ratio. While this relationship may not always hold, we should expect that it generally would because emerging market companies have higher costs of capital. And the flip side of a higher cost of capital is a higher *expected* return to the providers (investors) of that capital.

We also need to consider which of the three emerging market asset classes to use when building portfolios. How does one decide on allocating among the three? With the usual caveat that the data presented here represent a relatively brief period, the historical evidence *suggests* that if investors are going to accept the high risks of investing in emerging markets, they might consider taking on the incremental risk of small-cap and, especially, value stocks within those same emerging markets. Once again, let's look at the data for the period from 1989 through 2007 (**TABLE 4.4**).

As the table shows, emerging market value stocks provided the highest returns and produced the highest Sharpe ratio. Emerging market small-cap stocks provided higher returns than did the large-cap stocks, but produced the same Sharpe ratio. Also, note that the correlations of emerging market small-cap and value stocks with emerging market large-cap stocks are very close to 1.00, making them relatively good substitutes.

Table 4.4   Comparing Large-Cap, Small-Cap, and Value Emerging Market
             Stocks, 1989–2007

	Annualized Return (%)	Standard Deviation (%)	Sharpe Ratio	Correlation with S&P 500	Correlation with MSCI EAFE Index	Correlation with Fama-French Emerging Markets Index
Fama-French large-cap emerging markets*	15.9	32.3	0.48	0.29	0.69	1.00
Fama-French small-cap emerging markets*	16.9	35.9	0.49	0.23	0.64	0.98
Fama-French value emerging markets*	19.7	36.5	0.56	0.22	0.72	0.96

*The Fama-French benchmark portfolios represent distinct asset classes, which are based on academic definitions.

It appears that investors in the emerging market small-cap and value stocks, as compared to large stocks, get greater returns, a bit more effective diversification (in general, slightly lower correlations to the S&P 500 and the MSCI EAFE Index), and more efficient portfolios (higher Sharpe ratios) than investors who use only a large-cap emerging market strategy. Thus, investors both willing and able to take the risk of investing in emerging markets should consider allocating at least some (if not a high percentage) of their emerging market allocation to the small-cap and especially value asset classes.

RECOMMENDED VEHICLES

From an implementation standpoint, the preferred choices are index funds, exchanged-traded funds (ETFs) that replicate broad-based indexes (not single-country vehicles), and the passive asset class funds of DFA. The evidence shows that active investing has fared very poorly in emerging markets, with the majority of funds underperforming the benchmark index. The returns results are so poor that the majority of funds that existed at one time have already disappeared. There are very few funds with even ten-year track records. One reason for the failure of active management in this supposedly inefficient asset class is the aforementioned obscenely high costs of trading. Therefore, we recommend the following (expense ratios as of July 2008):

- Vanguard's Emerging Markets Stock Index Fund (VEIEX). It has an expense ratio of 0.37 percent.
- The iShares MSCI Emerging Markets Index Fund (EEM). It has an expense ratio of 0.74 percent.
- DFA's Emerging Markets Portfolio (DFEMX). It has an expense ratio of 0.6 percent.
- DFA's Emerging Markets Small Cap Portfolio (DEMSX). It has an expense ratio of 0.78 percent.
- DFA's Emerging Markets Value Portfolio (DFEVX). It has an expense ratio of 0.60 percent.
- DFA's Emerging Markets Core Equity Portfolio (DFCEX). It has an expense ratio of 0.65 percent.
- DFA's Emerging Markets Social Core Equity Portfolio (DFESX). It has an expense ratio of 0.66 percent.

For those investors who are seeking exposure to emerging market small-cap stocks or value stocks, or both, and who do not have access to DFA's funds, there is only one passively managed alternative as of this writing—WisdomTree's Emerging Markets SmallCap Dividend Fund (DGS). It has an expense ratio of 0.63 percent.

The bottom line is that investing in emerging markets is highly recommended for disciplined investors who understand the nature of the risks.

WRAP-UP: EMERGING MARKETS

Investors in emerging markets take on considerable risk. The risks are well known and go well beyond the simple notion of volatility. Only those investors who have a strong commitment to staying the course should consider investing in the asset class. Otherwise, they will likely end up selling low in the almost inevitable panics that occur from time to time—when most investors become convinced that emerging markets are more likely to submerge than emerge—and buying high when euphoria takes over.

The typical emerging market fund invests in such countries as Argentina, Brazil, Chile, the Czech Republic, Hungary, Indonesia, India, Israel, Malaysia, Mexico, the Philippines, Poland, South Korea, Taiwan, Thailand, and Turkey. And some also invest in Russia and China. Investing in these countries involves increased risks relative to investments in the United States and other developed countries. Given the long list of countries and the potential for various types of risk arising, it is likely that on a regular basis investors will be faced with news from at least one country that will give them cause to reflect on why they have invested in such a risky asset class—or even cause them to panic. Only investors who can ignore the noise should consider investing in this asset class. Investors who have the strong stomach and the discipline required can *expect* to be rewarded with both higher returns and a diversification benefit, resulting in a more efficient portfolio. However, they should also accept that *expectation* is different from *guarantee*.

INTERNATIONAL SMALL-CAP STOCKS

Small-cap stocks, wherever they are located, are risky, exhibiting high volatility. Since risk and *expected* return are related, they should provide high *expected* returns.

As shown in TABLE 4.5, international small caps, the stocks of small companies in the developed markets, also have a lower correlation with U.S. equities (0.38) than do international large caps (0.59),

Table 4.5   Performance: S&P 500, MSCI EAFE, and International Small-Cap Stocks, 1970–2007

	Annualized Return (%)	Standard Deviation (%)	Correlation with S&P 500
S&P 500	11.1	16.6	1.00
MSCI EAFE Index	11.6	21.6	0.59
International small-cap stocks*	16.6	29.0	0.38

*Dimensional Fund Advisors International Small Cap Index; data from Style Research Ltd.

the stocks of large companies in the developed markets. That makes them even better diversifiers of the risks of the domestic equity asset classes in a portfolio.

The logic for the lower correlation is clear and simple. Many large companies are global giants, selling their products and services all over the world. Thus, while they tend to perform mostly like domestic companies in terms of returns, clearly their earnings will be affected by global conditions. On the other hand, many smaller companies are more dependent on the conditions of their local economies. Thus, their returns are driven more by local, idiosyncratic factors. This makes them more effective diversifiers than international large-cap stocks.

As an example, the performance of two giant global pharmaceutical companies like Merck and Roche are likely to be more highly correlated, because their products are sold all around the globe, than the performance of two small-cap domestic restaurant chains whose products are sold only in their home countries.

As we should expect, risky international small-cap stocks provided higher returns than either U.S. or international large-cap stocks, and they exhibited significantly higher volatility.

Using a data series provided by DFA (that gives us thirty-eight years of data), we will examine how the addition of international small-cap stocks affects the overall risk and return of a portfolio.

SAMPLE PORTFOLIOS

To see how the addition of international small-cap stocks affects the risk and return of a diversified portfolio, we will consider several different asset allocations (TABLE 4.6). Portfolio A is our base case of 70 percent S&P 500 and 30 percent MSCI EAFE Index. Portfolio B splits the 30 percent international allocation between large-cap and small-cap stocks. Portfolio C shifts the 30 percent international allocation entirely to international small-cap stocks.

The portfolio that included only the international small-cap stocks produced the highest return and the highest Sharpe ratio. While that does not necessarily mean that investors should allocate all of their international equity allocation to small-cap stocks

Table 4.6 Sample Portfolios: International Small-Cap Allocations, 1970–2007

Portfolio	Allocation	Annualized Return (%)	Standard Deviation (%)	Sharpe Ratio
A	70% S&P 500 and 30% MSCI EAFE	11.5	16.3	0.41
B	70% S&P 500, 15% MSCI EAFE, and 15% international small-cap*	12.4	16.5	0.47
C	70% S&P 500, 30% international small-cap*	13.3	17.0	0.53

*Dimensional Fund Advisors International Small Cap Index; data from Style Research Ltd.

(although that case could be made if they were willing to take the incremental risks), it presents a strong case for at least including a significant allocation.

It is also worth reviewing the results of combining an allocation to each of the three international asset classes of large-cap, small-cap, and emerging markets (**TABLE 4.7**). Portfolio A is 70 percent S&P 500 and 30 percent MSCI EAFE Index. Portfolio B is 70 percent S&P 500, 10 percent MSCI EAFE Index, 10 percent international small caps, and 10 percent emerging markets.

The benefits are clear.

RECOMMENDED VEHICLES
Unfortunately, there are very few good investment alternatives available in the asset class of international small-cap stocks. DFA does have passive funds for both international small-cap and small-cap value stocks. As of this writing, the other low-cost, passive alternatives are the ETFs of WisdomTree. The ticker symbol

Table 4.7 Sample Portfolios: Risk and Return, 1988–2007

Portfolio	Allocation	Annualized Return (%)	Standard Deviation (%)	Sharpe Ratio
A	70% S&P 500 and 30% MSCI EAFE	10.8	15.6	0.48
B	70% S&P 500, 10% MSCI EAFE, 10 % international small-cap, and 10% emerging markets	12.1	15.8	0.55

of their international small-cap ETF is DLS. They also offer the Europe SmallCap Dividend ETF (DFE) and the Japan SmallCap Dividend ETF (DFJ). All three have expense ratios of 0.58 percent. (Expense ratios as of July 2008.) Our preference is always for broader diversification.

The other alternative is to select an actively managed fund. Investors who make that choice should be sure to select one that has low costs and low turnover and that sticks to its knitting (avoids style drift). Low turnover is especially important because the cost of trading in international small-cap stocks is significantly greater than it is for large-cap stocks. We suggest considering Vanguard's International Explorer Fund (VINEX).

SUMMARY

Once investors begin to think of extending their investment journey beyond the five major domestic asset classes (small-cap and large-cap growth stocks, small-cap and large-cap value stocks, and real estate) and international large-cap stocks, they begin to think about alternative investments such as hedge funds, venture capital, and junk bonds. While these alternatives might be "interesting," superior alternatives are available in the form of emerging market equities and both international small-cap and small-cap value stocks. Each offers higher expected returns, for those seeking them. In addition, their unique risk characteristics make them excellent diversifiers of the equity risks of U.S. investments. They are even good diversifiers of the risks of international large-cap stocks. Thus, every investor, from the aggressive to the risk averse, should at least consider some allocation to these asset classes. The more economic risks investors are willing to accept, the more they can allocate to these asset classes (while allocating less to international large-cap stocks).

Fixed Annuities   5

NOT ALL ALTERNATIVE investments are as exciting as commodities. In fact, the tried and true investments with the greatest long-term success are often downright boring! Perhaps the most boring of all alternative investments are fixed annuities.

A fixed annuity is a contract sold by an insurance company. The contract guarantees a fixed periodic payment over the life of the annuitant(s). The payments can begin either immediately, for an immediate annuity, or at some point in the future, for a deferred annuity.

A fixed annuity is *not* an investment vehicle. The issuer of the contract, the insurance company, is taking the investment risks. The only investment risk borne by the purchaser of the annuity is the risk of default by the issuer of the contract. In contrast, variable annuities, which we discuss in Chapter 17, are investment vehicles.

To explain immediate fixed annuities, we will first contrast them with deferred variable annuities. With a deferred variable annuity, investors place—either today or over a period of time—a portion of the annuity money in underlying mutual-fund-like investments called *subaccounts*. These subaccounts generally hold portfolios of stocks, bonds, or a combination of both. The money then grows—hopefully—over time. Withdrawals begin, free of penalty, starting at age fifty-nine and a half. No taxes are due until withdrawals begin. When money is withdrawn, investment gains, if any, are taxed at ordinary income rates. Those who are familiar with nondeductible IRAs can see that, from a taxation standpoint, a deferred annuity is similar to a nondeductible IRA. An immediate fixed annuity works in a much different fashion.

With an immediate fixed annuity, investors give an insurance company a lump sum of money. In exchange, the insurer agrees to pay them a fixed amount of money on a periodic basis (for example, monthly, quarterly, or annually). The quoted periodic payment is net of costs. Investors can choose to receive these payments over different lengths of time. With a single-life annuity, they receive payments for as long as they are alive. The way this product works makes many people think of immediate annuities as "life insurance in reverse."

For a joint-life annuity with survivorship, payments are made as long as one of the two annuitants is alive. In addition to being able to choose single-life or joint-life payments, annuitants can also specify whether they want payments to continue for a certain period of time—regardless of whether they are alive. For example, they could purchase a single-life annuity with guaranteed payments for ten years. For joint-life annuities, investors can also specify what percentage of the annuity payment the surviving annuitant would receive after the first annuitant passes away.

The only difference between an immediate fixed annuity and a deferred fixed annuity is that, with the latter, payments begin at a predetermined date in the future. For example, a sixty-five-year-old couple might feel that they have sufficient assets to comfortably fund a retirement until age eighty-five. However, they run the risk of living beyond eighty-five and possibly outliving their financial assets. Thus, they might consider purchasing a deferred fixed annuity that would begin payments only if they reached the age of eighty-six. The deferral of the payment until that later date drives down the cost of the "longevity insurance." This enables investors to tailor the insurance to their specific needs.

How Long Do Payments Continue?

It is important to emphasize that payments continue only as long as the contract stipulates. If the buyer chooses the single-life option, payments will continue only as long as the annuitant is alive—no residual annuity value passes to his heirs. For a joint-life annuity with survivorship, payments continue as long as one of the two annuitants is alive. Once again, no residual annuity value passes to the annuitants' heirs. Therefore, if investors choose to annuitize, their heirs are exposed to the risk that a premature death will result in fewer assets being bequeathed. This risk is what prevents many from purchasing an immediate annuity.

DETERMINANTS OF PAYMENT SIZE

How much the insurance company agrees to pay depends upon a number of factors. The most important ones are as follows:

- **Age at the time of annuitization**—Everything else being equal, the older investors are at the time of annuitization, the more they can expect to be paid. The reason is simple: When the investor annuitizes at an older age, the insurance company will not have to pay for as long as it would have had the investor annuitized at a younger age. This same logic applies to joint-life annuities with survivorship.
- **The payment option selected**—Generally, the option that provides the highest payment is the single-life option with no guaranteed period of payments. Choosing joint-life with survivorship or opting for a period of guaranteed payments reduces the payment amount. The joint-life with survivorship option typically results in the largest reduction in the level of payments.
- **Percentage of payments guaranteed to the survivor**— With the joint-life with survivorship option, the higher the percentage of the payment that is guaranteed to pass to the survivor, the lower the original payment. For example, all else being equal, an annuity with a 75 percent survivorship payment would pay less than an annuity with a 65 percent survivorship payment. This is an important option to consider because living costs will typically decline (though not by 50 percent) when the first person dies. And the lower the survivorship percentage investors are willing to accept, the lower will be the cost of the annuity.
- **Interest rates**—The higher interest rates are at the time of annuitization, the higher the payments will be. This is

perfectly logical because insurance companies can afford to make higher payments when they can invest the premium amounts (that is, the lump sum exchanged for the annuity payments) at higher rates.

■ **The insurance company selected**—For the same annuitant and circumstances, payment levels will vary significantly from one insurance company to another. Therefore, it pays to shop around when purchasing an immediate annuity. However, beware of purchasing annuities from insurance companies with weak credit ratings. Low-rated companies are likely to be the ones that are paying higher rates because they need to do so to attract business. Since the decision to annuitize is irrevocable and credit risk increases as the length of the commitment increases, we do not recommend purchasing annuities from companies that have a rating of below AAA. The same recommendation would hold for the purchase of any long-term insurance, such as life, disability, and long-term care. Investors want to have the greatest chance of actually receiving the contracted benefit. The best way to do that is to buy only from a company with the highest credit rating.

Now that we have discussed some of the basic features of immediate annuities, let's move on to the question of why one would want to annuitize a portion of his or her assets in the first place.

THE BENEFITS OF ANNUITIZATION

For logical reasons we insure against many different types of risks. We buy insurance to protect our homes, cars, and lives. We also buy medical, dental, and disability insurance. And many people even purchase travel insurance. We buy insurance to transfer some or all of the risk (to the insurance company) that we prefer not to bear ourselves. Thus, the purchase of insurance is really about diversifying risks that we find unacceptable to bear on our own, because the costs of not being insured might be too great. The same logic applies to the purchase of fixed annuities.

At its most basic level, the decision to purchase an immediate annuity is a decision to insure against longevity risk—the risk that an investor might outlive his or her financial assets. Keeping in mind that the "cost" of outliving financial assets is extremely high, the purchase of fixed annuities makes sense for those individuals who run that risk. Those who run that risk should strongly consider transferring some of that risk to a financially strong insurer.

When evaluating longevity risk, consider that a healthy male (female) at age sixty-five has a 50 percent change of living *beyond* the age of eighty-five (eighty-eight) and a 25 percent change of living beyond the age of ninety-two (ninety-four). For a healthy couple, both of whom are sixty-five, there is a 50 percent chance that one will live beyond the age of ninety-two and a 25 percent chance that one will live beyond the age of ninety-seven.[1]

Immediate annuities protect against longevity risk because payments are guaranteed to continue for as long as the annuitants live or, if the investors choose a joint-life with survivorship option, as long as one of the annuitants is alive. Further—and this is important—the size of these payments will typically be higher than the level of withdrawals that one could safely take from a portfolio of traditional investments of similar risk, such as a bond portfolio. For example, **TABLE 5.1** shows first the annual, lifetime income that a sixty-year-old male could currently receive from a single-life-only immediate annuity with a $100,000 premium. In the second column is the amount that he could safely withdraw annually for thirty years from a $100,000 investment in a 30-year U.S. Treasury bond, if he were to spend the entire principal amount and all the earned interest.

Note that the annuity not only provides for approximately 20 percent larger payments, it also guarantees these payments for the entire

Table 5.1   Annuity Payout Compared to Treasury Bond Payout

	Immediate Annuity	Treasury Bond
Duration of payment	Entire life	30 years
Amount of payment	$7,824	$6,446

Note: Annuity payment comes from immediateannuity.com.

life of the annuitant. This contrasts with the limited 30-year period faced by the bond investor. Given the continuing improvements in medical technology and health care in general, it is entirely possible that a sixty-year-old male could live longer than thirty years. In this simplified example, an annuitant would have payments for the entire length of his life. On the other hand, a bond owner would have spent down all of the bond's principal and interest payments in thirty years.

Mortality Credits Make It Possible

How are insurance companies able to pay more than an individual can earn from a traditional investment of similar risk? The answer is one of the most important—but perhaps least understood—features of immediate annuities. The short answer is that those annuitants in the insurance pool who do not live to life expectancy are effectively subsidizing those who do. This is how insurance companies are able to provide better "returns"—while still earning a profit—than individuals can earn on similar investments. The difference is the result of what are called *mortality credits*.

The concept of a mortality credit is illustrated by the following example: Suppose that on January 1 we have fifty eighty-five-year-old males who each agree to contribute $100 to a pool of investments earning 5 percent. They further agree to split the total pool equally among those who are still alive at the end of the year. Also, suppose that we (but not they) know for certain that five of the fifty people will pass away by the end of the year. This means that the total pool of $5,250 ($5,000 principal plus $250 interest) will be split among just forty-five people. The result is that each person will receive $116.67, or a return on investment of 16.67 percent. If, instead, each person had invested independently of the pool, the total amount of money earned would have been $105, or a return on investment of 5 percent. The difference in returns is the mortality credit. What this example shows is very similar to how an immediate annuity functions. It also illustrates why it can be a good option for some individuals.

WHEN ANNUITIES CAN BE THE RIGHT CHOICE

The following example illustrates why fixed annuities can be an appropriate investment in the right circumstance. John and Jane Smith—both sixty-five years old—have identified some concerns and goals related to their retirement. First, they realize that their portfolio is of relatively modest size. When combined with their retirement income from Social Security, it is just enough to furnish them with sufficient income to provide for a comfortable retirement. They would like to be able to spend a bit more in retirement and would also like to have more "margin for error." However, they do not want to take any action that would increase their chance of running out of money during retirement.

Second, they are both concerned about the risk that they might live longer than expected and would not have sufficient assets to fund their desired spending in their later years. Further, they are worried that if they do live beyond their life expectancy, their two sons might have to help them financially. Their worst fear is that they would become financially dependent on their children.

Third, while they would like to leave a modest estate to their two sons, this goal is of minor importance relative to the goal of not becoming dependent on their children. They are also secure in the knowledge that their children have both been successful and have their financial affairs in good order.

The purchase of a fixed annuity would provide the Smiths the peace of mind they are seeking. The combination of the higher "return" (resulting from the mortality credits) and guaranteed payments for life helps the Smiths achieve their desired standard of living and decreases the risk of outliving their assets (and becoming a financial burden on their children). For the Smiths, these benefits outweigh the loss of liquidity and the potential reduction in the value of the estate should they die before their life expectancy.

Faced with the same situation, another couple might come to a different conclusion. There is not a one-size-fits-all answer. It is an individual decision that should be made by carefully weighing the costs and benefits.

EVIDENCE FROM ACADEMIA

Several academic papers have discussed the benefits of annuitization. Most have compared the ability of portfolios with and without immediate annuities to provide a certain level of income in retirement or have examined the probabilities that these portfolios would be exhausted prior to the end of the analysis. The portfolios without immediate annuities typically consist of diversified holdings of stocks and bonds. The portfolios with immediate annuities maintain a certain percentage, such as 75 percent, in traditional investments like diversified stocks and bonds and put the rest of the assets in immediate annuities.

The 2001 study, "Making Retirement Income Last a Lifetime," by John Ameriks, Robert Veres, and Mark J. Warshawsky, found that portfolios with immediate annuities ran out of money far less frequently than those that did not have them (**TABLE 5.2**). For example, the "growth" portfolio in the study—60 percent stocks, 30 percent bonds, and 10 percent short-term investments—ran out of money 20 percent of the time over thirty-five-year horizons and 27 percent of the time over forty-year horizons. Most people would consider these probabilities to be unacceptable. Thus, people in similar situations would have to consider working longer, saving more, or spending less to reduce their chances of running out of money. Annuities provide an alternative.

The study found that the "growth" portfolios with 50 percent in annuities (that is, for every $1 in the portfolio, $0.50 is annuitized and $0.50 is invested in the growth portfolio) ran out of money only 8 percent of the time over thirty-five-year horizons and 14 percent of the time over forty-year horizons—essentially cutting the risk of failure in half. This is a substantial reduction in risk that did not involve lifestyle changes, such as working longer or spending less.[2]

Table 5.2   Likelihood of Outliving Investable Assets

	35-Year Horizon	40-Year Horizon
Portfolio without a fixed annuity	20%	27%
Portfolio with 50% allocation to a fixed annuity	8%	14%

The 2003 study, "Allocation During Retirement: Adding Annuities to the Mix," found very similar results. Using historical data from 1972 through 2000, author William Reichenstein found that partially annuitized portfolios were prematurely exhausted less often than portfolios with no annuity component. His reasoning for using data starting in 1972 was that the early years of the period of the study were a time when the returns were very poor and inflation was high. This is just the type of scenario that can cause investment portfolios to "fail" (deplete all assets while the investor is still alive).

Reichenstein tested a balanced portfolio with 40 percent stock and 60 percent fixed-income investments. He then tested similar portfolios in which 25 percent and 50 percent of the portfolios were annuitized. The balanced portfolio ran out of money in the twenty-sixth year. The portfolio in which 25 percent was annuitized survived until the twenty-ninth year. And the portfolio in which 50 percent was annuitized was able to meet the withdrawal needs of the hypothetical investor for the entire period.[3]

These studies show that fixed immediate annuities can be valuable tools for investors looking to increase their retirement income and reduce their risk of running out of money. This is not surprising given the advantages of immediate annuities, including mortality credits and guaranteed payments throughout life.

WHEN TO PURCHASE A FIXED ANNUITY

In general, the research indicates that it is preferable to delay annuitization (see the Glossary) until the annuitants reach their mid-seventies or early eighties. The 2001 study, "Optimal Annuitization Policies: Analysis of the Options," by Moshe Milevsky, concluded that a sixty-five-year-old female has an 85 percent chance of being able to beat the rate of return from a life annuity until age eighty. For males the figure was 80 percent.[4]

There are two main reasons for this. The first is that the insurance company—in addition to covering its costs of marketing, underwriting, and issuing the contracts—is building in a profit. The second is that the insurance companies that issue these policies are aware that they are being adversely selected—the most likely buyers of longevity insurance are those who have a good reason to believe that they will live a longer-than-average life. Thus, unless they are highly risk averse, investors should probably not buy an immediate fixed annuity until approaching age eighty. Similarly, if an investor is considering buying a deferred fixed annuity, he or she should consider delaying payments until age eighty.

We do offer two caveats: There are risks in delaying the purchase of an immediate annuity. First, there is the risk that if life expectancy increases, the cost of the annuity will increase. A 2006 study, "Rational Decumulation," by David F. Babbel and Craig B. Merrill, calculated that a 1 percent annual improvement in mortality is associated with roughly a 5 percent increase in the price of an annuity, or a 5 percent reduction in monthly payouts.[5] Second, there is the risk that interest rates will fall, leading to lower monthly payouts upon annuitizing.

INFLATION-INDEXED IMMEDIATE ANNUITIES

Fixed immediate annuities are by far the most prevalent and best-known type of immediate annuity. However, they are not the *only* type of immediate annuity. Two other immediate annuity structures are inflation-indexed (or real) immediate annuities and variable immediate annuities. (See Chapter 17 for a discussion on variable annuities.) As we compare their payout structures, keep in mind that almost every feature, such as mortality credits and choice of benefit periods, of fixed immediate annuities are offered by inflation-indexed immediate annuities.

A relatively new product, inflation-indexed immediate annuities are easy to understand if one understands fixed immediate annuities. While inflation-indexed annuities offer a lower initial payment than fixed immediate annuities do, the payment is not fixed. Instead, it is adjusted—up or down—for the rate of inflation. The inflation adjustment is usually made at the first of each year, based on the percentage increase in inflation during the prior year.

The difference between the initial payments of fixed and indexed annuities depends on a number of factors, including the age of the investor at annuitization and the chosen index or level of indexation (for example, the consumer price index or a fixed 2 percent annual increase). The initial payment from an indexed annuity could be 30 percent less than one for an analogous fixed annuity, and in some circumstances the difference could be even greater. This reduced initial payment is in exchange for what could be much larger payments in the future. It is important that investors are comfortable with the difference in initial payout before purchasing an inflation-indexed annuity—the decision is likely to be irreversible.

The decision to choose the inflation-indexed annuity should depend on how adversely affected the buyer would be by *unexpected* inflation. The more negatively affected the buyer would be by *unexpected* inflation, the more she should consider this type of annuity.

Individuals also have the ability to choose a payment option for which the payments increase by a fixed percentage each year. Such an option offers some measure of protection against inflation— although payments may not grow as fast as the rate of inflation.

For example, if investors choose an option that inflates payments at 1 percent per year, inflation could easily exceed this value. Of course, by choosing a modest percentage increase, their initial payment will also likely be higher than if they chose to have the payments grow with the actual inflation rate. Again, it should be emphasized that inflation-indexed immediate annuities are a relatively new product, and it is important to fully understand all the terms of a particular inflation-indexed annuity before purchasing one.

SUMMARY

As they approach retirement, many individuals begin to consider whether they should annuitize at least some portion of their investable net worth. Despite the obvious benefits of a guaranteed lifetime income stream and the power of mortality credits, the decision is often a very difficult one for most people. The reasons for this are that the decision is irrevocable and if the annuitant dies prematurely his or her estate will have been depleted with little to show for it. Individuals are often paralyzed by the fear that, in hindsight, the decision will backfire.

While the loss of liquidity is permanent, and the risk of premature death is real, the positive attributes of fixed annuities make them an alternative that should be considered by many. Obviously, those who have enough net worth that they don't have to worry about running out of assets can self-insure (for example, use their financial assets to pay for long-term care) against longevity risk. However, for the rest of the world, transferring some longevity risk can be a prudent decision. Remember, investors can still run out of investable assets, but a lifetime annuity will last—well, a lifetime. So the decision is not just whether to annuitize, but also how much to annuitize. The more that gets annuitized, the greater the guaranteed payments, but less investable assets will be left.

Stable-Value Funds 6

At the end of the first quarter of 2004, money market accounts (a traditional safe harbor for investors) were yielding less than 1 percent, the lowest level in decades. Ten-year Treasury bonds were yielding less than 4 percent. If interest rates rose, longer-term bond prices could fall dramatically. Investors who were unwilling to, unable to, or had no need to take the risks of equity ownership were searching for safe investments that could provide higher-than-money-market yields without significant credit, price, or inflation risk.

Investors' search for incremental yield intensifies whenever interest rates fall to low levels. Fortunately, there is an investment vehicle that fits the bill, delivering somewhat higher returns without forcing the investor to take significant credit or inflation (price) risk. The product is called a *stable-value fund*. Stable-value funds are also called *interest-income*, *principal-preservation*, or *guaranteed-interest* funds.

Stable-value investments are fixed-income investment vehicles offered through defined-contribution savings and profit-sharing plans, 529 college savings plans, and individual retirement accounts (IRAs). The assets in stable-value funds are generally very high-quality bonds and insurance contracts that are purchased directly from banks and insurance companies that guarantee to maintain the value of the principal and all accumulated interest. They deliver the desired safety and stability by preserving principal and accumulated earnings. In that respect, they are similar to money market funds, but they offer higher returns.

Stable-value options in participant-directed defined-contribution plans allow participants access to their accounts at full value for withdrawals and transfers. However, since these plans are often purchased within retirement plans that have their own withdrawal restrictions, there might be withdrawal restrictions. In addition, the stable-value fund itself may impose restrictions.

Unique Risk and Return Characteristics

A 2004 study, "Why Investors Want Stable-Value Funds," by the Stable Value Investment Association, covering the twenty-year period ending in 2002, found that stable-value funds outperformed 30-day Treasury bills by 3.2 percent a year (8.9 percent versus 5.7 percent). And they achieved that return with only slightly greater risk. Stable-value funds experienced an annual standard deviation of 2.3 percent, just slightly higher than the 2.1 percent experienced by Treasury bills. And their return virtually matched the return of the Lehman Intermediate Government/Credit Index—and it did so while experiencing less than one-half of the volatility.

The study found another positive attribute of stable-value funds—they exhibited very low correlation with stocks. Their correlation with the S&P 500 Index was just 0.2. Compare that to the correlation with equities of the Lehman Intermediate Government/Credit Index at 0.3 or the correlation with equities of 1-month Treasuries at 0.4.[1]

The evidence demonstrates that stable-value funds produced higher returns than short-term instruments and did so with similar risk. They produced returns similar to those of intermediate-term instruments, but with less risk. We can conclude, therefore, that stable-value funds offer unique risk-return characteristics that allow investors to create portfolios that are more efficient at delivering returns for a given level of risk. This helps explain why they are included in two-thirds of employee-directed 401(k) and 403(b) plans, representing more than 33 percent of assets that, according to the Stable Value Investment Association, totaled about $400 billion in value by 2006.[2]

To gain an understanding of these vehicles, we will look at the types of investments they make and how they are able to offer stability of value yet provide attractive returns.

INVESTMENT PORTFOLIOS

Until recently, most stable-value vehicles were structured as guaranteed investment contracts (GICs). These are contracts issued by financial institutions—typically a highly rated insurance company, though it could also be a bank—guaranteeing investors a fixed rate of return. It is worth noting that in the 1980s several insurers (such as Executive Life, Mutual Benefit Life, and Confederation Life) financed by high-yield bonds sold GICs to retirement plans and then went under. However, even in these three cases, which represented less than 1 percent of the stable-value market, investors were *eventually* made whole.[3]

The result is that while stable-value funds may still hold insurance company–issued GICs (or similar instruments) as well as cash equivalents, today most stable-value assets are structured as *synthetic GICs*, also known as *wrapped bonds*. Synthetic GICs are created by the purchase of short- to intermediate-term bonds, including U.S. government and agency bonds, mortgages, and asset-backed securities. The bonds purchased are generally of the highest-credit-quality ratings (AAA and AA). Some vehicles include a provision for a very limited allocation, such as 10 percent, to lower-rated bonds. In addition, provisions are often made for the portfolio to invest in futures, options, and forward currency contracts. The portfolio is then protected from fluctuation in value by the purchase of insurance "wrappers." If the market value of a stable-value portfolio falls below the book value of the portfolio, the insurer pays the difference, keeping the fund's value stable. The wrapper allows the stable-value vehicle to fix its net asset value at, say, $10 a share (similar to a money market fund). This is why returns are relatively stable.

However, a stable-value fund is not a money market fund, and there can be no assurance that the fund will be able to maintain a stable value over time. Also, note that if a fund holds derivative positions, it can be more volatile than a money market fund and less liquid than traditional securities. The potential greater volatility of these instruments could lead to greater losses.

Typically the insurance wrapper costs the fund from 0.05 percent to 0.1 percent, depending on the credit quality of the portfolio, the structure of the wrapper, and the supply-demand conditions of the market for this type of portfolio insurance. Because of the insurance wrapper, the returns for the funds come solely from their yield. Thus, there is no potential for capital gains and very little risk of loss to consider (unless the credit rating of the insurer and the underlying instruments are not of the highest investment grades).

RISKS

Stable-value funds appear to be a good deal for investors, providing returns similar to those of high-grade intermediate-term bonds with the volatility of a money market account. However, while the risks are minimal, the investments are not risk-free. The earnings of stable-value vehicles can be outpaced by inflation, their yields typically lag interest trends, and unlike money market funds that invest solely in U.S. government securities, they are not entirely immune to a credit blowup among the issuers of the bonds they hold. The 2007 crisis in subprime debt is a good example of the risks that investments in stable-value funds may entail. Although the insurers put their financial weight behind stabilizing the fund's net asset value (NAV)—"guaranteeing" that investors would never experience a loss in their invested capital—they do not shield the fund from credit problems. While credit blowups do not affect the NAV, credit problems can result in lower future yields for a stable-value fund. In addition, investors accept the credit risk of the insurance provider. Thus, it is important to analyze both the risk profile (credit rating, maturity, individual bond structure, and liquidity) of the individual securities held in the portfolio and the credit rating of the insurance providers. Many stable-value investment vehicles diversify (but do not eliminate) the credit risk of the insurance provider by purchasing contracts from several providers.

Costs

If the characteristics of stable-value funds are of interest, be sure to keep a particularly close eye on costs, as with any investment vehicle. Within defined-contribution plans such as 401(k)s and 403(b)s, such annual expenses average less than 0.5 percent, but in IRAs the fees are likely to be as high as 1 percent, according to the Stable Value Investment Association.

Restrictions

Most stable-value offerings place restrictions on when or how often investors can withdraw cash from the fund. For example, they may limit the number of withdrawals that can be made during a specified time period. Consequently, they typically don't offer the same degree of liquidity or ready access to one's cash as do money market funds. Note that the liquidity restrictions allow the stable-value funds to invest in less-liquid, longer-term, and higher-yielding investments. For example, most stable-value funds have a weighted average duration of between one and a half and four and a half years.[4] As an additional restriction, some plans force investors to move their withdrawal amount into an equity fund, instead of another fixed-income investment, which prevents investors from shifting their stable-value assets into the bond market whenever it looks as though interest rates might decline or into money market funds whenever it looks as though interest rates might rise. Also, if the investment vehicle is inside a retirement plan, it will be subject to the rules of that plan.

Returns Change Slowly Over Time

A stable-value investment vehicle typically contains a number of GICs and individual bonds. Each time a contract or bond matures, the principal sum is paid back to the fund. The fund must then reinvest the proceeds in a new contract or bond at whatever interest rate is prevailing at the time. If rates are going down, the current rate will be lower than the rate that was being earned previously, and the return to the stable-value fund will gradually decline. Similarly, if current rates are higher than the rate on the matured contract, the stable-value fund's return will gradually increase. Most stable-value managers choose to ladder or diversify the maturities of the contracts held within the stable-value fund to smooth these changes. Because book value accounting returns are much more stable and the correlation of stable-value funds to equity holdings is lower than it is for bond funds, stable-value funds are excellent diversification tools for a portfolio.

Cash Flows Can Affect Returns

If large sums of money flow into a stable-value fund when interest rates are high, and small sums of money flow into a stable-value fund when interest rates are low, everyone in the fund enjoys higher-than-average returns because more money is invested in contracts that continue to pay high rates until their maturity date. The reverse is also true.

The timing of the cash flows is typically the main concern for the manager of the stable-value fund. If the manager didn't have the ability to accurately forecast contributions and withdrawals, managing the fund for stable value would become very difficult. In addition, the cost of the insurance wrappers would certainly increase (withdrawals would rise whenever interest rates increased and losses would be incurred). This is why stable-value funds are only available in tax-exempt or tax-deferred account environments with heavy withdrawal restrictions. The complete investment freedom of a taxable-account environment has proven to be too great a hurdle to overcome.

Summary

Well-designed stable-value funds are like the old reliable family trip to the beach. They are appropriate for all investors who allocate some portion of their portfolio to fixed-income assets. The three major benefits are as follows:

- Returns are higher than those of similar, high-quality short-term investments, but the risk is less.
- Returns are comparable to those of high quality, intermediate-term investments, but the risk is smaller.
- Returns are less correlated with the returns of equities than are the returns of intermediate-term bonds with equities, making them superior diversification tools.

With these benefits in mind, we offer the following recommendations:

- A significant amount of due diligence should be undertaken on the creditworthiness of both the underlying investments and any insurance contracts, as well as on any restrictions on withdrawals.
- The vehicle should carry contracts with multiple, high-quality insurers (insurers that carry at least a rating of AA or the equivalent from one of the major rating agencies).
- More than 90 percent of the portfolio should be covered with insurance contracts.
- At least 90 percent of the vehicle's assets should be in investment-grade bonds that are rated at least AA.
- The average maturity and duration of assets should be short-term (for example, not longer than about three years). This helps ensure that the fund won't be stuck with longer-term, low-yielding bonds if rates start to rise. This is especially important for investors, such as retirees, who are highly sensitive to the risk of unexpected inflation.
- If the portfolio uses derivatives, the investor should thoroughly understand how they are used and whether any leverage is involved.
- The fund's management team should have a record of producing returns that are competitive with its stable-value peers or an appropriate bond market index.
- Costs are critical. Therefore, consider only very low cost vehicles, preferably with annual expenses under 0.5 percent.

An example of a stable-value product that should be considered is the TIAA Traditional Annuity, available in many 403(b) accounts and in the TIAA-CREF IRA. This product is backed by the claims-paying ability of TIAA-CREF, a highly rated (AAA) insurance company, and it carries no sales or surrender charges.

PART 2

The Flawed

High-Yield (Junk) Bonds   7

THE SEARCH FOR higher returns often leads investors to the world of high-yield bonds, also called *junk bonds*. Junk bonds have lower credit ratings (below BBB from Standard & Poor's and below Baa from Moody's) and higher yields than more creditworthy securities. Those higher yields, of course, are compensation for an investor's willingness to take incremental risks. **TABLE 7.1** describes the risks connoted by each rating in more detail.

Note that Moody's describes any bond with a rating of Ba or below as *speculative*—differentiating it from a sound investment. Logically, the more speculative (risky) the investment, the greater the yield needs to be to entice investors to assume this incremental risk.

A fixed-income instrument plays three primary roles in a portfolio: to serve as a liquid reserve in the event of emergencies; to generate a stable cash flow; and to provide the portfolio with stability, allowing investors to take equity risk.

As we will demonstrate, junk bonds are too risky and too exposed to equity risk to serve these purposes. However, they do possess two other characteristics that should be analyzed before deciding against this asset class.

First, junk bonds offer the potential for high returns. Second, they also exhibit nonperfect correlation (a correlation of less than 1) with equities, U.S. government securities, and the securities of corporate bonds with the highest credit ratings (AAA and AA). This suggests the possibility that junk bonds might have some diversification benefits.

Table 7.1 Credit Ratings for Standard & Poor's and Moody's

S&P 500	Moody's	Description of Risk
AAA	Aaa	Almost riskless, just below U.S. Treasury obligations. Future changes *unlikely* to impair debt rating.
AA	Aa	High quality. Future changes *may* impair rating.
A	A	Good quality. *Susceptible* to impairment of rating.
BBB	Baa	Medium quality; lowest investment grade. Have *some speculative characteristics*.
BB	Ba	*Speculative*; noninvestment grade.
B, CCC, CC	B, Caa	Very speculative.
C	Ca	Extremely speculative.
D	C	Default.

For example, for the period from 1980 through 1992, SEI Capital Markets Research found that the twenty-month correlation of high-yield bonds and intermediate government bonds was 0.59, and their correlation with the S&P 500 Index was just 0.46. Alternatively, the correlation of the returns on government bonds and investment-grade corporate bonds was 0.95.[1]

The almost perfect correlation of government bonds and investment-grade bonds is evidence that the latter contain virtually no equity component. Therefore, most of the return on investment-grade bonds is explained by the return on government bonds. Since government bonds have no credit risk, the only thing explaining their return is interest-rate risk. Thus, we can also conclude that almost all of the returns of high-credit-quality fixed-income instruments derive from term risk. However, this is decidedly *not* the case for high-yield bonds.

EXPLAINING THE LOW CORRELATION

It is easy to understand why high-yield bonds exhibit relatively low correlation with investment-grade bonds. First, the higher yield of low-grade bonds makes their duration shorter. Thus, they are less sensitive to movements in interest rates than investment-grade bonds are. And their *effective* duration is lower, because callable low-grade bonds are often called earlier—they have weaker call protection than investment-grade bonds.

Furthermore, their credit ratings are more likely to rise. Low-grade bonds are also more sensitive to changes in stock prices than are investment-grade bonds (which, with rare exception, respond only to changes in interest rates). Treasury bonds, of course, *only* respond to changes in interest rates.[2] High-yield bonds also maintain a low correlation with equities because of their bond characteristics (that is, their sensitivity to interest rates).

That being said, low correlations alone are not enough to tell us whether the higher yield is a sufficient reason for investing in this asset class, nor do they determine the diversification benefit of adding a high-yield-bonds allocation to a portfolio. The following sections tackle each of these subjects in more detail.

IS HIGHER YIELD WORTH HIGHER RISK?

As stated earlier, junk bonds offer higher yields than more creditworthy bonds because they are inherently riskier. To understand whether the higher return is worth the increased risk, we need to find out more about what risks are being compensated in the spread (the difference in yield) between junk bonds and Treasury bonds or highly rated corporate debt—the kind of fixed-income instruments we recommend.

A major 2001 study, "Explaining the Rate Spread on Corporate Bonds,"[3] by Edwin J. Elton, Martin J. Gruber, Deepak Agrawal, and Christopher Mann, posed three pertinent questions:

- How much of the spread between corporate and Treasury bonds is explained by expected losses from defaults? Some percentage of corporate bonds is likely to default, and defaults generally result in recovery rates below 100 percent. Furthermore, the lower the credit rating, the lower the recovery percentage. Investors must be compensated for the greater expected losses.
- How much of the spread is explained by the tax premium? Interest on U.S. government securities is not taxed at the state or local level. However, interest on corporate debt is taxed. Investors must be compensated for the tax differential.

■ Is the incremental risk of corporate bonds systematic (non-diversifiable) or unsystematic (diversifiable)? Investors are compensated with risk premiums for systematic risks, but they are not compensated for unsystematic risks.

The study's conclusions regarding these questions can be summarized this way:

■ The difference in tax treatment and expected default losses does not adequately explain the spread. For example, the authors found that expected losses account for no more than 25 percent of the corporate spread. In the case of a 10-year A-rated corporate bond, just 18 percent of the spread was explained by default risk. The difference in tax treatment accounted for 36 percent of the spread. In other words, default risk accounts for a *surprisingly small* fraction of the premium in corporate rates over Treasuries. There must be another source of risk premium demanded by investors.

■ The Fama-French three-factor model (see the Glossary) explains as much as 85 percent of the spread that is not accounted for by taxes and expected default loss. This means that most of the spread is compensation for three risks: the risk of the overall stock market; the risk of small (versus large) companies; and the risk of value (versus growth) companies. The lower the credit rating—and the longer the maturity—the greater the explanatory power of the model (its inherent accuracy). Thus, much of the expected return on high-yield debt is explained by risk premiums associated with equities, not debt. These risks are systematic risks that cannot be diversified away.

A 2006 study, "Personal Taxes, Endogenous Default, and Corporate Bond Yield Spreads," by Howard Qi, Sheen Liu, and Chunchi Wu, focused on the tax issue and found that personal taxes explain almost all of the spread between shorter-term high-grade bonds and Treasuries. That is exactly what we should expect, because there is almost no credit risk in short-term, high-quality bonds. Taxes explain about 60 percent of the spread for longer-term, high-quality bonds. This is logical, as the credit risk of corporate bonds—even high-grade ones—increases with time. But the picture is quite different for high-yield bonds: Personal taxes explain about 60 percent of the spread for shorter-term bonds and less than 40 percent for long-term bonds.[4]

These findings demonstrate three important facts. First, corporate debt contains very little risk that is not explained by other factors. As we have seen, most of the returns are explained by term risk, taxes, and equity risks. Second, despite its low correlation with other portfolio assets, high-yield debt provides almost no unique benefit in terms of portfolio diversification. Third, it also helps explain why corporate bond spreads *appear* to be so large. (There is a tax component, as well as an equity component, in the security.)

THE IMPORTANCE OF EQUITY RISK

HYBRID SECURITIES AND ASSET ALLOCATION

If, for example, investors are considering a 60 percent equity and a 40 percent fixed-income portfolio based on their risk tolerance, they might be advised to allocate one-fourth of their fixed-income holdings to high-yield debt (10 percent of the portfolio). However, that would create a problem, because high-yield debt is really a *hybrid* instrument. While it is considered debt, it has equity-like risk characteristics. (The three-factor model partly explains the returns.)

Since high-yield debt is really about taking on equity risk, the investors will actually be holding a portfolio that has more equity risk than would a 60 percent equity, 40 percent fixed-income portfolio. *As the results of the aforementioned study show, the lower the credit rating and the longer the maturity of the debt, the more equity-like the high-yield security becomes.*

That high-yield bonds are hybrid securities is also supported by the findings of "Comovements of Low-Grade Debt and Equity Returns of Highly Leveraged Firms," a 1994 study by Hilary Shane that evaluated 208 low-rated bonds and an index of the stocks of the issuers represented in the bond portfolio. Shane concluded, "Significant positive correlations of the all-inclusive, low-grade bond portfolio with the matched equity portfolio and with the Treasury bonds support the intuition that low-grade bonds are hybrid securities."[5]

Evidence Supported by Theory

The case that an equity component in high-yield bonds makes them hybrid securities is also supported by theory. "In effect, a corporate bond is a combination of a pure interest-rate instrument and a short position in a put (see the Glossary) on the issuer's equity. The put is triggered by a decline in the value of the issuer's assets to less than the value of its liabilities, resulting in a default—putting the equity to the bondholders. For a highly rated company, the put is well out of the money and is not likely to be exercised.

"Consequently, the option has a negligible impact on the price movement of the bonds, which is more sensitive to interest-rate fluctuations. However, the possibility of a high-yield bond default is a realistic enough prospect to enable the equity put to materially affect the bond's price. With the equity-related option exerting a greater influence on its price movement, the high-yield bond tracks government bonds—pure interest-rate instruments—less closely than does the investment-grade bond."[6]

Do High-Yield Bonds Have a Role?

As stated before, fixed-income instruments serve three main roles in a portfolio: a reserve for emergencies, a reliable source of cash flow, and a stable foundation for a portfolio that allows investors to take equity risk.

The risks of high-yield bonds make them inappropriate for consideration for meeting the first two objectives—safety of principal and stability of income. While it is true that high-yield debt has non-perfect correlation with equities, the correlation of the highest-rated bonds with equities is even lower. Thus, investing in high-yield debt isn't necessary to obtain the diversification benefit. In addition, the correlation of high-yield bonds with equities may increase at just the wrong time—when the risk of equities shows up. In other words, junk bonds don't mix well with the inherent risks of equities.

Several other issues impact the decision on whether high-yield securities should play a role in the portfolio. They include liquidity, asset location, and the distribution of returns.

ILLIQUID SECURITIES

High-yield bonds are generally illiquid instruments, and the lower the credit rating, the more illiquid the instrument is likely to be. For example, a typical U.S. high-yield index includes about 1,500 securities, with only about 25 percent of them trading at least once per month.[7] The less liquid an asset class, the greater the trading costs will be, including not only the costs of bid-offer spreads, but also market-impact costs. In addition, in times of crisis, the markets for illiquid assets can virtually dry up; buyers disappear and sales can only be made if the seller is willing to accept a severe discount. (It's like trying to sell a condominium in a glutted market when prices are falling.)

As a result, investors in high-yield bonds demand an incremental risk premium. Thus, a liquidity premium must explain part of the differential in yields between high-yield bonds and Treasuries. Unfortunately, this liquidity risk rears its ugly head most in times of crisis, just when equity prices are under pressure. This leads to high correlation with equity prices just when investors need low correlation—again illustrating that correlations are not static values.

OTHER NEGATIVE CHARACTERISTICS

Unfortunately, high-yield bonds also have other negative qualities—ones that are rarely discussed and therefore little known. For example, they often carry call provisions. Investors generally think of the call feature in terms of the risk that the bond will be called if interest rates fall, and this is true for high-grade bonds. However, for lower-rated bonds, the call feature creates an additional risk. The risk is that the credit rating of the issue will improve sufficiently for the issuer to call the bond and issue a new bond with a higher rating, which lowers interest costs.

A similar risk is created by what is known as a *clawback* provision. This refers to the fact that some high-yield securities allow the issuer to call a predetermined amount of the bond, if the issuer is able to do an equity offering. The good news for investors in a clawback scenario is that the investment risk is reduced. However, that doesn't do investors any good if it's *their* bond that is called.

Another issue related to illiquid assets is often overlooked: Illiquidity *artificially* induces what is known as *positive serial correlation* (also known as *autocorrelation*) of returns. Serial correlation is the correlation of a variable with itself over successive time intervals. A "real-world" example will clarify the concept.

Imagine that a person needs to sell his home to take a job in another town. How would he determine the price at which he should list his home? Typically, he would look at the sale prices of similar properties. But what if no sales had occurred in the past year? And what if economic conditions had changed dramatically during that period? Would the last sales price truly reflect current valuations for the homes in his neighborhood? If he believed those prices were accurate, he would be assuming that prices had been stable. Of course, both assumptions are likely to be incorrect.

The calculation of the value of an index—or the value of the assets in a portfolio—that prices bonds for which there has been no active market will include prices that are either outdated (stale) or are based on what is known as *matrix pricing* (an attempt to estimate the market price by evaluating the prices of bonds that have *similar* risk characteristics, but that have traded more recently).

If estimates are based on prices that are outdated, the true price is probably different. Thus, the price may be overstated or understated. Both outdated prices and matrix pricing tend to give the appearance of greater price stability than is actually being experienced, if the securities had actually traded.

Thus, illiquidity and the resulting autocorrelation lead to an underestimation of volatility and of the real risks of an asset class. The result is that for portfolios of illiquid securities, reported returns will tend to be smoother than true economic returns, thus understating volatility and overstating risk-adjusted performance measures, such as the Sharpe ratio. The issue of serial correlation and its implications is important to keep in mind when considering any illiquid investment (including emerging market bonds, venture capital, and hedge funds, which we discuss in later chapters).

DISTRIBUTION OF RETURNS MATTERS

Yet another risk-related issue exists that should be considered before investing in high-yield bonds. Risky or illiquid assets tend to have a distribution of returns that exhibits *skewness* and excess *kurtosis*. We will define these terms first and then explain why it is necessary to understand their implications.

Skewness measures the asymmetry of a returns distribution when the historical pattern does not resemble a normal bell curve. Negative skewness occurs when the return values less than the mean are fewer but *farther* from the mean than the values greater than the mean. This pattern suggests a greater potential for large losses.

For example: The return series of –30 percent, 5 percent, 10 percent, and 15 percent has a mean of 0 percent. There is only one return less than 0 percent and three higher, but the one that is negative is much farther from 0 than the positive ones. Positive skewness occurs when the values greater than the mean are fewer but *farther* from the mean than are the values less than the mean. So there is greater potential for large gains.

In general, people like assets with positive skewness, as evidenced by their willingness to accept low, or even negative, expected returns for assets that exhibit this characteristic. The classic example is a lottery ticket, which has *negative* expected returns, but has *positive* skewness. As we all know, there are precious few who win the lottery (a positive outcome) and an enormous number who lose (a negative outcome). However, for buyers of lottery tickets, the benefit of a large, but unlikely, positive outcome is much greater than the cost of a small, but highly likely, negative one.

On the other hand, most people do not like assets with negative skewness. This explains why people generally purchase insurance against low-frequency events, such as disability or fires. While these events are unlikely to occur, they carry the potential for large losses.

The problem for investors is that high-yield debt exhibits negative skewness. Mark Anson researched the period from January 1990 through June 2000 and found that high-yield bonds—as measured by the Salomon Smith Barney High Yield Composite Index—exhibited skewness of –0.43, similar to that exhibited by stocks. For the same period, the S&P 500 had skewness of –0.50.[8]

High-yield debt returns also exhibit high kurtosis. Kurtosis is a measurement of the degree to which exceptional values that are much larger or smaller than the average occur more frequently (high kurtosis) or less frequently (low kurtosis) than in a normal (bell-shaped) distribution. High kurtosis results in exceptional values that are called *fat tails*. Fat tails indicate a higher percentage of very low and very high returns than would be expected with a normal distribution. Conversely, low kurtosis results in *thin tails*.

The following example provides an illustration of high kurtosis:

Suppose that the average monthly return for an asset, over a period of thirty years (360 months), was 1 percent, with a 2.5 percent standard deviation of monthly returns. If the distribution of returns were approximately normal, then about 2.5 percent of the monthly returns—or about nine of the 360 monthly returns—should be –4 percent or less (calculated as the average return minus two standard deviations). The same number of monthly returns should be 6 percent or more (the average return plus two standard deviations). If, instead, it happened that twelve of the 360 monthly returns were –4 percent or worse, and fifteen of the 360 monthly returns were 6 percent or better, that would indicate high kurtosis for the distribution of monthly returns of that asset. Now, consider the findings of research done by Mark Anson. For the period January 1990 through June 2000, the kurtosis of high-yield bonds (as measured by the Salomon Smith Barney High Yield Composite Index) at +4.2 was three times that of the +1.4 kurtosis of the S&P 500. "The high kurtosis figure for high-yield debt reflects the significant risk of downgrades, defaults, and bankruptcies," writes Anson.[9]

When combining the data on skewness and kurtosis, it is easy to see that high-yield bonds have a lot in common with equities, which is why they offer equity-like risk premiums. However, they have not provided investors with a good long-term "bang" for their buck.

HIGH-YIELD BONDS AND EFFICIENT FRONTIER MODELS

It is important for investors to understand that not all distributions of returns are normal. If the distribution is not normal, then skewness and excess kurtosis may be present. In that case, investors looking *only* at the standard deviation of returns, the most commonly used measure of risk, receive a misleading picture of the riskiness (it understates the risks) of the asset class.

This creates problems for investors and advisers using *efficient frontier models* (see the Glossary) to help them determine the "correct," or most efficient, asset allocation from a universe of risky assets. The reason is that efficient frontier models are based on *mean-variance analysis* (see the Glossary), which assumes that the returns distribution is completely described by mean and variance.

In other words, those relying on efficient frontier models are relying on the assumption that investors do not care whether an asset exhibits skewness or kurtosis. If that assumption is correct, and investors are not bothered by skewness and the risk of a negative fat tail, then, indeed, the use of mean-variance analysis is appropriate. However, this assumption is too simplistic, as many, if not most, investors do care about skewness (especially negative skewness) and kurtosis.

If an asset exhibits nonnormal distribution, as do high-yield bonds, mean-variance analysis using the standard deviation as the measure of risk is only a good first approximation of the optimal portfolio. This is because mean-variance analysis does not completely reflect investors' true preferences. It may underestimate risk, and the result could be an overallocation to the asset class. And, as we have seen, not only are high-yield bond returns *not* normal, but the distribution of their returns is negatively skewed with fat tails—exactly the opposite of what investors prefer.

INFLATION RISK

An appropriate reason to consider an alternative asset class is that its inclusion would hedge some of the risks of the other assets in the portfolio. Since stocks and bonds are negatively correlated with inflation, a good match would be commodities and Treasury inflation-protected securities (TIPS), as both offer positive correlation to inflation.

Because high-yield bonds are hybrid instruments with characteristics of both stocks and bonds, we should expect that they would also have negative correlation with inflation. That is what Mark Anson's research on high-yield bonds found. For the period from 1990 to 2000, the S&P 500 had a correlation with inflation of about –0.25. The negative correlation of high-yield bonds with inflation was even greater, exceeding –0.3.[10] This provides further evidence that high-yield bonds do not mix well with other traditional portfolio assets.

ASSET LOCATION

Investors holding high-yield securities in taxable accounts receive their incremental risk premium in the form of interest payments that are taxed at ordinary rates. If an investor holds that same type of distress risk in the form of equities—owning the stocks of risky companies instead of their debt—the return will be in the form of long-term capital gains. These are taxed at lower rates, as are dividends. However, because high-yield debt carries equity-type risks, holding these securities in a tax-deferred account can have negative implications.

Whether in the form of stocks or high-yield debt, it is preferable to hold equity risk in a taxable account for the following reasons:

- Holding equity risk in taxable accounts creates the potential for a step-up in the asset's cost basis upon death. As a result, while estate taxes must be paid, the heirs avoid any income tax on the appreciated stock, because the cost basis becomes the value at the time of death.
- Holding equity risk in taxable accounts allows for tax-loss harvesting. The more volatile the asset, the more valuable the benefit. And high-yield bonds are more volatile than investment-grade bonds.
- Holding equity risk in taxable accounts allows for the gifting of securities to charities at the full value, thus avoiding taxes on the gains.

These benefits are lost when an investor holds equity risks inside a tax-deferred account, whether the equity risk is in the form of a bond or a stock.

THE NEED FOR DIVERSIFICATION

One of the beneficial characteristics of Treasury securities is that for U.S. investors there is no need for diversification of credit risk because there is no credit risk. All of the risk is interest rate risk. As they move down the spectrum from Treasuries to individual investment-grade bonds and then to junk bonds, investors begin to take on risk that can be diversified away (the idiosyncratic risks of the individual companies).

However, investors are not compensated with higher expected returns for taking diversifiable risks. When the credit rating is lower, the investment is more equity-like. Therefore, the need for diversification increases as an investor moves down the credit spectrum. The implication in terms of portfolio construction is that when moving beyond Treasury bonds, prudence dictates the need to diversify credit risk.

With high-grade corporate (or municipal) bonds, because credit risk is minimal, a small number of individual securities—perhaps as few as ten to twenty—provide sufficient diversification. In the category of junk bonds, the need for diversification greatly increases. For most investors the only way to obtain sufficient diversification of the risks of investing in speculative securities is through a mutual fund. And that means incurring expenses that can be avoided by limiting investments to Treasuries or high-quality bonds. Thus, some of the risk premium built into the prices of high-yield debt will be eroded by the resulting incremental costs.

THE HISTORICAL EVIDENCE

While junk bonds do carry *higher yields* than investment-grade securities, the question is, have investors actually earned *higher returns*? In other words, what has been the realized return after credit losses and the impact of calls and clawbacks?

Table 7.2 Has Credit Risk Been Rewarded?

Asset Class	Mean Return (%)	Standard Deviation (%)
7 to 10 Year Treasury Bonds	9.6	6.5
7 to 10 Year AAA/AA Bonds	9.6	5.7
7 to 10 Year A/BBB Bonds	9.6	5.3
7 to 10 Year High-Yield Bonds	8.8	7.7

Source: *The Journal of Portfolio Management* (Winter 2004)

TABLE 7.2 presents the results of the 2004 study, "Which Risks Have Been Best Rewarded?" by Antti Ilmanen, Rory Byrne, Heinz Gunasekera, and Robert Minikin.[11] The study covers the relatively brief period from 1985 through 2002, so it is important to not draw far-reaching conclusions that might be limited to a specific period.

At least for this period, the striking result is that the negative impact of credit risk, calls, and clawbacks resulted in a reduction in returns. The reduction in returns also occurred while producing greater volatility—not a good combination.

Because the results might be specific to a period of time, when considering this data we should also consider that the period in question was one of the best for U.S. economic performance. We did not experience any serious recession like that of the Great Depression or the one that occurred in 1973 and 1974. This should have been a period when credit risk was highly rewarded. However, the period does end with high-yield spreads at levels that are high from a historical perspective.

Spreads did retreat significantly beginning in 2003, as a result of defaults falling to just 4.66 percent in 2003. This was below the thirty-three-year average of 5.35 percent, and down sharply from the record 12.8 percent rate experienced in 2002. In addition, the recovery rate rose sharply from about 25 percent to about 45 percent. This combination led to high-yield bonds producing returns in excess of 30 percent in 2003—their best performance ever relative to U.S. Treasuries.[12]

We can also look at a more recent study, "Original Issue High-Yield Bonds," covering the period from 1997 through 2006.[13] This study took the unique approach of breaking the high-yield market into two subcomponents: original issue (OI) bonds and fallen angels (FAs)—bonds initially rated as investment-grade that were subsequently downgraded. The study produced some surprising results.

Using data from the Merrill Lynch High Yield Master II Index, author Martin Fridson found that an apparent anomaly exists in the market and that only the FAs produced significantly higher returns. In fact, OI bonds returned just 5.8 percent per year, barely outperforming the 5.7 percent per year return of a security with a comparable maturity, the 10-year Treasury. The reason was that OI bonds deteriorated in price by almost 3 percent per year. (The high coupon was illusionary.)

It was only the FAs that provided the significantly higher returns of 10.4 percent per year, benefiting from a rise in price of almost 2 percent per year. Fridson found that the difference in returns between the OI bonds and the FAs could not be explained by either differences in maturities or credit risks, nor were they explained by extreme differences in particular years. (Note that the overall return of high-yield bonds was 6.6 percent per year.)

It is important to note that Fridson's findings cover a period that ended with spreads on high-yield bonds at historically low levels. For example, at the end of 2002, the spread between 10-year Treasuries and B-rated bonds was 6.7 percent. By the end of 2006, the spread had fallen by more than half to just 3.0 percent, and by the end of 2007, the spread had once again widened, approaching 5 percent. Thus, if the study was extended through 2007, the picture for high-yield bonds would have looked even worse than the one Fridson uncovered.

Fridson attempted to explain the anomaly of the failure of OI high-yield bonds to deliver appropriate risk-adjusted returns. One obvious explanation is that the market in high-yield bonds is not very liquid, making it difficult to short "overpriced" OI high-yield bonds and to take an equivalent long position in the FAs. Along the same lines, the credit derivative market in junk bonds is just not developed enough to allow for arbitrage—so the anomaly persists.

Another explanation is that investors were unaware of the difference in performance between OI bonds and FAs. Fridson pointed out that, in fact, high-yield managers have generally disdained FAs, because they typically offer weaker covenants than OI bonds. Note that their weak covenants result in greater risk and, therefore, help explain the risk premium FAs earn.

Fridson offered four other possible explanations for the anomaly:

- **Focus on security selection**—Even if managers were aware of the data, they might still have invested in the segment based on the belief that they, as individuals, could deliver above-average performance and could avoid the bonds that drag down performance. Remember, active managers must believe they are able to do so consistently, or they would have no reason to exist.

- **Dependence on new issues to deploy funds**—Typically, a high-yield fund will want to be fully invested. Because FAs represent less than 30 percent of the high-yield market, it is hard to stay fully invested if a high-yield manager excludes over 70 percent of the investable universe.

- **"Lottery ticket" effect**—Even when high-yield bonds produce relatively low returns over long periods, they often produce extremely high returns over brief periods. For example, the Merrill Lynch High-Yield Master II Index returned over 25 percent in 2003. Thus, at any point in time, active managers may perceive the opportunity to "win the lottery." The large upside potential outweighs an average outcome that is unattractive.

- **The mirage of a remedy based on yield, rather than return**—Unfortunately, the evidence suggests that the yield is insufficient to compensate for the future declines in price that OI bonds experience.

Fridson concluded that the "problem" might result from the fact that the initial findings used to market high-yield bonds to investors in the late 1970s were based on the performance of the FAs. Prior to that point, there was not much of a market, if any, for OI high-yield bonds. Unfortunately, the subsequent new issues market has failed to replicate this performance.

A well-known Vanguard fund also offers almost thirty years of evidence to consider.

VANGUARD HIGH-YIELD CORPORATE FUND

In late December 1978, Vanguard opened the Vanguard High-Yield Corporate Fund (VWEHX), a high-yield corporate-bond fund. Like most of Vanguard's products, the fund is low cost, with an operating expense ratio of just 0.25 percent (as of July 2008).

- This fund also has an Admiral Share class (VWEAX), a lower-cost version (with an operating expense ratio of 0.13 percent) of the regular shares. The fund is diversified, minimizing unsystematic (diversifiable) risk. As of March 2008, the fund held 236 securities, and the top ten holdings represented less than 14 percent of assets. The fund had an average *effective* maturity of about eight years, and the average credit rating was BB. (See also Chapter 1.)

For the period from 1979 through 2007, the fund provided investors with a return of 9.01 percent per year. For the same period, the Lehman Brothers Intermediate Credit Bond Index—an index of *investment-grade* bonds with maturities of one to ten years—returned 8.88 percent per year, almost matching the return of the Vanguard fund without taking the credit risks of junk bonds. Thus, although the spread between high-yield bonds and investment-grade bonds can often be quite wide, the incremental return *realized* by investors was just 0.13 percent. This demonstrates that investors should never confuse yield with returns.

But, as we've said, returns are not the only considerations. The correlation of returns also plays an important role in determining the risk and return of a portfolio. As noted before, the correlation of high-yield debt to equities is much higher than the correlation of either Treasuries or investment-grade debt to equities. For the period from 1979 through 2007, the correlation of the Vanguard High-Yield Corporate Fund to the S&P 500 was 0.54. The correlations of the Lehman Brothers Intermediate Credit Bond Index and the Lehman Brothers Treasury Bond Index to the S&P 500 were much lower at 0.26 and 0.20, respectively. Thus, high-yield debt was a less effective diversifier of the risks of equity holdings.

In addition to the higher correlation to equities, the annual standard deviation of the Vanguard High-Yield Corporate Fund was 8.70 percent. This compares to a standard deviation of 5.64 percent for the Lehman Brothers Intermediate Treasury Bond Index (1–10 years) and 6.56 percent for the Lehman Intermediate Credit Index. The combination of higher correlations with equities and higher volatility is a negative characteristic of high-yield debt. The bottom line is that even if high-yield debt provides somewhat higher returns than investment-grade debt, the use of more creditworthy assets might result in higher overall portfolio returns, or at least a higher risk-adjusted return (that is, a higher Sharpe ratio). A look at some alternative portfolios offers further insights about evaluating returns, as compared to other characteristics, of a security.

MORE EFFICIENT ALTERNATIVES

For those seeking greater returns than those offered by investment-grade securities, there are superior alternatives to high-yield debt. TABLE 7.3 provides the historical evidence of four alternative strategies, all of which produced the same return—but did so with less volatility.

By using Portfolio B, we were able to completely eliminate the risks and negative features of high-yield bonds, while only increasing our exposure to stocks by 1 percent. The result was a portfolio that produced the same return with less volatility.

Portfolio C also improved the efficiency of the portfolio. The addition of investment-grade bonds (combined with the elimination of junk bonds) allowed us to reduce our equity exposure from 60 to 56 percent, while maintaining the same portfolio return. However, volatility was reduced by 5 percent.

Table 7.3   Annualized Returns and Standard Deviations for Alternative
Strategies, 1979–2007

Portfolio	Annualized Return (%)	Standard Deviation (%)
60% CRSP (1–10 Index)/30% Lehman Intermediate Government Bond Index/ 10% Vanguard High-Yield Corporate Fund	11.5	10.3
61% CRSP (1–10 Index)/39% Lehman Intermediate Government Bond Index	11.5	10.1
56% CRSP (1–10 Index)/44% Lehman Intermediate Credit Bond Index	11.5	9.8
40% CRSP (1–10 Index)/9% Fama-French Small Value Index/51% Lehman Intermediate Government Bond Index	11.5	8.4

Portfolio D produced even more interesting results. By eliminating our exposure to credit risk and adding a small allocation to small-cap value stocks, we were able to significantly increase the allocation to safer government bonds. The net result was a portfolio that produced the same returns, but experienced 18 percent less volatility. Thus, we were able to eliminate the negative features of junk bonds, maintain the return of the portfolio, and considerably improve the efficiency of the portfolio. Portfolio D was also the most efficient at providing returns relative to risk.

SUMMARY

Investing in high-yield bonds offers the appeal of higher yields and the potential for higher returns. Unfortunately, the historical evidence is that investors have not been able to realize greater risk-adjusted returns with this type of security. It appears that the inherent flaws of high-yield bonds have resulted in investors assuming risks that are simply not worth taking. The following summarizes the shortcomings of high-yield bonds covered in this chapter:

- Exposure to equity risks in a tax-inefficient manner.
- Small amount of unique risk, resulting in only a small diversification benefit.

- Returns that exhibit negative skewness and excess kurtosis.
- Negative correlation with inflation.
- Need to pay a mutual fund to obtain sufficient diversification, resulting in costs that reduce the expected return.
- Asymmetric risk created by the presence of calls and clawbacks. Exacerbating the problem is that low-grade bonds generally offer weaker call protection than high-grade bonds do. In addition, they are more likely to be called, because the credit quality of low-grade bonds is more likely to rise.[14]
- Not playing any of the key roles that fixed-income investments should assume in a portfolio—providing liquidity for emergencies, creating a consistent cash flow, or reducing the overall risk of the portfolio in an efficient manner.

Investors should also consider another important negative characteristic of high-yield bonds. One reason investors accept price risk when they extend the maturity of their bond holdings beyond the short term is that longer-term bonds provide a hedge against deflation. Another is that they hedge reinvestment risk that occurs during periods of falling interest rates. Unfortunately, the default risk of high-yield bonds emerges during periods of deflation, and the reinvestment risk shows up during periods of falling interest rates, because of the presence of the call option. Thus, just when the benefits of longer maturities are needed, they disappear for holders of longer-term high-yield bonds.

David Swensen, the highly regarded chief investment officer of the Yale Endowment, stated, "Well-informed investors avoid the no-win consequences of high-yield fixed-income investing."[15] We certainly agree. Thus, for those seeking greater returns than those offered by investment-grade securities, we recommend considering other, superior alternatives. For example, investors could increase either their overall equity allocation or their specific allocations to the riskier asset classes of small-cap and value stocks. At the very least, investors holding high-yield debt should adjust their allocations, recognizing that they are taking some incremental equity risk.

Finally, because diversification assumes greater significance as one moves to bonds with lower credit ratings, those wanting to speculate with high-yield bonds should only consider doing so through a low-cost mutual fund, like the one offered by Vanguard. There is no other efficient way to obtain a sufficient degree of diversification.

Private Equity (Venture Capital) 8

T HE TERM *private equity* is often used to describe various types of privately placed, as opposed to publicly traded, investments. Within the broad category of private equity are three major subcategories: venture capital, leveraged buyouts (LBOs), and mezzanine financing. Even the name of this alternative asset class is tantalizing because of its allusion to privately available opportunities. Individual investors may even yearn to be "players" in an arena dominated by institutional investors such as the Yale Endowment. This may explain why private equity is among the most popular alternative investments for individuals.

The private equity market has grown tremendously over the past twenty-five years. In 1980, investors had committed $5 billion to this alternative investment. By 2004, that figure had swelled to a total of $300 billion.[1] According to the National Venture Capital Association, 248 venture capital firms raised a total of $35.9 billion of new funding for private equity in 2007.[2] What accounts for this spectacular growth?

ORIGINS

The original source of the term *venture capital* (VC) is unknown. However, it is generally accepted that the VC industry, as we know it today, was launched in 1946, when General Georges Doriot, Ralph Flanders, Karl Compton, Merrill Griswold, and other partners organized American Research and Development Corporation to invest in the illiquid equity or equity-related securities (i.e., convertible preferred stock) of early stage, pre-initial public offering (IPO) firms. These businessmen and civic leaders were concerned about the ability of the U.S. economy to recover from the Great Depression. They believed if they could provide the required capital, small, innovative firms seeking to upgrade and expand their operations could contribute to economic growth and provide a source of significant capital gains.[3]

Today, VC firms are typically partnerships that pool resources to raise capital to invest in a relatively small number of different opportunities. The typical VC partnership invests in just fifteen to twenty different companies. Larger partnerships might expand that figure to twenty-five to thirty firms. In addition to providing capital, VC firms often help businesses develop their management teams, and they frequently take seats on their boards. In many cases, the VC firms make a board seat a condition of their investment.

VC is usually the second or third stage of a traditional start-up financing sequence—one that begins with the founding entrepreneurs putting up the initial funding. The next round of funding may come from what are called *angel investors*. Generally, an angel investor is someone who has a personal relationship with the entrepreneur or who possesses industry-related experience and is willing to accept the high degree of risk associated with start-ups.

THE ATTRACTION

Private equity excites many investors, offering the opportunity for spectacular returns (although, as with most investments, both individuals and the media tend to emphasize stories with happy endings). Naturally, it is reasonable to assume that high-risk, illiquid investments are priced to deliver higher expected returns than publicly traded securities as compensation for the greater risk.

In general, private equity investors have been rewarded with high returns, but returns alone are an insufficient reason for considering this or any investment. Investors should also ask: Have the high *absolute* returns been sufficient to compensate investors for the significant incremental risks entailed?

THE HISTORICAL EVIDENCE

According to Venture Economics (a research firm that provides information and analysis on the private equity industry), private equity overall returned 13.8 percent for the twenty-year period ending June 30, 2005.[4] During the same period, both the S&P 500 Index and microcap stocks (the smallest two deciles of stocks as defined by the Center for Research in Security Prices at the University of Chicago) returned 11.2 percent. Large-cap value stocks returned 12.2 percent and small-cap value stocks returned 16.0 percent.[5] Thus, while the returns of private equity capital outperformed those of the S&P 500, microcap stocks, and large-cap value stocks, they underperformed small-cap value stocks by a significant margin.

Data from Venture Economics also allow us to examine the returns of three subsectors of the private equity market: VC, LBOs, and mezzanine financing. LBOs involve acquiring businesses using mostly debt and a small amount of equity, with the debt being secured by the assets of the business. Mezzanine financings are late-stage venture capital investments, usually the final round of financing prior to an IPO.

As later-stage investments, mezzanine financings are less risky than earlier-stage investments. Thus, capital provided in mezzanine financings is typically less costly than the capital for investments that occur at an earlier stage. On the whole, according to the Venture Economics data, VC (the riskiest of private equity investments) just matched the 16 percent return of small-cap value stocks. And, as we would expect, because of its greater risk, early-stage VC (that is, seed capital) provided the highest return—20.2 percent. Later-stage VC, despite the still significant risks, actually underperformed the returns of small-cap value public equities, returning 13.8 percent. LBOs also returned 13.8 percent, and mezzanine financing returned just 9.1 percent.[6]

These findings are consistent with those of the 2005 study "Private Equity Performance: Returns, Persistence, and Capital Flows," by authors Steven Kaplan and Antoinette Schoar. The study covers private equity funds that were launched from 1980 through 1997, although the data covers the period ending in 2001. The authors found that, net of fees, the average private equity fund had returns roughly equal to the return of the S&P 500.[7]

Kaplan and Schoar's research covered the period that included one of the greatest private equity booms in history—the Internet/dot-com era. Thus, it would be helpful to also examine the returns from an earlier period. A 1992 study, "Venture Capital at the Crossroads," by William D. Bygrave and Jeffry A. Timmons, covering the period from 1974 through 1989, found that the average internal rate of return (IRR) from venture capital was 13.5 percent.[8] (The IRR is the discount or interest rate that makes the net present value of an investment equal to zero.) This was virtually identical to the 13.3 percent return from the S&P 500. However, this was significantly below the return of the three other benchmarks—microcap stocks returned 17.5 percent; large-cap value stocks returned 18.0 percent; and small-cap value stocks returned 23.7 percent.

We also have the results of a 2002 study, "The Returns to Entrepreneurial Investment: A Private Equity Premium Puzzle?" by Tobias J. Moskowitz and Annette Vissing-Jorgensen, covering the period from 1952 through 1999. The authors concluded that private equity investing provided returns similar to those of public equity markets. They noted that the finding was surprising, given the greater risks of private equity investing. For example, they found that after ten years the survival rate of private firms was only about 34 percent. There was a high risk of a total loss.[9]

Finally, we have the results of the 2007 study, "The Performance of Private Equity Funds," by Oliver Gottschalg and Ludovic Phalippou. They researched the performance of six thousand private equity deals and about one thousand buyout funds, using data collected from investors in 852 private equity funds whose funds were raised before 1993—to be sure the funds had sold all their assets. Their findings are quite interesting.

Gottschalg and Phalippou found that *before* accounting for fees and carried interest (profit sharing), the average private equity fund outperformed the S&P 500 by 3 percent per year. However, after accounting for fees, the average private equity fund *underperformed* the S&P 500 by 3 percent per year.[10]

In sum, it appears, from the results of the research, that private equity strategies have provided returns that have not been fully commensurate with the risks involved. Among the considerations are that private equity investors forgo the benefits of liquidity, transparency, broad diversification, and the access to daily pricing that mutual fund investors enjoy. Also keep in mind that private equity investments typically entail long lockout periods, during which investors cannot access their capital. In addition, there are other aspects of the asset class that investors should consider carefully.

CHARACTERISTICS OF PRIVATE EQUITY RETURNS

Studies have found that private equity returns exhibit the following characteristics:

- **Extreme positive skewness in returns**—The median return of private equity is much lower than the mean (arithmetic average) return. Their relatively high average return reflects the small possibility of a truly outstanding return, combined with the much larger probability of a more modest or negative return. In effect, private equity investments are like options (or lottery tickets): They provide a small chance of a huge payout, but a much larger chance of a below-average return.[11]

- **High standard deviation of returns**—The standard deviation (volatility) of private equity is in excess of 100 percent. This compares to the standard deviation of the S&P 500 of about 20 percent, and the standard deviation of small-cap value stocks (based on the Fama-French U.S. Small Value Index) of about 35 percent from 1927 through 2007. A 2002 study, "Venture Capital and Its Role in Strategic Asset Allocation," covering the period from 1960 through 1999, found that VC had an annual arithmetic average return of 45 percent. The high standard deviation of 116 percent reduced the annual arithmetic average return of 45 percent to an *annualized* return of just 13 percent. The authors—Peng Chen, Gary T. Baierl, and Paul D. Kaplan—concluded, "The variance of VC investment is so high that the estimated average compounded annual return for VC investment is actually lower than for U.S. small-cap stocks and comparable to U.S. large-cap stocks and international stocks."[12]

High volatility is a potential negative that investors might prefer to avoid. Highly risk-averse investors might choose to avoid securities with this characteristic, even if they carry high-risk premiums.

VENTURE CAPITAL VERSUS PUBLICLY TRADED SECURITIES

A 2005 study, "The Risk and Return of Venture Capital," by John H. Cochrane, covering the period from January 1987 through June 2000, looked at 16,613 financing rounds involving 7,765 companies and concluded that the risks of, and returns to, VC were similar to those of the smallest Nasdaq stocks. These are stocks defined by small market capitalizations that are illiquid and thinly traded. (For some of them, there are many months with no trading at all.) Furthermore, they exhibit traits similar to those of venture capital—extreme skewness and high volatility.

However, despite their greater risks, VC did not provide any higher return than comparable publicly traded equities. Cochrane reached the following conclusion: "The fact that we see a similar phenomenon in public and private markets suggests that there is little that is special about venture capital."[13]

INEFFICIENT DIVERSIFICATION

In addition to the risks of extreme skewness and volatility, investors must consider that because of its inability to broadly diversify across hundreds or even thousands of stocks (as do index funds or passive asset-class funds), private equity investing—be it VC, LBOs, or mezzanine financing—involves accepting the risk that such investments might produce a wide dispersion of returns.

For example, the California Public Employees' Retirement System (CalPERS), generally considered among the most sophisticated of institutional investors, invested in a venture capital fund called Beacon Group III-Focus Value Fund in 1996. As of year-end 2004, the fund was down almost 30 percent. CalPERS also invested in Inroads Capital Partners 1995 Fund. The fund produced a loss of almost 25 percent through 2004.[14]

Investors should consider that while CalPERS diversified its exposure to private equity investments across many funds, it is unlikely that the typical individual investor would be able to accomplish similar diversification. Thus, it is unlikely that the returns that individual investors received over the period would have been similar to the 13.8 percent return averaged by all private equity funds. Without such diversification, investors must accept the risk that the funds they invest in might generate poor results. Therefore, one of the risks individual investors are accepting, probably without giving it appropriate consideration, is an *uncompensated* risk—because it could be diversified away.

BIAS IN THE DATA

Unfortunately, despite the less than favorable results, the data from much of the aforementioned research are likely to contain an upward bias. Another study mentioned earlier in this chapter, "The Performance of Private Equity Funds," attempts to correct for this bias.[15] The bias results from what the authors called *living dead* investments. In other words, the residual values reported in studies often include inactive funds—those with an age above the typical age limit of funds (that is, ten years) that show no sign of any recent activity within the past four years, such as distributions or cash calls. As a result, accounting values may not reflect market values. Poorly performing funds have an incentive to postpone liquidation to artificially raise their reported return. Thus, the authors suggest, the residual value of these funds is overstated (and should likely be written off).

Studies (such as the one by Kaplan and Schoar) that include only liquidated funds have a "winners" bias. Once the authors of the paper corrected for this bias, they found that the return of private equity funds raised between 1980 and 1996 lagged the return of the S&P 500 by 3.3 percent per year. They also found that about one-quarter of the funds had negative IRRs and that few funds produced very high returns—the distribution of returns was similar to that of a lottery ticket.

PERCEPTION VERSUS REALITY

While private equity investing combines high risk and high *expected* return, the returns investors have actually realized do not appear to have compensated them fully for the incremental risks. For example, the high returns could reflect, at least to a significant degree, a premium for the extreme illiquidity of private equity investments. Highlighting the lack of liquidity is a finding from the 2003 study, "The Cash Flow, Return and Risk Characteristics of Private Equity," by Alexander Ljungqvist and Matthew Richardson. The study found that the IRR for the average private equity fund did not turn positive until the eighth year.[16] Once we account for the cost of capital, it is easy to see that it is only at the end of a fund's life that any excess returns are realized.

Given the evidence, it appears that the real winners from private equity investments are the sponsors of private equity funds. They collect large fees (typically 2 percent or more per year, and at least 20 percent of the profits), regardless of whether their funds deliver on their "promise" of market-beating returns. This result should not be a surprise, as the previously discussed academic studies have found that, *after* fees, private equity provided returns comparable to those of the most risky of public equities. That means that *before* fees private equity earned above-market returns (alpha). Note, however, that the alpha went to the fund, not the investors! In a sense, this is actually a logical outcome. If there is any alpha, we should expect most, or even all, to be earned by the scarce resource (skillful managers), not the abundant resource (investor capital). The study by Kaplan and Schoar found evidence that these top-performing funds often raised their "carried interest" (profit sharing) from 20 percent to 30 percent.

PRIVATE EQUITY'S ROLE IN A PORTFOLIO

When the merits of private equity investing are evaluated on a stand-alone basis, it appears that investors have not been appropriately compensated for the incremental risks. However, we should not evaluate investments strictly on a stand-alone basis. Instead, we should analyze how adding them to the portfolio affects the risks and expected returns of the entire portfolio. One determining factor is the correlation of returns of the new asset with the returns of the other assets within the portfolio.

The aforementioned study, "Venture Capital and its Role in Strategic Asset Allocation," found that the correlation between VC investments and large-cap stocks was virtually zero. This appears to be consistent with the notion that the risk of VC investments derives almost entirely from investment-specific (unsystematic) risk. This is risk that is often independent of overall stock market performance. Using an efficient frontier model (see the Glossary), the authors determined:

- For the minimum-variance equity portfolio, the allocation to venture capital was about 2 percent.
- For the equity portfolio that had the same standard deviation as the S&P 500, the allocation was 4 percent.
- For the equity portfolio with the maximum Sharpe ratio, the allocation was 9 percent.

The authors concluded, therefore, that despite the extreme skewness and high volatility of VC, it is justifiable to make an allocation of between 2 and 9 percent of a diversified equity portfolio to VC.[17] We are skeptical of that claim, however. It seems to us that because VC firms depend on the public markets to fund their exit strategies, both venture funds and private equity funds depend on a buoyant market for public securities for their success.

If the IPO market dries up because there is a bear market in public securities, it seems unlikely that private equity funds will be able to provide high returns. Thus, we can conclude that during bear markets, when the risks of equity investing appear, the correlations of returns of private equity with the returns of public equities are likely to turn highly positive. In other words, just when low correlation becomes important, correlations become high.

NONMONETARY EXPLANATIONS FOR PRIVATE EQUITY INVESTING

There are many possible nonmonetary reasons an individual might consider investing in private equity. One of the most common is a high tolerance for entrepreneurial risk taking. Often one requirement of senior-level employment at a start-up is a significant personal investment. There are also many people who derive large nonmonetary benefits from self-employment and being their own boss, which may lead them to invest in starting up their own business. Additionally, tax advantages are often associated with self-employment.

Another possible reason for investing in private equity is the urge to make a difference in the world. For example, many people invest in medically related ventures based on a personal connection: investors might know or be related to someone fighting a specific illness. The desire to accelerate the development of a cure or treatment is a perfectly valid reason for considering making an investment in a company. However, investors should be completely clear on the reasons they are making the investment, should take into account the true nature of the risks, and should be certain the risks are affordable. From the outset, it's important not to have the wrong reasons for making the investment.

Perhaps a personal example would help demonstrate this point. After his grandmother died of complications from diabetes, Larry personally invested in two start-ups that focused on managing the care of, or treating, diabetics. Unfortunately, neither one did well, and both investments were eventually written off.

SUMMARY

For most investors, private equity investing is an unattractive proposition because of its lottery-like characteristics, its lack of liquidity, and the difficulty of effectively diversifying its risks. While private equity capital has generally provided high returns, investors have not been appropriately compensated for all of the incremental risks they incur, and this means they should proceed cautiously, if they are going to proceed at all. So why has there been such a huge flood of investments in private equity? The following are likely explanations:[18]

- Lack of investor knowledge on either the absolute returns on private equity or the relative returns available on similar, but far more liquid, public securities.
- Investor overconfidence in their ability to choose the few winning investments. Overconfidence is a well-documented and common human trait. Professors Brad Barber and Terrance Odean have conducted several studies on this phenomenon, including "Boys Will Be Boys: Gender, Overconfidence, and Common Stock Investment."
- The previously mentioned nonmonetary benefits that private equity can provide.
- Investors who prefer an asset with extreme positive skewness, even though this preference could result in lowering the returns of investments with this characteristic. This is one explanation, for example, of why riskier small-cap growth stocks have produced no higher returns than safer large-cap growth stocks.
- The success of a few high-profile institutional investors, such as the Yale Endowment.

From a purely investment viewpoint, the more prudent strategy appears to be to take equity risks in the public markets, using passively managed funds that deliver the returns of their respective asset classes in a low-cost, tax-efficient manner. However, those among the minority of investors who like skewness—and are willing to trade both the high likelihood of poor returns and a significant likelihood of the total loss of their investment for the small probability of a huge payoff—might consider allocating a small percent of their equity allocation to private equity.

However, before doing so, they should carefully consider the following advice from David Swensen, of the Yale Endowment: "Understanding the difficulty of identifying superior hedge-fund, venture-capital, and leveraged-buyout investments leads to the conclusion that hurdles for casual investors stand insurmountably high. Even many well-equipped investors fail to clear the hurdles necessary to achieve consistent success in producing market-beating, active management results. When operating in arenas that depend fundamentally on active management for success, ill-informed manager selection poses grave risks to portfolio assets."[19]

Those who decide to "venture" into VC should remember that, due to the extreme volatility and skewness of returns, it is important to diversify the risks. This is best achieved by investing indirectly through a private equity fund, rather than through direct investments in individual companies. Because most such funds typically limit their investments to a relatively small number, it is also prudent to diversify by investing in more than one fund.

In addition, the evidence suggests that there is learning—older, more experienced funds tend to have better performance—and there is some persistence in performance. Thus, investors should choose a firm with a long track record of superior performance.[20]

One final word of caution: It is extremely important to engage in thorough due diligence for each investment before making any private equity investments. At the very least, this would involve a thorough background check on all the principals and checking the firm's track record in the field. Clearly, private equity is a case of *caveat emptor*—let the buyer beware.

Covered Calls 9

INVESTORS ARE ALWAYS interested in increasing returns without having to accept more risk. Therefore, they are attracted to covered calls by marketers' assurances that this elusive combination is within reach. The real question is whether writing covered calls represents an efficient investment strategy, or if there are better ways to achieve the same objective. To answer these questions, we'll compare covered calls to a similar passive strategy. However, let's begin with some helpful definitions.

A *call* is an option contract that gives the holder the *right*, but not the *obligation*, to buy a security at a predetermined price on a specific date (known as a *European call*) or during a specific period (known as an *American call*). A *covered-call* strategy involves the investor's writing (selling) a call option on stocks that are already in his or her portfolio. In doing so, the seller of the option gives up all of the potential for appreciation above the option strike price, but, in exchange, receives an up-front premium. If the call expires without being exercised, the portfolio return is based on the call premium and the value of the stock that the call writer still owns. Alternatively, if the call is exercised, the call writer receives the call premium and surrenders the stock at the strike price.

It is important to note that one of the "costs," besides transactions fees and taxes, of a covered-call strategy is the lost upside opportunity. Essentially, the covered-call investor is trading the upside potential of the equity investment for an up-front fee and reduced exposure to downside risk (based on the size of the call premium).

Marketers of covered-call strategies use the Sharpe ratio to demonstrate the efficiency of the strategy. As discussed previously, the Sharpe ratio is a measure of the return earned above the rate of return on riskless short-term U.S. Treasury bills relative to the risk taken. In this case, risk is measured by the standard deviation of returns.

While the Sharpe ratio is a useful risk-reward measurement tool, it relies on standard deviation as *the* measure of risk. However, while standard deviation does measure the volatility of returns, volatility is not the *only* kind of risk. As discussed in Chapter 7, investors care not only about volatility, but also about other characteristics of the distribution of returns, including skewness. And they generally try to avoid assets characterized by negative skewness, such as junk bonds and hedge funds.

This leads to two fundamental questions: What impact does a covered-call-writing strategy have on the potential distribution of returns? And does it shift the distribution away from a "normal" one (that is, a bell curve), reducing the usefulness of measures that include the Sharpe ratio?

A 2005 study, "Covered Calls: A Lose/Lose Investment," by Karyl B. Leggio and Donald Lien, covering the period between February 1987 and December 1995, found that while a covered-call strategy did produce a lower standard deviation than did an indexing strategy, it eliminated the upside potential and produced *negative* skewness of returns, the kind that investors dislike.

For example, a strategy of 1-month covered calls produced a negative skewness of 4.6, versus a negative skewness of just 1.1 for a buy-and-hold indexing strategy.[1] The negative skewness of the covered calls brings into question the relevance of the Sharpe ratio for this strategy.

While it is true that a covered-call strategy does reduce kurtosis (see the Glossary), the problem is that it eliminates the potential for the good fat tail (the highly positive return), while having no impact on the risk of the bad fat tail (the extremely negative return). This approach only reduces the size of the bad fat tail by the amount of the premiums collected. Risk-averse investors would much prefer that the reverse be true—that a covered call eliminated the risk of the left fat tail (which is a result of a bear market) while accepting a smaller right fat tail (which is a result of a bull market).

Unfortunately, covered-call strategies also have other negative characteristics.

TAXES MATTER

For taxable accounts, covered-call strategies result in tax inefficiencies, because the option premiums generate income that is taxed at rates above those for long-term capital gains. On the other hand, for long-term investors, the capital gains that are lost when options are exercised (because the stock was above the strike price of the option) would have been taxed at long-term capital gains rates.

TRANSACTIONS COSTS

Compared to passive strategies, covered-call strategies entail high transactions costs. The high turnover results in costs related to both commissions and bid-offer spreads, and possibly market impact costs as well.

AN ALTERNATIVE STRATEGY

The stated objective of any covered-call strategy is to capture the upside potential of equities, while reducing the downside risk. Yet we believe that investors can accomplish this objective in a more tax-efficient manner. Instead of writing covered calls, investors could reduce their allocation to equities and increase their allocation to fixed-income assets, while at the same time increasing their exposure to value and small-cap stocks (riskier stocks with higher expected returns). Historically, such an approach would have resulted in less volatility—as well as less downside risk—while producing returns in a more tax-efficient manner. In addition most of the potential upside is maintained. The following example illustrates this approach:

Consider two portfolios covering the period from 1973 through 2007. Portfolio A is 60 percent large-cap stocks (the Fama-French U.S. Large Cap Index) and 40 percent Lehman Brothers Intermediate

Treasury Bond Index (1–10 years). Portfolio B is only 44 percent equities, and is 56 percent fixed income. The 44 percent equity allocation is split equally, with 11 percent allocated to each of large-cap stocks, large-cap value stocks the (Fama-French U.S. Large Value Index), small-cap stocks (the Fama-French U.S. Small Cap Index), and small-cap value stocks (the Fama-French U.S. Small Value Index).[2] The fixed-income portion is invested in the same Lehman Brothers Treasury Bond Index. **TABLE 9.1** illustrates the results.

Portfolio B, despite having a significantly lower equity allocation, produced both higher returns and a higher Sharpe ratio. Portfolio A experienced more years of negative returns and a larger loss in the worst single year. From any perspective, Portfolio B produced higher returns with less risk. Although it is never a certainty that history will repeat itself, investors seeking to improve the efficiency of their portfolios should consider this alternative, instead of a covered-call strategy.

Unfortunately, we cannot compare the above results to the outcome of a covered-call strategy, as no long-term historical data series on covered-calls strategies exists. However, a covered-call strategy might conceivably be a more prudent choice for investors who place little to no value on the lost upside potential, but place a high value on the *limited* downside protection that is obtained (the premiums received). In addition, because of the negative tax consequences of this strategy, an investor would need to be holding the underlying equities in a tax-advantaged location, such as a 401(k), a

Table 9.1 Comparing Alternative Portfolio Strategies, 1973–2007

	Portfolio A (%) 60% Equity/40% Bonds	Portfolio B (%) 44% Equity/56% Bonds
Annualized return	10.0	10.7
Standard deviation	11.2	9.7
Years with negative returns	7	5
Worst year	−13.7	–7.6
Average return during years with negative results for either portfolio	−5.8	–4.3

profit-sharing plan, or an IRA. And remember that a taxable account would be the preferred location for those investors who can choose where to hold their equities.

SUMMARY

While covered-call strategies appear to promise "a free lunch" of increased returns with less risk, investors who care about more than the volatility of returns will not find this an efficient strategy. Even for investors who value the attributes of a covered-call strategy, there is a more efficient way of achieving the same objective. The same goal can be accomplished by reducing the equity allocation of the portfolio, which provides important downside protection, while expanding the percentage of value stocks, thereby increasing the expected return from the equity portion of the portfolio.

Socially Responsible
Mutual Funds 10

INVESTORS CAN CHOOSE to demonstrate their opposition to certain business activities by opting not to buy products or services from companies that they feel are engaging in practices that violate their values, ethics, or beliefs. Additionally, they can decide not to invest in such companies. For example, in the eighteenth century, the governing bodies of several U.S. religious groups would only issue loans to companies that did not distill alcohol, produce or distribute tobacco, or operate gambling facilities.

More recently, in the 1970s, after the global outcry over South African apartheid, many individual and institutional investors sold their investments in any multinational companies doing business in or with that nation. Although economic sanctions against South Africa ended in 1993, investors continued to expand this practice by applying the same moral standards to all companies, wherever they operated in the world.

Today, this values-based approach is referred to as *socially responsible investing* (SRI). And while SRI is not generally thought of as an alternative investment in the same category as hedge funds or commodities, it represents a thoughtful alternative for many investors.

DEFINING SRI

SRI has been referred to as "double-bottom-line" investing. The implication is that investments must not only be profitable, but must also meet investors' personal standards. Some investors don't want their money to support companies that sell tobacco products, alcoholic beverages, or weapons, or that rely on animal testing as part of their research and development efforts. Other investors may also be concerned about social, environmental, governance, labor, or religious issues. It is important to note that SRI encompasses many personal beliefs and does not reflect just one set of values. Therefore, it is no surprise that each socially responsible fund relies on its own carefully developed "screening" system.

For example, consider the "gay benefits" issue. Some funds specifically exclude companies like Walt Disney for maintaining gay-friendly employee benefits policies. On the other hand, the Meyers Pride Value Fund (which merged into the Citizen's Value Fund in September 2001) only invested in companies that offered domestic partner benefits and supported policies that prohibited discrimination against homosexuals.

There are also funds designed for Catholics (Ave Maria Mutual Funds), Muslims (Amana Mutual Funds Trust), Presbyterians (New Covenant Funds) and Christians of all faiths (the Timothy Plan). Our capitalist system excels at responding to the growing demand for customized approaches to investing.

RAPID GROWTH

TIAA-CREF began offering a socially responsible fund in 1990. Since then, assets dedicated to SRI have grown rapidly. According to the Social Investment Forum, total SRI assets in the United States rose from $639 billion in 1995 to $2.71 trillion in 2007, which represents 11 percent of the total assets under professional management tracked in *Nelson Information's Directory of Investment Managers.*

While institutions, with $1.9 trillion in assets, are clearly the largest participants in the SRI market, mutual funds dedicated to SRI have exploded in popularity, growing from $12 billion in assets in 1995 to $202 billion in 2007, far outpacing overall mutual funds growth nationwide.[1]

Investors even have a choice between active and passive (index) strategies. In the case of the socially responsible index funds, the management of the fund designates its own index. For example, the

Domini Social Equity Fund, one of the largest SRI funds, with $892 million of assets under management as of April 2008, originally relied on an index of four hundred socially acceptable stocks (as compared to the S&P 500 Index). Unfortunately, given the historical evidence on the poor and inconsistent performance of actively managed funds, the fund received shareholder approval to switch to an active approach as of November 30, 2006. The fund also has a high expense ratio of 1.08 percent.

One passive alternative is the Calvert Social Index Fund. As of March 2008, the fund had $84 million in assets under management and held 636 issues. The Class A shares of the fund have an expense ratio of 0.75 percent. Unfortunately, they also carry a 4.75 percent load. Additionally, the minimum investment is $5,000.

DOES SOCIALLY RESPONSIBLE INVESTING COME AT A PRICE?

Thanks to the 2003 study "Investing in Socially Responsible Mutual Funds," by Christopher C. Geczy, Robert F. Stambaugh, and David Levin, we now know that SRI does come at a price.[2] But just how large a price one pays for social responsibility depends on how investors allocate their equity investments to various equity asset classes.

The study focused on thirty-four no-load equity funds that could provide at least three years of data on returns, expenses, and turnover. The sample and its subsets were large enough to represent the socially responsible universe in a meaningful way. The authors came to the following conclusions:

1. Passive investors pay a price of about 0.5 percent per year when investing in socially responsible broad-market index funds. Socially responsible funds have higher costs because of the cost of developing and implementing the screens. The Domini Social Equity Fund's expense ratio (1.08 percent) is much higher than the expense ratio of a low-cost S&P 500 fund or an exchange-traded fund (ETF). Naturally, higher costs translate into lower returns.

The returns of one of the most popular SRI funds offer compelling evidence. For the period from 2003 through 2007, the Domini Social Equity Fund returned 10.1 percent per year, compared to a gain of 12.7 percent for the Vanguard 500 Index Fund. Thus, we can say, at least in this case, "the cost of being socially responsible" was actually 2.6 percent per year.

Historically, small-cap and value stocks have provided risk premiums over large-cap and growth stocks. Most socially responsible funds are large-cap funds that tend to have a growth orientation based on their screening process. Thus, socially responsible investors who would otherwise prefer to gain exposure to small-cap and value stocks sacrifice higher expected returns. Additionally, they lose out on the diversification benefits of allocating portions of their portfolio to those two asset classes. The study found that for these investors the cost of being socially responsible rose to as much as about 3.5 percent per year, depending on the amount of exposure the investor opted for in the riskiest asset class (small-cap value).

2. Socially responsible investors also may be accepting other risks. Because the funds are not fully diversified (that is, they generally screen out what are known as "sin" stocks), they are taking uncompensated risk—risk that can be diversified away. Accepting this risk increases volatility and the dispersion of returns.

In the case of broad market indexes, this problem is relatively minor. For example, according to Morningstar Principia, as of February 2008 the Calvert Social Index Fund held 636 stocks, providing significant diversification. However, it is basically a large-cap growth fund. The problems related to this situation are magnified when investors seek to invest in other asset classes, such as small-cap value.

It should be noted, for instance, that we could not identify any socially responsible funds that invest in international small-cap or value stocks, or any real estate–based SRI funds. However, in August 2006, Dimensional Fund Advisors (DFA) opened the first socially responsible emerging market fund—

the Emerging Markets Social Core Equity Portfolio. The bottom line is that investors who do not invest in anything but SRI vehicles are likely to be missing out on important diversification benefits.

THE "PRICE" OF PRINCIPLES

One way to look at the relative underperformance of the Domini fund, and SRI funds in general, is that it represents the *price* of investing according to your principles. Some might conclude that the cost is worth it, while some might decide that the cost is too great. Another alternative is to consider how that same performance differential could be used to support personal beliefs or values.

For example, investors could invest in the aforementioned Vanguard funds instead of the Domini fund and donate the difference in returns to their favorite charitable causes. They could also increase their allocation to other asset classes with higher expected returns, and further diversify the risk of their portfolio. Doing so would provide two distinct benefits. The first is a tax deduction for the donation. And if donating appreciated shares, capital gains taxes are avoided. The second benefit is that the choice of causes is now completely in the investors' hands.

Obviously, this is a personal decision and one for which there is no single, right answer. The goal of this book is to ensure that investors consider all the issues and alternative strategies, as well as their implications.

SUMMARY

Investors who want to "do good" by investing in socially responsible funds should recognize that they are likely paying a considerable price in the form of lower expected returns. These lower expected returns should not come as a surprise, because in addition to the higher fees that reduce returns, the demand for SRI drives up the stock prices of companies that pass social screens. This lowers the cost of capital for these firms. The flip side of a lower cost of capital is a lower expected return to investors.

The reverse is true for companies that fail to pass through the screens. Their cost of capital increases. Thus, their investors now have a higher expected return. In addition to accepting lower expected returns, socially responsible investors should remember that they are also accepting somewhat greater portfolio risk due to inefficient diversification.

The cost of SRI, in the form of lower expected returns, should be weighed against the value placed on the desire to be socially responsible. Those interested in SRI can find a current list of socially responsible mutual funds at www.socialinvest.org. This list includes both domestic and international funds, as well as both equity and bond funds.

Precious Metals Equities   11

In Chapter 3, we discussed the three methods of investing in commodities: (1) direct investment in the commodities, (2) investment in collateralized commodity futures (CCFs), and (3) investment in the equities of commodities-related producers. Precious metals equities (PMEs) represent a narrower subset of the third alternative. Specifically, PMEs are the stock investments in companies that mine gold, silver, and platinum. The spectacular returns of 2001, 2002, and 2003, when PMEs returned 39.4 percent, 61.5 percent, and 62.9 percent, respectively, led many investors to ask whether they should consider including PMEs in their equity allocation.

To determine if the PME world merits consideration, we should revisit the same important questions we asked before about deciding on any investment:

- How risky is the asset class?
- What is the expected return of that asset class?
- What is the correlation of that asset class to the rest of the assets in the portfolio? (How does its inclusion affect the overall risk of the portfolio?)

RISK

PMEs are exposed to the risks of equity investing. Thus, we would naturally expect that PMEs would provide returns similar to those of other equities. Unfortunately, in the long run, they have provided returns below those of the overall equity market.

RETURNS

While the data are not as robust as they are for other asset classes, useful PME data are available. Based on a return series provided by Global Financial Data, author William Bernstein estimated that for the period from 1942 through 1996, the annualized return to PMEs was about 9.5 percent.[1] During the same time period, the S&P 500 Index returned 14.0 percent per year. Additionally, data on PMEs from the industry portfolios series available on professor Kenneth French's website indicate that for the period from July 1963 through December 2007, PMEs returned 7.6 percent per year. However, for that same period, the S&P 500 returned 10.6 percent per year.

Alternatively, the data for Vanguard's Precious Metals and Mining Fund also show that from its inception on May 23, 1984, through December 31, 2007, the fund returned 9.6 percent per year, but for roughly the same period, the S&P 500 returned 12.9 percent per year. Correlations with other assets in the portfolio are also relevant and play a key role.

CORRELATIONS

The good news is that a 2005 study by Ibbotson Associates, covering the period from 1970 through 2004, found that "hard assets," such as precious metals and natural resource equities, had low correlations with both U.S. equities (0.34 for small-cap stocks and 0.29 for large-cap stocks) and international equities (0.36).[2] In addition, hard assets were negatively correlated with intermediate-term bonds (−0.25) and positively correlated with inflation (0.22). This makes hard assets a good diversifier of the risks of both nominal return bonds and inflation.

THE HEDGING VALUE OF PME

It is important to note that, *on occasion*, PMEs have provided some stability to a portfolio—acting like a good anchor in a storm by keeping the ship safe in the harbor. This can be seen in TABLE 11.1.

While PMEs did, on average, rise 12.6 percent during the eight negative years for stocks, PMEs actually rose in just four of those years. In addition, PMEs suffered severe losses in four of those years

Table 11.1   Years of Negative Returns for the S&P 500 Index (1970 to 2007)

Year	Return of S&P 500 Index (%)	Return of Precious Metals Equities* (%)
1973	−14.7	+88.1
1974	−26.5	−20.3
1977	−7.2	+16.3
1981	−4.9	−33.2
1990	−3.1	−17.6
2000	−9.1	−33.7
2001	−11.9	+39.4
2002	−22.1	+61.5
Average Return	**−12.4**	**+12.6**

*Fama-French data (includes companies that mine gold and silver)

(one-half the time). Even worse, in three of those four years, PME holdings would have exacerbated the damage done to portfolios from equity holdings.

Looking at PMEs' value as a hedge against fixed-income assets, we find the following: In the two years during the period from 1973 through 2007 that the Lehman Brothers Treasury Bond Index (1–30 years) produced negative returns—1994 (−3.4 percent) and 1999 (−2.5 percent)—PME provided returns of −20.6 and +6.2 percent, respectively.

Positive Attributes of PME

There are two other possible reasons why investors might want to consider including a small allocation to PMEs in their portfolio. First, PMEs do provide a good hedge against inflation (and, thus, the risk of owning longer-term bonds). During inflationary periods, hard assets—such as precious metals and real estate—tend to perform well. For investors for whom inflation is a considerable risk (such as retirees), an allocation to PMEs or other hard assets is worth considering.

Second, there could be a large rebalancing (diversification) bonus. The low correlation of PMEs with other portfolio assets, along with their high volatility, means that if investors have the discipline to rebalance their portfolio when allocations drift significantly from the plan, the contribution of the PMEs' return to the total return of the overall portfolios will be larger—perhaps far larger—than their weighted average return. William Bernstein, in an article in his online publication, *Efficient Frontier*, estimates that the rebalancing bonus might be as large as 5 percent.[3]

OTHER CONSIDERATIONS

There are other major issues regarding PMEs that should also be considered. The first is psychological. Landmark studies by Nobel Prize–winner Daniel Kahneman, as well as books on investor behavior by Gary Belsky and Thomas Gilovich (*Why Smart People Make Big Money Mistakes—and How to Correct Them*) and Jason Zweig (*Your Money and Your Brain*) have found that emotions play a significant role in determining the ultimate returns of a portfolio.

As noted, PMEs constitute a highly volatile asset class, often experiencing severe drops. And those severe drops test investor discipline to stay the course. All too often, investors panic and sell after a severe drop. Thus, they are not there for the recovery. For example, for the period from 1963 through 2007, the PME industry portfolio fell more than 35 percent five times, and once lost nearly 70 percent. Also, because they are considered a "safe harbor" investment, PMEs tend to experience long periods of very low returns during periods of economic and political stability, and short periods of very high returns in times of crisis. It should be noted that it is in these periods of crisis that investors have the greatest need to generate high returns.

Tellingly, for the period from 1981 through 1992, the return of PMEs was –1.3 percent annualized versus 14.7 percent for the S&P 500. An even more dramatic situation occurred during the period October 1980 and August 1998, when the PME index lost almost 54 percent of its value, producing a nominal loss of 4.2 percent per year and an inflation-adjusted loss of 7.7 percent per year. Additionally, for the period October 1980 and December 2004, PMEs' real return was −0.3 percent.[4]

Investors with the patience to stay the course for more than twenty years, buying additional PMEs along the way to keep the portfolio's asset allocation in balance, were *ultimately* rewarded with the large gains of 2001 through 2003. We can conclude that investors must have both great discipline and strong stomachs, staying the course for a decade—or even perhaps even multiple decades—to reap the benefits of their patience. "Know thyself" is an important tenet of successful investing in this and other asset classes.

Another important consideration relates to implementation. Unfortunately, there are no passively managed funds available for investors who want to choose a PME allocation. This presents four significant problems. First, since we know that the average actively managed equity fund underperforms its benchmark by almost two percent per year on a pretax basis, investors are not likely to be fully rewarded for the risks of investing in PMEs. The Vanguard Precious Metals and Mining Fund should logically perform better than the average actively managed fund, because its expense ratio is well below average—an almost index-like 0.35 percent. The problem is that the operating expense ratio is not the only expense of active funds; trading costs must also be considered.

The second problem is that actively managed funds are likely to be less tax efficient than passively managed ones.

The third issue is that there are very few stocks in the PME asset class. In most years, the Fama-French PME benchmark portfolio contains as few as ten to fifteen stocks. With a portfolio that contains such a small number of holdings, investors are not sufficiently diversifying the unsystematic and uncompensated risk of owning individual PME stocks. Other asset classes typically contain hundreds, if not thousands, of individual stocks.

The fourth obstacle is, perhaps, the greatest. To address the issue of the large cash inflows the Vanguard Precious Metals Fund received (likely due to investors chasing the high returns of 2001 through 2003), Vanguard closed the fund to new investors in June 2002. To accommodate demand and reopen the fund, Vanguard allowed the fund to expand its mandate to include nonprecious metals. The reason? There were just not enough PME stocks to buy without creating large market impact costs and limiting the percentage holdings in any one company to an acceptable level. So, instead of limiting the fund to PME stocks, Vanguard changed the name of the fund to Vanguard Precious Metals and Mining Fund. It now invests in companies engaged in activities related to gold, silver, and platinum *and* in companies engaged in activities related to diamonds, nickel, copper, zinc, and other base or common metals or minerals. The result is that the fund has changed its nature, and the historical data we rely on to make decisions are no longer of much, if any, value. What's more, as of February 2, 2006, Vanguard once again closed this fund to new investors.

To summarize, while the historic risk and reward profile of PMEs is not particularly attractive on a stand-alone basis, its low correlation to both domestic and international equities, and to intermediate bonds, makes it at least worthy of consideration. This is especially true for investors who are significantly affected by inflation risk. The problem remains that there is no truly effective way to invest in this asset class.

Therefore, all things considered, we cannot identify a compelling reason to include PMEs in a well-diversified portfolio. On the other hand, those attracted by the diversification benefits PME can provide, and with a great deal of patience and discipline, might consider a small allocation (perhaps 5 percent) to Vanguard's fund—should it reopen to new investors.

IMPLEMENTING THE STRATEGY

Although strategies themselves have no costs, implementing them does. To access the asset class of PME, the best alternative is the Vanguard Precious Metals and Mining Fund (as noted previously, currently closed to new investors) with its reasonable expense ratio of 0.35 percent. For the period from 1988 through 2007, the fund returned 9.9 percent per year and experienced a standard deviation of 31.4 percent. During the same period, the S&P 500 returned 11.8 percent per year and experienced a standard deviation of just 16.6 percent.

However, the Vanguard fund did provide a diversification benefit, as can be seen in the fund's negative correlation (-0.11) with the S&P 500. The only other diversified PME fund with at least a ten-year track record and an expense ratio of less than 1 percent is the Franklin

Gold and Precious Metals Fund. For the same period, the Class A shares of the fund, which has an expense ratio of 0.93 percent (as of July 2008) and carries a load of 5.75 percent, returned just 8.4 percent and experienced a standard deviation of 28.1 percent. The fund's correlation with the S&P 500 was −0.06.

In addition to these diversified funds, two funds limit their exposure to PMEs strictly to gold producers and meet the dual criteria of having at least a ten-year track record and an expense ratio of less than 1 percent. The American Century Global Gold Fund has an expense ratio of 0.67 percent (as of July 2008). For the period from September 1988 (inception August 17, 1988) through December 2007, the fund returned 5.4 percent per year, and its annualized standard deviation was 33.4 percent. During the same period, the Vanguard Precious Metals and Mining Fund returned 11 percent per year, and its annualized standard deviation was 27.1 percent. By comparison, the S&P 500 returned 11.8 percent per year, and its annualized standard deviation was 13.6 percent. However, the American Century Global Gold Fund did demonstrate a negative correlation (−0.26) with the S&P 500, thus offering a significant diversification benefit.

The other PME fund to consider is Fidelity's Select Gold, with an expense ratio of 0.81 percent (as of July 2008). For the twenty-year period ending December 2007, it returned 7.6 percent per year, with a standard deviation of 29.3 percent. During the same period, the Vanguard Precious Metals Fund returned 9.9 percent per year, and its standard deviation was 31.4 percent. By comparison, the S&P 500 returned 11.8 percent per year, and its standard deviation was 16.6 percent. However, it is important to note that the Fidelity Select Gold Fund also exhibited negative correlation with the S&P 500 (−0.25).

SUMMARY

While the PME asset class does offer some positive attributes—the hedge against the risks of inflation, and to a lesser extent its hedge against the risks of equities—better alternatives exist. For investors seeking the diversification attributes of PMEs, PIMCO's Commodity Real Return Strategy Fund (or an exchange-traded fund, an exchange-trade note, or the equivalent) is a better alternative than a precious metals or precious metals and mining fund. Although CCFs provide a similar hedge against the risks of inflation, they have historically provided a better hedge against the risks of equities. This can be seen in the following CCF performance data:

■ In the eight years from 1970 to 2007 when the S&P 500 experienced negative returns, on average PMEs rose 12.6 percent, but managed to provide positive returns in just four of the eight years, while incurring substantial losses in the other years. On the other hand, CCFs rose in six of the eight years, providing an average return of 22.6 percent. In addition to their superior hedging characteristics, CCFs provided superior returns.

The bottom line? PMEs continue to be an alternative investment with limited appeal.

Preferred Stocks   *12*

I n Chapter 6, we discussed why investors who need or want more income than can be earned through short-term fixed-income investments should consider stable-value funds. The relatively high yields of preferred stocks make them another candidate that investors in similar situations typically consider. However, while preferred stocks offer relatively high yields, in general, they possess enough negative attributes to make them inappropriate choices for individual investors.

Standing behind debt holders in the credit lineup, preferred stocks are technically equity investments. They provide a specific dividend that is paid before any dividends are paid to common stockholders. While preferred shareholders receive preference over common equity holders (hence the term *preferred*), in the case of a Chapter 11 bankruptcy, all debt holders would have to be paid off before any payment could be made to the preferred shareholders. If a company were to be liquidated, both preferred and common stockholders would generally receive nothing.

Unlike with shares of common stock, which may benefit from the potential growth in the value of a company, the investment return on preferred stocks is mainly a function of the *fixed* dividend yield (although there are some variable preferred stocks available). A difference between conventional bonds and preferred stocks is that conventional bonds have a fixed maturity date, while preferred stocks may not.

LONG MATURITIES

Preferred stocks are either perpetual (have no maturity) or they are generally long term, typically with a maturity of between fifteen and thirty years. In addition, many preferred stock issues with a stated maturity of thirty years include an issuer option to extend for an additional nineteen years. Investors considering purchasing perpetual preferred stock should ask themselves the following question: Would a prudent investor purchase a bond from the same company paying the same interest rate with a 100-year maturity? The answer is almost certainly no. Why not? Because the *credit risk* on a bond of such long maturity is likely to be too great.

The long term of preferred stocks with a stated maturity also creates another problem. The historical evidence on the risk and rewards of fixed-income investing demonstrates that longer maturities have the poorest risk-reward characteristics—the lowest return for a given level of risk (with risk being defined as volatility, or standard deviation).

RISKS AND REWARDS OF LONG MATURITIES

Consider the following evidence: For the period from 1973 through 2007, the Lehman Brothers Intermediate Treasury Bond Index (1–10 years) returned 7.84 percent and did so with a standard deviation of 5.38 percent. The comparable figures for the longer-maturity Lehman Brothers Treasury Bond Index (1–30 years) are a return of 8.22 percent and a standard deviation of 6.51 percent. While providing 4.8 percent higher returns, the longer maturity index experienced 21 percent greater volatility.

Now consider the following alternative: Investors willing to accept a greater amount of volatility than that produced by Lehman Brothers Intermediate Treasury Bond Index could add a small allocation to stocks instead of extending maturity to try to increase returns. TABLE 12.1, covering the period from 1973 to 2007, illustrates that a strategy of adding a small allocation to equities was a more efficient way (resulting in higher returns with less volatility) of improving returns than extending maturity.

Table 12.1   Alternative Portfolio Strategies 1973–2007

Allocation	Annualized Return (%)	Standard Deviation (%)
100% Lehman Brothers Intermediate Treasury Bond Index	7.84	5.38
100% Lehman Brothers Treasury Bond Index (1–30 years)	8.22	6.51
90% Lehman Brothers Intermediate Treasury Bond Index (1–10 years)/10% S&P 500	8.27	5.54
80% Lehman Brothers Intermediate Treasury Bond Index (1–10 years)/20% S&P 500	8.68	6.16

CALL RISK

Unfortunately, the long maturities typical of preferred stocks are not the only problem with these securities. They typically also carry a call provision. With few exceptions, U.S. Treasury debt has no call provision. Thus, almost all U.S. government debt (as well as all noncallable debt instruments) carries what is called *symmetric price risk*. If interest rates rise, bond prices will fall. If rates fall, bond prices will rise.

As an example, a 1 percent rise or fall in interest rates will result in an approximately 1 percent change in the price of the bond for each year of duration. This is not the case with callable preferred stock. If rates rise, the price of the preferred stock will fall. However, if rates fall, and the issuer is able to do so, it will call the preferred stock and replace it with either a new preferred stock issue at lower rates, less-expensive conventional debt, or perhaps even equity. Thus, investors face *asymmetric risk*. They get the risk of a long-duration product when rates rise. However, because of the call feature, when rates fall, the gains are limited to those that would be realized from an instrument of shorter maturity. As a result, preferred stocks rarely trade much above their issue price.

It is important to note that almost all callable preferred stocks are callable at par. Therefore, there is extremely limited upside potential (virtually none, if the call date is near) if the security is purchased at par. Call protection is vital to income-oriented investors, because callable instruments present *reinvestment risk*, the risk of having to reinvest the proceeds of a called investment at lower rates. Through calls, investors lose access to relatively higher income streams. Thus, part of the incremental yield of preferred stocks relative to a noncall-able debt issuance of the same company is compensation for giving the issuer the right to call the debt, should the rate environment prove favorable or the credit standing of the issuer improve.

The other source of the incremental yield of preferred stocks is *credit risk*.

CREDIT RISK

As is the case with corporate bonds, preferred stocks are rated by the three major credit-rating agencies (Standard & Poor's, Moody's, and Fitch), making it easy to check their credit quality. However, as is also the case with corporate bonds, the rating needs to be constantly monitored. While all preferred stocks are not in the junk category, they seldom receive high credit ratings.

Given the lower cost to the issuer of tax-deductible conventional debt, and the fact that equity preferred dividends are not deductible for the issuer, one has to ask why companies issue preferred stock in the first place. This is especially true when, traditionally, preferred shares have been rated two notches below the issuer's rating on unsecured debt. (The lower credit rating increases the cost.) The ultimate answer may not be reassuring to those seeking safe investments.

One reason preferred stock is often issued is that the company has already loaded its balance sheet with a large amount of debt, and it would risk a downgrade if it piled on even more. Some companies also issue preferred stock for regulatory reasons. For example, regulators might limit the amount of outstanding debt a company is allowed to have.

In October 1996, the Federal Reserve allowed U.S. bank holding companies to treat certain types of preferred stocks (called *hybrid preferred stocks*) as Tier 1 capital for capital adequacy purposes. An additional reason for issuing preferred stock is that it can be structured to look like debt, from a tax perspective, and equity, from a balance-sheet perspective. Instruments structured in this manner are called *trust preferreds.*

Finally, investors should be aware that in times of financial distress, the payment of preferred dividends could be deferred. On the other hand, bond interest payments represent a contractual obligation and failure to pay sets the wheels in motion for reorganization or bankruptcy and liquidation.

Another risk related to buying preferred stocks has to do with the call feature. The call feature is not only related to interest-rate risk, as most investors assume, but also to changes in the company's credit rating. Issuers with low credit ratings and high-yielding preferred stocks will likely call the preferred stock if their credit status improves. They would then replace the preferred stock with a now higher-rated conventional corporate bond (which provides tax deductibility).

Of course, if the company's credit deteriorates, it will not call the preferred stock (but the price of the preferred stock will fall due to the deteriorated credit). Again, the investor faces an asymmetric risk—one of the reasons for the higher yield. Risk and expected return are always related. Whether the higher yield eventually translates into higher returns—and for how long—is a question that only a clear crystal ball could answer.

LONG MATURITIES AND CALL RISK

Longer-term maturities with fixed yields do provide a hedge against deflationary environments. The problem with long-maturity preferred stocks is that the call feature negates the benefits of the longer maturity in a falling-rate environment. Thus, the holder does not benefit from a rise in price that would occur with a noncallable fixed-rate security in a falling-rate environment.

It is also worth repeating that if the issuer is unable to call the preferred stock, the reason is likely to be a deteriorating credit rating, putting the investor's principal at risk. Given that preferred stock issuers are often companies with weaker credit ratings, and distressed companies are the ones most likely to default in deflationary environments, the benefit of the high-yielding longer maturity (which should rise in price in a falling-rate environment) is unlikely to be realized by the holders of these callable instruments.

Thus, the risks of preferred stocks reveal themselves at the worst possible times for investors.

Dividend Suspension

As was noted earlier, even if a company does not go into bankruptcy, because preferred stocks are considered equities, it can suspend the payment of preferred stock dividends. It is also essential to understand that unless the preferred is a *cumulative preferred stock* the company is not obligated to make up any of the missed dividends. However, the company must make up the missed dividends of cumulative preferred stocks before it declares any dividends to its common stockholders.

Preferential Treatment for Corporate Buyers

Are there any good reasons to buy a preferred stock? The answer is "yes"—but only for certain types of investors. Corporate buyers of preferred stock receive favorable tax treatment on the dividends of preferred stock, with most of the dividend not subject to taxes. U.S. corporate stockholders can exclude up to 70 percent of the dividend from their taxable income provided they hold the shares at least forty-five days. This favorable tax treatment creates demand for the product. Individuals get no such favorable tax treatment.

The bottom line is that investors who buy preferred stocks because of their higher yield—possibly combined with the fear of equity investing—are assuming additional risk. Because the market is efficient at pricing risk, higher yields entail greater risk. These risks may include perpetual life (or very long maturity), a call feature, low credit rating, and deferrable dividends. In addition, there is the depressed yield due to demand from corporations that receive favorable tax treatment.

Other Considerations

There are three other reasons to consider avoiding preferred stocks. First, there are no low-cost index funds or passive asset-class funds that provide investors with the most effective way to diversify the credit risks of individual issuers. Second, buying individual issues involves trading costs, the lack of diversification, and the need to constantly monitor credit ratings. Third, the typical lengthy maturity of preferred stocks increases credit risk. Many companies might present modest credit risk in the near term, but credit risk increases over time.

Tax Advantages

Preferred stocks can have an advantage *relative* to taxable bonds if they are both held in taxable accounts. The dividend on *some* preferred stocks is treated like the dividend from equities in that it is considered qualified dividend income (QDI) and is eligible for the lower capital gains tax rate. This is currently 15 percent in most cases, as opposed to interest on bonds, which is taxed at the higher ordinary income tax rates. Note that dividends from real estate investment trust (REIT) preferred stocks do not qualify for the preferred tax treatment.

Summary

The risks incurred when investing in preferred stocks make them inappropriate investments for individual investors. They can also be extremely complex instruments, making it difficult to analyze the risks. And one of the rules of prudent investing is to avoid complex securities because the complexity is likely to favor the issuer.

As we have discussed, a stable-value fund is a good alternative for investors seeking more income and represents the preferred choice. Alternatively, those needing higher returns and willing to accept equity risk can simply increase their allocation to equities, as it will be a more efficient way of improving returns. Those still considering investing in preferred stocks should consider only those that carry an AAA rating (or perhaps AA if the remaining maturity is relatively short). The reason is that the longer the maturity, the greater the credit risk. In addition, investors choosing preferred stocks with a rating below the highest investment-grade ratings (AAA/AA) begin to take on more equity-like risks—risks that are better taken in the equity market where they can be more effectively diversified.

Those purchasing preferred stock should buy cumulative preferred stocks, to benefit from additional dividend protection. And finally, if the preferred stocks are going to be held in a taxable account, investors should be sure that the dividends are "qualified" dividends, so they enjoy the lower capital gains rate.

Convertible Bonds   13

CONVERTIBLE BONDS ARE hybrid securities that have character-istics of both stocks and bonds. The attraction of convertible bonds as alternative investments is that they seem to offer the best of both worlds to the risk-averse investor—the upside potential of equities and the safety of corporate bonds. However, as discussed previously, there are no free lunches in the world of investing (with the exception of diversification). Investors should gain an under-standing of all of the issues related to convertible bonds before deciding if they should play a role in their portfolio.

As the name implies, a convertible bond gives the holder the option—the right, but not the obligation—to exchange a corporate bond for a predetermined number of shares of common stock in the issuing company. It is the tantalizing right, but not the obligation, to convert a bond to equity that creates the perception that an investor can enjoy the best of both worlds. If the stock does well, the holder can convert to equity, but if it does poorly, the investor retains the safety of the bond and the coupon payment. Not surprisingly, the market recognizes this option has value and assigns a "price" for this flexibility—the interest rate on the convertible bond would be less than it would be on a similar nonconvertible debt issue.

As for the conversion price, it is typically set well above the cur-rent market price. Two key factors determine how much the option to convert is worth: (1) how far the conversion price is above the current price and (2) how volatile the stock is. The more volatile the stock, the more the option to convert is worth, because there is more upside potential.

The Realities of Convertible Bonds

Upon further review, convertible bonds start to lose their best-of-both-worlds appeal. First, as we have discussed, because of the inherent value of the conversion option, convertible bonds provide a lower yield than nonconvertible bonds of similar credit and maturity. Second, they are only as safe as the underlying credit of the issuer.

As discussed in previous chapters, the bonds of companies below the highest investment grades of AAA and AA actually contain equity-like risks. And if the stock of a convertible bond issuer is doing poorly, the safety of the interest and principal payments may also be put in jeopardy, as there is an increasing risk of downgrades that will have a negative impact on valuation, as well as default. Thus, the investor might have the worst of both worlds—a below-market coupon and a deteriorating credit rating. Clearly, the free lunch is not free at all.

Considerations

Many convertible bonds come with a call feature, giving the issuer the right to call in the bonds prior to maturity. This means that investors might be forced to convert their bonds into common stock when the timing is least favorable for investors. This scenario would likely occur when the price of the stock is higher than the conversion price, so the call feature effectively places a cap on potential capital appreciation. The result? While the downside risk continues, the upside potential is effectively capped.

In every case, calls are features that favor the issuer. If either interest rates were to fall sharply, or the company's credit rating were to improve so it could issue cheaper (perhaps nonconvertible) debt, the issuer would likely exercise the call.

Another negative is that convertible bonds are usually subordinated debentures (debt whose interest and principal is paid only after other higher-ranking debt has been paid).

That means in the event of bankruptcy, unsubordinated debts must be paid off first. A further consideration is that the conversion price is typically well above the current market price for the common stock of the issuer. Thus, the stock price must rise significantly before the break-even point for conversion is reached.

One of the supposed benefits of convertible bonds is that they exhibit low correlation with both stocks and bonds. Of course, this must be true because they are hybrid securities containing some elements of both asset classes. However, low correlation is only a necessary—but an insufficient—condition for considering an investment. In other words, a low correlation with stocks and bonds should not be the *only* consideration, let alone the deciding factor.

SHIFTING ASSET ALLOCATION

The majority of a portfolio's risk and return is determined by its asset allocation, so it is critical to maintain control over this aspect of its investments. A problem with convertible bonds is that investors are always dealing with a shifting asset allocation. The amount of equity risk and bond risk investors actually hold depends on where the stock price is trading relative to the conversion rate stated in the bond.

If the current stock price is well above the conversion price, investors basically no longer hold a bond. Instead, they hold an equity security—the convertible bond will virtually move in tandem with the stock price.

On the other hand, if the stock price is well below the conversion price, then investors basically hold a debt instrument—the convertible bond will trade more like a bond than a stock. And if investors hold a mutual fund (in our opinion, the only prudent way to invest in convertible bonds), it will be impossible to determine the equity-to-fixed-income ratio at any point in time.

The remaining maturity and credit ratings are also important factors in determining just how much equity and fixed-income risk investors actually hold by owning convertible bonds. As these factors shift, asset allocations will shift as well. The result is that holding convertible bonds in a mutual fund, or a separate account, causes a loss of control over the risks and expected return of the overall portfolio.

ASSET LOCATION

Another significant problem for individual investors is that the hybrid nature of convertible bonds creates a dilemma in terms of the asset-location decision. As we have discussed, the preference is to hold tax-inefficient bonds in tax-advantaged accounts and tax-efficient equities in taxable accounts. Since convertible bonds are hybrids, and investors don't know which type of asset they will eventually be holding, there is a distinct possibility that a security will be matched to the wrong type of account.

COMPLEXITY

Convertible bonds are complex instruments. As we have discussed, the more complex the instrument, the more likely it is that the inherent complexity favors the issuer, not the buyer. The more complex the security, the more likely it is that a sophisticated institutional investor will be able to exploit these advantages and, as a result, the individual investor will suffer. With about 95 percent of all trading in convertible bonds being driven by hedge funds and other large institutional investors, the competition for these securities among individual investors is extremely intense.[1] Therefore, investors even considering convertible bonds should only do so if they are going to purchase them through a mutual fund.

With almost all trading in convertible bonds being done between institutional investors, one has to ask who active managers can exploit so that they can outperform and justify their expenses. In fact, the extreme level of competition has led many convertible funds to shut down.

A good example is that on August 4, 2008, Citicorp announced that it was shutting down Tribeca Convertible (its $400 million convertible bond hedge fund) and returning the remaining assets to investors.[2] The need to diversify both the credit and stock risks involved with convertible bonds also leads us to conclude that a mutual fund is the only appropriate investment vehicle for these securities. However, this requirement also results in an additional layer of expenses in the form of management fees and trading costs that buyers of Treasury securities can avoid, because buying them directly from the Treasury eliminates the need for diversification (because there is no credit risk in Treasury securities).

SUMMARY

While convertible bonds offer some interesting features, we cannot recommend them for individual investors. In fact, because of issues like shifting allocation, the asset-location dilemma, and call risks, individual investors should avoid them.

If the reason for buying convertibles is to seek higher returns than nonconvertible bonds can provide, consider either increasing equity allocations or increasing exposure to equity classes with higher expected returns, such as small-cap stocks, value stocks, and emerging market stocks. If, instead, the reason for buying convertibles is to reduce the overall risk of the equity portfolio, it is wiser to purchase nonconvertible investment-grade bonds.

Emerging Market Bonds **14**

D URING THE 2000–2002 bear market for equities, emerging market bonds proved to be one of the top-performing asset classes. Although the global equities markets—including emerging market equities—suffered, many emerging market bond funds delivered double-digit returns, a trend that continued from 2003 through 2006. This led to a rush of investment dollars chasing the latest "hot" asset class.

Today, the question for prudent investors is whether emerging market bonds are an appropriate building block for a globally diversified portfolio. Or are investors experiencing just another case of "recency"—the tendency to assign too much importance to recent experience, while ignoring the lessons of long-term historical evidence? Let's examine the issues to consider to make the wisest decision.

RISKS

Investing in international bonds exposes the investor to a mixture of risks that are different for each country. A country's unique set of risks (for example, political, economic, and cultural) make up what is collectively called its *sovereign risk*, the risk of a country defaulting on its debt. U.S. Treasury bonds entail no risk of default for U.S. investors. Default risk, however, is a real threat in emerging markets. Countries have defaulted on "foreign-denominated" debt, because of their inability to generate sufficient foreign currency to repay their obligations.

Because of these inherent risks, emerging market debt is a risky asset class, characterized by extreme volatility. In fact, for the period from January 1991 through September 1999, emerging market debt exhibited greater volatility (approximately 20 percent) than emerging market equities (although returns were higher as well).[1] Emerging market debt is similar in nature to high-yield bonds and possesses some of the same characteristics that risk-averse investors find unattractive about the high-yield asset class.

First, the securities markets for emerging market debt are not liquid. This means that not only are trading costs high, but also that markets can dry up in times of crises. Buyers virtually disappear, and trades can only be made if the seller is willing to accept a substantial markdown. There may even be times when sales cannot be made at any price.

Unfortunately, in the case of emerging markets, crises are not infrequent occurrences and can have negative consequences for all investors, even those who stay the course. The problem is that other investors in a fund may flee, forcing expensive turnover to meet redemptions. The collective actions of some investors in a fund can impose high costs on all shareholders.

Second, portfolios of illiquid securities have reported returns that tend to be smoother than their true economic returns, resulting in the understatement of volatility and the overstatement of risk-adjusted performance measures such as the Sharpe ratio (see the Glossary).

Third, investors who experience a period of high returns can also make the mistake of being fooled into thinking the asset class isn't risky. Then, one day the risk appears, and all the "excess" returns that were previously earned can disappear overnight.

Fourth, emerging market bond returns exhibit negative skewness (see the Glossary). For example, for the period from January 1991 through September 1999, emerging market bonds exhibited a negative skewness of 1.9.[2] This is roughly five times the negative skewness exhibited by domestic high-yield bonds during the 1990s.[3]

Fifth, emerging market bond returns exhibit high kurtosis (a larger-than-normal proportion of extreme returns), and risk-averse investors prefer a distribution with low kurtosis. Having both nega-tive skewness and high kurtosis is a sign of a highly risky asset class—complete with the potential for significant losses.

Recalling our discussion of high-yield bonds, remember that if an asset exhibits *nonnormal* distribution (such as with high-yield bonds and emerging market bonds), mean-variance analysis using standard deviation as the measure of risk is only a good *first ap-proximation* of the optimal portfolio. It does not completely reflect investors' true preferences. On the flip side, because investors pre-fer to avoid assets with these characteristics (that is, negative skew-ness and excess kurtosis), these securities must be priced to provide high expected returns to attract capital.

RETURNS

Keep in mind that the available data for emerging market bonds is derived from the JPMorgan EMBI Global Index (an index of the dollar-denominated debt of more than thirty countries). The index's short time frame (covering 1994 through 2007) makes it difficult to make any judgment on the overall attractiveness of the asset class.

It is also important to note that the decade prior to the 1990s was one of turmoil and default.[4] Therefore, returns may be biased, reflecting recovery from depressed levels.

The 2000 paper "Re-Emerging Markets," by authors William Goetzmann and Philippe Jorion, found that equity markets in emerging countries that re-emerge after a period of dormancy gen-erate returns for an initial period that are greater than their long-term expected returns. The same upward bias is also evident in emerging market bonds. Thus, it is likely that the aftermath of the debt renegotiation and market liberalizations that took place fol-lowing various crises in emerging markets drove returns above their sustainable long-term average for a period. We should, therefore, be careful about interpreting the data and not assume that future returns will remain as strong.[5]

As an example of why we should not consider future returns to be similar to those in the past, consider that in September 1999 the spread (the incremental yield above the yield on U.S. Treasury debt

Table 14.1   Emerging Market Bond Returns, 1994–2007

Year	JPMorgan EMBI Global Index Annual Return (%)
1994	−18.35
1995	26.38
1996	35.24
1997	11.95
1998	−11.55
1999	24.18
2000	14.41
2001	1.36
2002	13.12
2003	25.65
2004	11.73
2005	10.73
2006	9.88
2007	6.28
Annualized Return	10.58
Standard Deviation	14.45

of comparable maturity) on the sovereign debt of emerging market countries was about 10 percent.[6] By 2007, the figure was only a small fraction of that. It is difficult to earn much greater returns when beginning with such low yields.

As **TABLE 14.1** shows, emerging market debt has provided equity-like returns with equity-like risks (volatility). In comparison, for the same period, the S&P 500 Index returned 10.52 percent per year and exhibited a standard deviation of 18.12.

CORRELATIONS

An asset class that is risky in isolation may be less so in the context of the overall portfolio if it exhibits low correlations. On the positive side, because emerging market bonds possess some unique characteristics, *on average* they exhibit low correlation with other asset classes, including U.S. and international equities, and even emerging market equities.

Emerging market bonds tend to exhibit low correlation during periods that are characterized by tranquility in the economies and politics of emerging market countries. During such periods, the returns of emerging market bonds are explained to a high degree (more than 60 percent) by the returns of emerging market equities and the returns of long-term U.S. Treasury bonds.

Unfortunately, the correlation of returns tends to increase during times of crisis. At these times, the returns for emerging market debt are linked to the performance of emerging market equities, U.S. equities, and high-yield debt, and the explanatory power of these three asset classes rises to over 70 percent.[7] The result is that investors in emerging market bonds face the possibility of shifting allocations—a strong negative, as it means losing control over the risk of the portfolio.

This is especially important because the allocations shift in the wrong direction at the wrong time (to more risky assets in times of crisis). Obviously, this is an undesirable time for the risk to show up in the portion of an investor's portfolio that is supposed to be reducing the overall portfolio risks to an acceptable level.

Increasing correlation of emerging market debt with equities is especially likely to occur in response to a global capital markets crisis. As discussed in the section on emerging market equities in Chapter 4, what became known as the Asian contagion was triggered by a currency crisis that began in Thailand in July 1997. The crisis eventually spread throughout much of Asia and affected Hong Kong, Indonesia, Malaysia, the Philippines, and Singapore. Like a highly transmissible disease, it traveled around the globe and swept up other emerging markets, including those of Brazil and Russia.

As a result, in August 1998, JPMorgan's Emerging Market Bond Index fell almost 26 percent.[8] In the same month, emerging market equities, as measured by the MSCI Emerging Markets Index, fell almost 29 percent.

Just when investors need low correlation, the correlation shows its nasty tendency to rise, and emerging market bonds begin to trade more like emerging market equities. Thus, we see a similar story in terms of what occurs with U.S. high-yield debt; in times of crises, debt issues with low credit ratings become highly correlated with the equity of the issuer. In emerging markets, the lower the credit rating of the country, the greater the correlation of returns with the country's equity markets.[9]

However, it is important to note that during times of crises (when all risky assets tend to fall and their correlations rise), even countries with strong sovereign credit ratings are not immune to flights to quality; their bonds act more like equities. During the summer of 1998, for instance, the sovereign debt of some Asian emerging markets was not spared despite having investment-grade ratings.[10]

POTENTIAL POSITIVES

The main attraction of emerging market bonds is their high coupon. However, investors need to remember the following:

- The high coupon is also a reflection of the high risk for these securities.
- The high coupon does *not* equal the expected return. The risk of default and expected losses should be considered carefully.
- The high coupon compensates investors not only for the significant credit risk entailed, but also for the lack of liquidity and the high trading costs that are incurred when the bonds are bought or sold.
- The risks of emerging market bonds tend to show up just when equity assets in a portfolio are experiencing distress.

ADDITIONAL CONSIDERATIONS

- Typically, the main purpose for including fixed-income assets in an overall portfolio is to allow investors to limit the amount of their equity risk to a comfortable level. However, emerging market bonds are *not* an asset class that can be relied on to help investors sleep well during periods when equity markets are experiencing distress.
- Since the returns for emerging market debt occur in the form of current income, the asset class is a tax-inefficient one. Thus, this asset class should be held in a tax-deferred account, although this also has some negative implications. First, because of the high volatility of the asset class, there are likely to be

opportunities to harvest tax losses, and this can only be done in a taxable account. Second, there are also other tax benefits of holding equities in taxable accounts, namely the potential for a stepped-up basis for heirs and the ability to donate appreciated shares to charities, thus avoiding all taxes.

- Another consideration related to this asset class is that actively managed funds—at least in theory—can exploit market mispricings. One problem for actively managed funds in this asset class is that the asset class is the exclusive domain of sophisticated institutional investors, including mutual funds, hedge funds, pension plans, and investment banks. Thus, there does not seem to be a likely group of investors with a lack of knowledge that can be exploited to help offset these high operating costs.

- It is unlikely that the high returns experienced from 1999 through 2003 can be repeated (see Table 14.1). First, during the crisis of 1998, the spread between the yields on emerging market debt and U.S. Treasury debt dramatically widened. Since the crisis was resolved in a favorable manner, spreads narrowed. While this narrowing can continue, at some point spreads will likely widen because of the risky nature of the asset class. Thus, a narrowing of the spread should be treated as a one-time gain, not a permanent risk premium. Second, the yield on U.S. Treasury securities fell dramatically between 2000 and 2003. Since emerging market debt trades at a spread over U.S. Treasury debt, its yields fell in tandem with U.S. Treasury yields. This, too, must be treated as a one-time event, not an ongoing source of return premium.

- There are no passive, low-cost investment vehicles that allow investors to implement an emerging market bond strategy. Thus, some of the risk premium is lost to expenses, and investors are not fully compensated for taking risk. Currently, the only choices available are actively managed funds. Actively managed funds tend not only to be high cost and high turnover, but also typically to have concentrated (risky) holdings.

Table 14.2   An Overview of Emerging Market Bond Funds

Fund	Operating Expense Ratio (%)	Turnover (%)	Top Ten Holdings as Percent of Total Assets (%)
Goldman Sachs Emerging Markets Debt (A)	1.23	48	55
MFS Emerging Markets Debt (A)	1.33	125	32
Payden Emerging Markets Bond (A)	0.80	129	40
PIMCO Emerging Markets Bond (A)	1.25	238	27
T. Rowe Price Emerging Markets Bond (A)	0.98	577	36

Source: Morningstar as of January 31, 2008

TABLE 14.2 illustrates the operating expense ratio, the turnover rate, and the top 10 holdings as a percent of total assets for five popular funds. It is especially important to note the turnover rates, because this asset class's low levels of liquidity can lead to high trading costs (both bid-offer spreads and market impact costs). Note that all of the data are for the Class A shares of the fund.

SUMMARY

While emerging market bonds can't be recommended, they do have some positive attributes—high expected return combined with low correlation with both high-credit-quality U.S. debt securities and U.S. and international equities. On the other hand, there are also considerable negatives for investors (especially risk-averse investors) to consider, including high volatility, the risk of large losses, the potential for correlations to rise at the wrong time, tax-inefficient returns, and the high costs of implementing an emerging market bond strategy.

The bottom line is that the negatives appear to outweigh the positives. At best, emerging market bonds may be more appropriate as a substitute for emerging market equities than they are for U.S. fixed-income investments.

While the inclusion of emerging market bonds in a portfolio is not recommended, for those who believe the combination of high expected returns and some unique risk characteristics outweigh the negatives, we offer the following suggestions:

- Because of the high-risk nature of the asset class, any allocation to emerging market bonds should be considered an allocation to equities—*not* fixed income.
- Choose the active fund with the combination of the lowest expense ratio and, because trading costs are high in this asset class, the lowest historical turnover. Also keep in mind that the past turnover of actively managed funds may not be a good predictor of future turnover.

PART 3

The Bad

Hedge Funds *15*

REX SINQUEFIELD, RETIRED cochairman of Dimensional Fund Advisors (DFA), made this important observation: "Just because there are some investors smarter than others, that advantage will not show up. The market is too vast and too informationally efficient."[1]

Thus, while it is possible that hedge fund managers may be investment experts, the presence of special skills is one—but not the only—condition necessary for success. Trading costs, management fees, administrative fees, incentive fees, and tax inefficiency are all costs that are borne by investors in hedge funds. To make matters worse, investors accept the risks of potentially poor diversification of assets. Therefore, the question becomes this: Do hedge fund managers have enough skill to compensate for all the costs (and incremental risks) incurred?

The 2001 study "Hedge Fund Performance 1990–2000: Do the 'Money Machines' Really Add Value?" by Harry M. Kat and Gaurav S. Amin, investigated whether hedge funds did indeed offer investors a superior risk-adjusted return profile.[2] Because hedge fund returns may exhibit a high degree of nonnormality (that is, fat tails) as well as a nonlinear relationship with the stock market—rendering the use of traditional performance measures questionable—the study used a dynamic trading-based performance measure that does not require any assumptions about the distribution of fund returns.

The study covered thirteen hedge fund indexes and seventy-seven individual funds.

Summary of Hedge Fund Performance 1990–2000

- Twelve of the thirteen indexes (92 percent) showed signs of inefficiency, with the average efficiency loss (risk-adjusted return) on these twelve indexes amounting to 3.0 percent per year. In practical terms, this means that the same returns could have been achieved with much less risk.

- Of the seventy-seven funds studied, seventy-two (94 percent) showed signs of inefficiency, with the average efficiency loss amounting to 7.0 percent per year. Only five funds offered superior performance, with an average efficiency gain of just 1.5 percent per year.

- All fifteen of the event-driven funds showed signs of inefficiency, with an average efficiency loss of 3.8 percent per year.

- Of the twenty-eight global hedge funds, twenty-four (86 percent) showed some level of inefficiency, with an average cost of 8.5 percent per year.

- Of the eleven market-neutral funds studied, ten (91 percent) showed some level of inefficiency. For this group, the average efficiency loss was 6.8 percent per year.

The authors reached the conclusion that, even without taking into account the significant survivorship bias that exists in hedge fund data, their results clearly contradict the claim that hedge funds generate superior investment results on a stand-alone basis.

The study also considered the possible benefits of diversifying across hedge funds and found that there was an average efficiency gain over individual hedge funds of 3.7 percent per year—the hedge fund indexes performed significantly better than the individual funds. This result indicates that inefficiency costs can be reduced by investing in a portfolio of hedge funds instead of a single fund. Combining different types of funds seems to offer additional gains. After combining all thirteen indexes into an equally weighted portfolio, the efficiency loss would drop to 1.8 percent per year—a sizeable loss nonetheless.

The study also found that the diversification benefits touted by a fund-of-funds approach were more than offset by the incremental expenses incurred by adding another layer of fees. Despite the extra layer of diversification, the three fund-of-funds indexes were 1.6 percent less efficient than the average non-fund of funds and 5.2 percent less efficient than the average non-fund-of-funds index.

Based on these findings, one would expect funds of funds to generate results similar to those obtained for the non-fund-of-funds indexes. But these results strongly suggest that the fees charged by fund-of-funds managers outweigh the efficiency gains of additional diversification and potentially superior fund selection. Therefore, although smaller investors have little choice, larger investors should think twice before outsourcing their hedge fund portfolio management.

The authors concluded: "Our results make it clear that the main attraction of hedge funds lies in the weak relationship between hedge fund returns and the returns on other asset classes. It is interesting to note, however, that this is primarily the result of the general type of strategy followed by many hedge funds and not special manager skills. Any fund manager following a typical long/short type strategy can be expected to show low systematic exposure [to the market], whether he has special skills or not. *This leads us to the question of why investors should pay those high fees if the main attraction of hedge funds is not a manager specific feature.*" (Italics are the authors'.)

The inevitable answer? Most investors don't understand what they are buying or what they are paying.

Keep in mind that the sales pitches made by purveyors of hedge funds focus mainly on the supposedly (but not apparently) superior skills of the managers.

These findings are consistent with those of other published studies on hedge fund investing. Clearly, hedge funds make for inefficient investment vehicles. One might conclude, as Warren Buffett did, that they are not investment vehicles at all, but simply "compensation schemes," likely to enrich only the fund owners, managers, and those promoting their use. Investors should be especially cautious regarding reported returns data—the data do not appropriately reflect the risks of hedge fund investing, and they are likely to be biased in favor of hedge funds.

Even a fund-of-funds approach, advocated by many investment advisers and Wall Street investment firms (because of the high fees they generate), still leaves investors with highly inefficient investments. The data suggest that for those investors seeking diversification from domestic equities, the more efficient way to achieve such diversification is to invest in low-correlating asset classes, such as international small-cap value, emerging markets, real estate, and Treasury inflation-protected securities (TIPS). All of these asset classes can be accessed through low-cost, passive investment vehicles.

Exclusive Nature

Hedge funds are one of the most popular choices for intrepid investors who seek excitement and the proverbial "pot of gold at the end of the rainbow." At least for individual investors, hedge funds represent a relatively new option among alternative investments. This chapter is the longest in the book because hedge funds are characterized by many complex issues. In addition, much of the mystique surrounding hedge funds needs to be explored to distinguish myth from reality.

Hedge funds represent a rapidly growing specialized niche within the investment fund arena. In 1990, there were 530 hedge funds with about $50 billion in assets. However, it took just fifteen years for those figures to exceed 8,000 hedge funds and $1 trillion in assets,[3] and by the end of 2007, the industry had grown to $1.7 trillion.[4]

Apparently, the exclusive nature of the hedge fund "club" creates an aura that seems to attract investors the way swim-up bars attract guests at all-inclusive resorts. In addition to their "sex appeal," hedge funds lure investors with the ever-present hope of market-beating returns. Their historically low correlation with such indexes as the S&P 500 Index also boosts this appeal. But correlation is only one important condition for considering whether an investment should be included in a portfolio. It is not, however, a *sufficient* one.

For example, having a rental car already reserved on arrival at the airport can be an important condition for a successful family vacation. Yet, having a car large enough to accommodate all of the family's luggage can be even more critical. In investing, it is also important that returns are realized in a cost-efficient and tax-efficient manner (appropriate for the level of risk). Unfortunately, the historical evidence is that once the appropriate adjustments for risk are made and the biases in the data are eliminated, hedge funds have failed to deliver on their promise of superior risk-adjusted returns.

Before we look at the historical evidence, let's discuss how hedge funds are different from mutual funds.

WHY HEDGE FUNDS AREN'T MUTUAL FUNDS

Hedge funds differ from mutual funds in several key ways:

■ Management generally has a significant stake in the funds.

■ They are generally available only to high-net-worth individuals. In December 2006, the Securities and Exchange Commission (SEC) proposed raising the asset accreditation minimum for investors in hedge funds, private equity, and venture capital from $1 million to $2.5 million.

■ Unlike the typical broadly diversified mutual fund, hedge funds generally maintain concentrated positions in a few securities.

■ They have broad latitude to make large bets, either long or short (see the Glossary), on almost any type of asset, whether it is a commodity, real estate, currency, country debt, stocks, or other type of investment.

■ Management has strong financial incentives that can mean a multimillion-dollar payday. Fees typically range from 1 percent to 2 percent (or more) per year, plus 20 percent (or more) of profits. Note, however, that managers do not share in any losses!

■ Hedge fund management is subject to limited regulatory oversight. (But the huge losses that have occurred in recent years have brought increased scrutiny that might lead to increased regulation.)

However, the main selling point of hedge funds is their supposedly superior performance. So let's look at more of the actual data over time.

Facts Versus Fantasies

Following a flood of investor dollars into hedge funds, in 2003 the HFRX Global Hedge Fund Index (the leading industry benchmark) rose 13.4 percent. In both 2004 and 2005, the index rose just 2.7 percent. However, in 2006 the index rose 9.3 percent. And in 2007 the index rose just 4.2 percent.[5] Let's examine how those returns on hedge funds compared to the returns available from the public equity markets (TABLE 15.1).

As seen in the table:

■ In 2003 the HFRX Global Hedge Fund Index underperformed the various equity asset classes by from 14.5 percent to as much as 64.6 percent.

Table 15.1 Comparing the Return of Hedge Funds to the Returns of Publicly Traded Securities, 2003–2007

	2003 (% Return)	2004 (% Return)	2005 (% Return)	2006 (% Return)	2007 (% Return)	2003–07 (% Return)
HFRX Index	13.4	2.7	2.7	9.3	4.2	6.4
Domestic Indexes						
S&P 500	28.7	10.9	4.9	15.8	5.5	12.8
CRSP 9–10* (Microcaps)	78.0	16.7	3.6	18.1	−7.2	18.7
Large Value**	27.9	20.1	11.6	23.6	−12.2	13.5
Small Value**	64.1	21.4	9.1	25.0	−18.4	18.2
Wilshire REIT	36.2	31.3	13.8	36.0	−17.6	18.3
International Indexes						
MSCI EAFE	39.2	20.7	14.0	26.9	11.6	22.1
MSCI EAFE Small Cap	62.1	31.2	26.7	19.7	1.8	26.8
MSCI EAFE Value	46.0	24.9	14.4	31.1	6.5	23.8
MSCI Emerging Markets	56.3	26.0	34.5	32.6	39.8	37.5

*CRSP: Center for Research in Security Prices

**These Fama-French benchmark portfolios reflect historical returns based on academic definitions of asset classes.

- In 2004, the same index underperformed by from 8.2 percent to as much as 28.6 percent.
- In 2005, the hedge fund index underperformed by from 0.9 percent to as much as 31.8 percent.
- In 2006, the hedge fund index underperformed by from 6.5 percent to as much as 26.7 percent.
- In 2007, the hedge fund index underperformed the S&P 500 by 1.3 percent, and underperformed three of the international indexes by from 2.3 percent to as much as 35.6 percent. However, it did outperform the other four domestic indexes by from 3 percent to as much as 14.1 percent, and outperformed international small-cap stocks by 2.4 percent.
- For the full period, the hedge fund index underperformed by from 6.4 percent per year to as much as 31.1 percent per year.
- Investors in hedge funds earned returns below those of investors in the S&P 500 and dramatically less than investors who followed a strategy of broad global diversification using traditional asset classes.

Keep in mind that hedge funds were initially sold on the promise of superior performance. The universal sales pitch was that the proven investment skills of hedge fund managers virtually guaranteed superior performance. Given the data in Table 15.1, it is no surprise that the story has now changed from investing in hedge funds for superior performance to investing in them for their diversification benefits. As will be shown, that story doesn't hold up either.

Let's look at some respected studies covering earlier periods:

- The 1999 study, "Offshore Hedge Funds: Survival and Performance, 1989–95," by Stephen J. Brown, William N. Goetzmann, and Roger G. Ibbotson, found that most of the funds had underperformed the S&P 500.[6]
- A *Forbes* article by columnist David Dreman presented a performance index of 2,600 hedge funds (1,500 domestic and 1,100 international) for the period from January 1993

through October 1998. After subtracting fees, the average annualized return of the hedge funds was 13.4 percent, trailing the 19.9 percent return of the S&P 500 by 6.5 percent.[7]

■ The 2006 study, "The A, B, Cs of Hedge Funds: Alphas, Betas, and Costs," by Roger G. Ibbotson and Peng Chen, covering the period from January 1995 through March 2006, found that the average hedge fund had returned 8.98 percent per year, lagging the S&P 500 by 2.6 percent per year. Equally important, this study includes the bear market of 2000 to 2002 (the type of market during which hedge funds are supposed to perform the best).[8]

HEDGE FUND RISKS

At the same time investors in hedge funds were earning below-market returns, they were (in many cases) assuming far more risk—although they were probably unaware they were doing so. Let's take a closer look at some of the incremental risks:

Lack of liquidity—Investors in mutual funds have access to their funds on a daily basis. Hedge fund investors typically must accept long lock-up periods. In addition, redemption rights—the ability to withdraw assets from the fund—can be suspended, as was the case with the 2006 failure of Amaranth Advisors, a high-profile hedge fund.

Transparency—Mutual fund investors enjoy transparent investment strategy, and, therefore, know the risks taken by the funds' managers. This is not the case for hedge fund investors, which is an important point because investments are not like hot dogs—it's essential to know what's inside.

Loss of control of asset allocation and thus portfolio risk—Asset allocation determines the majority of the risk and return of a portfolio. Investors in passively managed funds can take full control of their risk. However, the freedom and range of investment choices that hedge fund managers have can cause investors to lose control over their asset allocations.

Nonnormal distribution of returns—Hedge funds exhibit characteristics that risk-averse investors dislike, and the majority of investors are risk averse. Hedge funds exhibit both negative skewness (the opposite of a lottery ticket, where most people lose, but losses are small, and a few winners win big) and high kurtosis. Assets that exhibit high kurtosis produce exceptional returns (both high and low) with greater-than-normal frequency—the so-called *fat tails*. However, investors do not like the risk of exceptionally large losses, especially if they occur with greater-than-normal frequency.

Risk of "dying"—The risk of a hedge fund dying (shutting down) is so great that a 2005 study, "Hedge Funds: Risk and Return," by Burton G. Malkiel and Atanu Saha, found that survivorship bias in the reported data on hedge fund returns creates an incredibly large upward bias of 4.4 percent per year. The same study found that there is a substantial attrition rate—less than 25 percent of the funds in existence in 1996 were still alive in 2004. The difference in returns between the live and defunct funds exceeded 8 percent per year (13.7 versus 5.4).[9] A 2002 study, "Hedge Fund Survival Lifetimes," by Greg N. Gregoriou covered the period from 1990 through 2001 and found that the median residual lifetime of a fund is just 5.5 years.[10] Perhaps hedge funds should come with their own "life insurance" policies.

Riskiness of the assets—Many hedge funds invest in highly risky assets, for which investors should be compensated. For example, a study by hedge fund AQR Capital Management, covering the six-year period through 2000, found that many hedge funds were taking on significantly greater risk by investing in illiquid securities.[11] In other words, the alphas (above-benchmark returns) reported by hedge funds are misleading, as they use inappropriate (less-risky) benchmarks. So the hurdles are set too low from the outset. Stated another way, there was no alpha in many cases—the incremental return was simply a risk premium.

Investors learned this lesson the hard way during the liquidity crisis of the summer of 2007, when subprime loans saw their values "submerge." The crisis quickly spread to all risky assets, and the prices of junk bonds, emerging market bonds, and other similar securities all fell sharply. It is also important to note that investing in illiquid securities means the Sharpe ratio of hedge funds is a misleading measure of their efficiency (the risk relative to the return).

Perhaps most importantly, the historical record demonstrates that hedge fund returns have not been commensurate with the risks. For example, as mentioned before, the 2003 study, "Hedge Fund Performance 1990–2000: Do the 'Money Machines' Really Add Value?" compared the fee-adjusted returns of seventy-seven hedge funds between 1990 and 2000 with the returns generated by a market benchmark with a similar risk profile. Seventy-two of the funds—more than 90 percent—failed to outperform their benchmarks.[12]

Tax inefficiencies—Due to high turnover rates, the average hedge fund produces returns in a tax-inefficient manner. On the other hand, investors have access to passive asset class funds that are specifically managed for tax efficiency.

Hedge funds don't combine well with equities—It's true that hedge funds generally have a low correlation with equities. Unfortunately, the correlation of hedge funds with equities can turn high at just the wrong time. For example, when things go wrong with the stock market, they also tend to go wrong with many, though not all, hedge funds. That's because falling stock prices are often accompanied by flights to quality, resulting in a widening of credit spreads and increasing liquidity premiums. Since the strategy of many hedge funds is to invest in distressed assets and to provide liquidity for other investors by investing in illiquid assets (the surest way to earn high returns is to take great risks), they are negatively affected by these flights to quality.[13] This is what occurred in the global financial crises of both 1998 and 2007.

No consistent performance beyond the randomly expected—
The aforementioned study, "Offshore Hedge Funds: Survival and
Performance, 1989–95," concluded that there was no evidence of
any persistent ability of managers in a particular style classification
to earn returns in excess of their style benchmark.[14] With no demonstrated persistence in performance, it is hard to see how one could
identify future top performers.

While investment management firms running funds of funds
(which provide investors the important benefit of diversification)
continue to tout their superior fund-manager selection skills, a 2003
study, "10 Things That Investors Should Know About Hedge
Funds," by Harry M. Kat, found no evidence of any such abilities.
For the period from 1994 through 2001, the average fund of hedge
funds underperformed an equally weighted portfolio of hedge funds
randomly selected from the sample by 3 percent per year.[15]

Agency risk—The compensation structure of hedge funds is geared
so that much (if not most) of the reward for managers occurs in the
form of incentive pay (usually 20 percent of profits). Thus, investors
take all the downside risk, but do not participate fully in the upside.
Agency risk occurs when a manager is approaching the end of a year
and has failed to reach the benchmark level above which incentive
compensation is paid.

This presents a clear conflict of interest in the form of unequal
incentives. If the manager takes large risks in an attempt to beat the
benchmark and wins, he or she will receive incentive pay. However,
if the manager fails, he or she loses nothing and still receives the
minimum fee. This creates an incentive for the fund manager to
take on greater risk in a game of "I Can Win, But I Never Lose."

What has happened in the past, leading to the eventual demise
of several hedge funds, is that a hedge fund trader has placed a big
bet that has lost. He or she then decides to double up in an effort to
earn back the loss. If the market keeps going against the trader, he
or she doubles up again until the "game" ends.

There is a second type of agency risk. Most hedge funds have a
clause that "protects" investors with what is known as a "high-water"

benchmark, or high watermark, that works in the following manner. After a year of negative performance, the fund cannot collect its incentive pay, unless it first "makes up" the negative performance.

For example, if a fund loses 10 percent in the first year, its incentive pay in the second year will only be calculated on the amount earned above the high watermark. Because of the effect of compounding, the fund would have to earn 11.1 percent in the second year to return to the high watermark.

The problem for investors is twofold. First, the same type of agency risk just discussed becomes an issue. To reach the high watermark and earn the incentive compensation, the fund manager may be tempted to take on greater risk than anticipated by investors.

The second problem is that after a bad year or two, when the chances of earning any incentive pay become small, the fund manager has the right to shut down the fund, returning all assets to investors. Thus, the high watermark that investors counted on never comes into play. The hedge fund manager leaves and starts up a new fund, with no high watermark to surpass.

Agency risk can also appear in the form of outright fraud, as was the case with the Bayou Group, a hedge fund firm that managed an estimated $400 million before its collapse.[16]

Biases in the data—When investors look at the performance of hedge funds, they need to be aware that the data are likely to be misleading—because of several biases, the returns are often overstated. The biases in the data include the previously mentioned survivorship bias (4.4 percent per year) and instant history (also known as *backfill*) bias. The aforementioned study, "Hedge Funds: Risk and Return," found that the backfill bias was over 5 percent per year.[17] There is yet another bias known as *self-selection bias*, which occurs when poorly performing funds choose not to report their performance. Unfortunately, we cannot know how much of a bias that adds to the data.

As studies have indicated, the biases are substantial. For example, the previously cited study, "The A, B, Cs of Hedge Funds: Alphas, Betas, and Costs," found that while funds that were live at the end of the period of the study returned 16.6 percent, correcting for survivorship and backfill bias reduced that to just 9.1 percent. These two biases alone had inflated returns by a whopping 7.5 percent.[18]

And we are not yet done. There is one more important, and large, bias in the data—liquidation bias. This phenomenon occurs in the data because funds that become defunct often fail to report their last returns. While it is impossible to know for certain the full impact of liquidation bias, "A Reality Check on Hedge Funds," a 2003 paper by Nolke Posthuma and Pieter Jelle van der Sluis, estimated the effect based on conversations with employees of Tass Research, the repository of the largest database on hedge funds (which is now owned by Lipper).

The assumption is that the hedge funds that terminated their reporting did so due to serious negative performance. After all, it is well known that many terminated funds are unable to return capital to investors.

The most famous example is Long-Term Capital Management (LTCM), discussed later in this chapter. It managed to lose 92 percent of its capital from October 1997 through October 1998, and did not report that loss to public databases.

The authors of the paper added one final month beyond the period for which returns were reported in order to estimate the impact of liquidation bias. They then created two scenarios; one with an estimate of a 50 percent loss, and the other with an estimated loss of 100 percent. An assumption of a 50 percent loss created a liquidation bias of about 3 percent. A 100 percent loss assumption created a liquidation bias of 6 percent.[19] In other words, if all the hedge funds that had been liquidated lost 100 percent of their assets, the average return to all hedge fund investors would have been overstated by 6 percent. Of course, that would be too extreme an assumption.

WISDOM AND EXPERIENCE, OR HOPE AND HYPE?

While investing in hedge funds does offer the hope of market-beating performance, investors should be aware of both the historical evidence on their actual performance and the risks of hedge funds—risks that are greater than those presented by mutual funds.

There have been several prominent hedge fund collapses in the past few years, and by taking a closer look at these scenarios, investors can see that even sophisticated investors who conducted thorough due diligence were badly burned. What follows are just some examples of how this can occur:

- "Our unique multifactor risk model acts as a road map for navigating risk and provides investors with alternative routes to reach their investment summit," said Steve Henderlite, a cofounder and principal of Trail Ridge Capital LLC, a hedge fund and fund-of-funds company. Trail Ridge was an investor in the Bayou Group, a hedge fund company that federal prosecutors called "a $300 million fraud."[20] Other prominent fund-of-funds firms also invested in Bayou, including Silver Creek Capital Management and Hennessee Group LLC (which *at the time* described its due diligence process on its website as a proprietary process that performed a unique in-depth evaluation of all the components of the hedge fund manager's organization, including its culture, philosophy, and other factors).

  Institutional investors were not alone in this debacle. Among the other investors in the Bayou Group hedge fund was Stern Investment Holdings, the investment firm founded by Edward Stern, the heir to the Hartz Mountain Corp. fortune.[21] Investors thinking about hedge funds should also carefully consider the following surprising fact: One of the investors in Bayou was a Certified Public Accountant (CPA) with a background in forensic accounting who had conducted extensive due diligence on the fund prior to investing.[22]

- In 2004, the Ohio Bureau of Workers' Compensation Fund lost $300 million on its investments (in a year when most markets provided positive returns). Among the losses was a $215 million loss resulting from the blowup of MDL Capital Management, which had invested in a hedge fund. An additional $50 million loss resulted from another "alternative investment"—rare coins funds.[23]

- According to the article "G-8 Meet to 'Manage' Hedge-Fund Crisis," by Lothar Komp and Nancy Spannaus, the Bailey Coates Cromwell Fund was founded in London in 2003 by Jonathan Bailey and Stephen Coates. "The fund was able to accumulate $1.3 billion in capital," the authors state, "and another $2 billion in bank credits. Bailey Coates was exposed, in particular, to bets on U.S. stocks."[24] Unfortunately, it found itself on the wrong side of such bets, losing more than 20 percent in just the first five months of 2005. The losses led to large withdrawals by investors. Note that in 2004, while the S&P 500 rose about 11 percent, this hedge fund earned about 5 percent.[25] In June 2005, less than two years after its inception, the firm announced its liquidation.

- Marin Capital Partners was a hedge fund that specialized in credit derivatives related to convertible bonds. At its peak, Marin had $2.2 billion in assets. In October 2004, the firm announced that it would limit investor withdrawals. After suffering losses on such investments as General Motors debt (which had been downgraded several times), Marin announced in June 2005 that it would liquidate and return its remaining capital to investors.[26] The fund cited a "lack of suitable investment opportunities" as one reason for closing the fund.[27] In other words, there weren't any (or enough) anomalies to exploit.

  Marin was not the only hedge fund that employed a convertible-bond arbitrage strategy to come to that conclusion. Other similar funds that closed were Alta Partners ($1.2 billion at its peak), run by Creedon Keller & Partners, and Lakeshore International Fund ($669 million), run by EBF & Associates. The *Wall Street Journal* reported that as of July 2005 the Goldman Sachs convertible arbitrage index had lost 23 percent of its capital since the start of that year.[28] And arbitrage is supposed to be a riskless proposition!

- Aman Capital Management Pte. was founded in September 2003 by top derivatives traders at Salomon Brothers and

UBS (the largest bank in Europe). The intent was to become Singapore's "flagship" in the hedge fund business. After suffering losses that may have been in the hundreds of millions, the fund's capital shrunk to just $242 million by the end of March 2005.[29] Then, just one month later, the fund may have lost more than $43 million, or 18 percent of its assets, by investing in derivatives based on the Korean Composite Stock Price Index.[30] In a statement published by London's *Financial Times* on June 20 of the same year, Aman Capital's managers acknowledged that "the fund is no longer trading," and that they would distribute whatever was left of the capital to investors. UBS is believed to have lost several hundred million dollars that the bank had invested in Aman Capital, and Temasek Holdings (Singapore's government investment agency) reportedly also lost a significant amount of money.[31]

It would be hard to find more sophisticated investors, but it also seems that UBS did not learn from this experience. In May 2007 the firm shut the doors of its own hedge fund, Dillon Read Capital Management, because it had lost $124 million. The bank announced that it would book a total loss of about $300 million once it accounted for all the costs associated with shutting the fund. The fund had managed more than $1.5 billion of outside investor assets and more than $3 billion of the firm's own capital.[32]

■ In January 2005, Institutional Investor's *Alpha* magazine placed Vega Asset Management in a tie for the largest European hedge fund, with assets of over $11 billion.[33] By July 2005, the *Wall Street Journal* reported that a combination of continued losses and investor withdrawals had caused the fund's assets to fall to $6.7 billion, dropping by $700 million in June 2005 alone.[34]

■ In the largest hedge fund collapse since LTCM, the sharp fall of natural gas prices in the summer of 2006 led to losses of over $6 billion (65 percent of the fund's assets) for investors in Amaranth.[35] Among those suffering great losses were "sophisticated" investors such as Morgan Stanley, the Goldman Sachs Group, and the multibillion-dollar San Diego County Employees Retirement Association. Ironically, just months earlier, the San Diego fund had boasted about its ability to make such investments directly.[36] Of even greater irony is that, in nature, the amaranth is a remarkably adaptable plant with a flower that never fades!

THE COST OF FOLLY

Despite the academic evidence and these high-profile tales of woe, hedge funds continue to gain assets. It seems that hype and hope are still triumphing over wisdom and experience. Even widely publicized examples, such as Julian Robertson's Tiger Management (assets fell from more than $22 billion in 1998 to $7 billion in 2000) and LTCM (whose failure not only cost billions, but almost caused a global financial crisis), are not stopping the wave of seemingly irrational behavior. To make matters worse, folly doesn't come cheaply; investors have to pay dearly for it.

The Tiger fund, for example, was formed in 1980 with $10 million in capital. The fund had a remarkable run, averaging more than 30 percent a year for the first eighteen years. By 1998, it had in excess of $22 billion under management, the vast majority coming from new investments. Over the next two years, however, the Tiger fund stumbled badly, losing more than $10 billion. The irony is that while the fund still showed a return of 25 percent per year over its life, investors in the fund may have actually lost money. This is a common occurrence—the *dollar-weighted* returns investors actually earn from their investments are less than the *time-weighted* returns reported by the very funds in which they invest. The reason is that they buy *after* periods of great performance, not ahead of them.[37]

Unfortunately, most individual investors are not aware of just how expensive hedge funds are when all the costs are considered. As noted earlier, the typical hedge fund includes a management fee of between 1 percent and 2 percent of net assets (though some are much higher), plus an additional incentive fee of 20 percent of profits (though some are much higher). However, hedge funds have something in common with icebergs. While it's the tip of the iceberg that we see, most of the berg itself is submerged. With hedge funds, the management fee and the incentive fee may only scratch the surface of total costs. Investors need to "look beneath the surface" to find the true costs of these funds.

Hedge funds often tack on additional charges for such items as administrative fees that cover expenses for accounting services, trader bonuses, operating expenses, and so on. A study by LJH Global Investments, a Naples, Florida, adviser to hedge fund investors, found that for about one hundred hedge funds the average bill for "other" expenses was 1.95 percent.[38] In addition to these expenses, many funds also include a sales load.

These fees also do not include the trading costs (bid-offer spreads and market impact [see the Glossary]) that all funds incur. Since the typical hedge fund has a high turnover rate, and many trade in illiquid securities, these additional expenses can be high. And they are never disclosed. (They simply reduce returns.)

Let's take a look at the impact that fees have on the returns investors earn. Let's assume that a *hypothetical* hedge fund earns 10 percent before any charges to investors. The fund would first subtract its fees (for example, 2 percent) and other expenses (for example, another 2 percent), leaving returns at about 6 percent. It then takes a cut of 20 percent of the profits, leaving investors with a return of just 4.8 percent, or 48 percent of the returns (100 percent of the risk, but only 48 percent of the profits in this example). The picture gets worse for investors who choose to invest through a fund of funds to reduce the risk of hedge fund investing: They incur an additional layer of high fees.

How High an Alpha Does a Hedge Fund Need?

The following is an example of a *hypothetical* hedge fund that charges investors a 2 percent fee, imposes additional costs of 2 percent, and takes a 20 percent share of profits. Historically, U.S. stocks have returned about 10 percent per year. For the purposes of our example, let's assume that rate will continue into the future. A passive buy-and-hold investor could access those returns by investing in a total stock market index fund with expenses of about 0.2 percent.

Table 15.2   Alpha Required by Hedge Funds Versus the Market

Hedge fund return	16.0%
Management fee	−2.0%
Other fees	−2.0%
Gross return	**12.0%**
Profit sharing (20%)	−2.4%
Net return	**9.6%**
Passive alternative	**9.8%**

Thus, the investor would earn a pretax return of 9.8 percent. This 9.8 percent return will serve as our benchmark against which we judge a hypothetical hedge fund.

Now, let's assume that our hypothetical hedge fund turns out to be a real star, producing a *gross* return of 16 percent (**TABLE 15.2**), which outperforms the market by 6 percent. What return does the investor earn? First, we have to subtract the 2 percent management fee, and then another 2 percent for other fees, leaving a return of 12 percent. Then the fund takes its 20 percent of profits (2.4 percent), leaving the investor with a pretax return of just 9.6 percent. (And it is important to note that these returns are likely to be taxed at higher rates than returns of an investor in passively managed funds.)

Thus, in this example, the fund manager must produce an alpha of *more than* 6 percent to simply match the pretax returns of the passive investor. (Investors using funds of funds incur further expenses, raising the hurdle to more than 8 percent.) If we eliminate any administrative fees, the alpha would still have to be in excess of 4 percent. (In the case of funds of funds investors, it would be more than 6 percent.)

Now consider the following example: Instead of investing in a total market index fund, our investor takes more risk and invests in a small-cap value index fund. Historically, small-cap value stocks have outperformed the S&P 500 by about 4 percent per year. So let's add that 4 percent to the 10 percent return of the market from our previous example; that results in a gross expected return of 14 percent.

Since expenses of investing in small-cap value stocks are a bit higher, let's subtract 0.5 percent for expenses, leaving us with a net return of 13.5 percent. That is our passive alternative. Now if our hypothetical hedge fund earns 21 percent (**TABLE 15.3**) before any expenses,

Table 15.3 Alpha Required by Hedge Funds Versus the Market

Hedge fund return	21.0%
Management fee	−2.0%
Other fees	−2.0%
Gross return	**17.0%**
Profit sharing (20%)	−3.4%
Net return	**13.6%**
Passive alternative	**13.5%**

after deducting 4 percent total expenses and the 20 percent profit sharing, the investor would net a pretax return of 13.6 percent.

As shown, if we use small-cap value stocks as the benchmark, the alpha hurdle has increased to 7 percent. (For funds of funds investors, the hurdles are even higher.) Given the historical record, it is hard to see why investors would invest in hedge funds, rather than other, less risky public-market alternatives. And keep in mind that all of these figures are *pretax*. Hedge funds, because of their high level of turnover, are notoriously tax inefficient.

The reason we use this example is that many hedge funds rely on the S&P 500 as a benchmark. To have higher expected returns, all one has to do is to take more risk—and, historically, one way to do so is to invest in small-cap value stocks.

How Funds of Funds Increase Hurdles to Outperformance
When planning a trip, we might decide to use the services of a travel agent because we value not only the convenience of her service, but also her expertise. With concerts or shows, we might use a service such as Ticketmaster, for which the value added might be either convenience or availability. In each case, we have to decide if the extra costs (if any) are at least offset by the value of the services. That's also a good way to think about a fund of hedge funds.

A significant portion of investments in hedge funds by individuals is through funds of funds. The reason is that while institutional investors may have sufficient assets to diversify across several hedge funds, individual investors may not (due to the high minimums many hedge funds set). However, while funds of funds do provide the benefits of diversification, they add their own expenses to the already high burden imposed by the hedge funds themselves. In return, it is supposed to add value by selecting hedge fund managers who will deliver future alpha that is more than sufficient to cover all of the expenses. The typical fund of hedge funds imposes its own charges of from 1 to 2 percent, may tack on additional expenses, and then takes its slice of the profits (perhaps 10 percent). It's important to factor in all of the expenses of the hedge funds themselves. Thus, total expenses could be as great as 6 to 8 percent and 30 percent or more of the profits.

Using the above example of a gross return of 10 percent, investors in a fund of hedge funds would earn net returns (the only kind investors get to spend) comparable to, if not below, the return on totally riskless Treasury bills. And as David Hsieh points out, there is yet another hurdle that hedge funds have to climb—alpha is a finite resource.

Hsieh, who researches the hedge fund industry, presented his findings at the CFA (chartered financial analyst) Institute's February 2006 hedge fund conference in Philadelphia. He told the audience that he was comfortable determining that for the entire hedge fund industry there was a finite amount of available alpha—roughly $30 billion each year.[39] The implication is that as more money enters the industry, there is less and less alpha to go around per hedge fund. This is not good news for hedge fund investors, because dollars have been flowing in at a rapid pace.

While we have no way of knowing how Professor Hsieh determined the $30 billion figure, let's assume that his estimate is correct. With our knowledge of the math, we can now determine what that means for the industry and for hedge fund investors, in general. Hsieh estimated that the industry had about $1 trillion under management.[40] Thirty billion dollars of alpha spread over $1 trillion of assets is 3 percent ($1 trillion × 0.03 = $30 billion) alpha for the industry.

As noted in the above example, simply to match the return of the market (while taking more risks), the average hedge fund must provide an alpha of about 6 percent, not 3 percent. The implication is that while some hedge fund investors may receive above-benchmark returns after all fees and expenses, the average hedge fund investor will earn returns net of all costs that probably approach those that can be earned on bank CDs.

It is also worthwhile to consider the following: Again, assume that Hsieh is correct that there is a finite amount of alpha, and it is $30 billion. Let's go back in time to when the hedge fund industry had just $300 billion under management. Then the industry-average alpha would have been 10 percent. Investors would have received above-benchmark returns and then poured more money into hedge funds. As a result, the alpha would become diluted to today's level of 3 percent.

It is also important to understand that the very act of exploiting mispricings makes them disappear. So, in fact, the alpha available to the industry would not be constant, but would shrink over time. Yet the evidence presented from earlier periods, when the industry was much smaller, showed negative alpha for hedge funds as a group— not the 10 percent alpha that one might have expected if Hsieh were correct. The bottom line? The evidence suggests that if there were ever any "easy pickings," with the increased competition, those easy pickings are long gone.

We have now seen the evidence on the persistent underperformance of hedge funds. Let's see why, despite their supposed advantages over mutual funds, this persistent underperformance has occurred.

THE "ILL-LOGIC" OF HEDGE FUNDS

There are really two types of hedge funds. Let's first discuss the type that is nothing more than an active mutual fund manager in disguise—who believes that markets have mispriced assets. The only difference is that hedge funds charge higher fees than do mutual funds. However, hedge funds do have a greater ability to concentrate assets in a few securities, and they also have the flexibility to short the market, taking advantage of "overpriced" securities.

Unfortunately, as we have seen, there is no "there" there. While some hedge funds have produced spectacular returns, on average the track records of hedge funds have been similar to those of actively managed mutual funds: On average they don't outperform after expenses, and there is no persistence in performance beyond that which is randomly expected.

In addition, their active trading styles make them tax inefficient. Furthermore, the most successful ones often discover that their very success creates the seeds of their own destruction—assets come rushing in and implementation costs rise, increasing the hurdle of outperformance. Therefore, even if there were skill involved, the hurdle of outperformance only increases with time. (By the time there is a sufficient track record to convince investors of the manager's skill, either the fund is closed to new investors or the hurdles created by new cash flows become large.) This is one explanation for the lack of persistence of outperformance. The other—and more likely— explanation is that the outperformance was the result of random good luck, which runs out eventually.

The second type of hedge fund is one that attempts to exploit arbitrage opportunities. *Arbitrage* can be defined as the process by which investors exploit the price difference between two securities that are exactly alike, by simultaneously buying one at a lower price and selling the other at a higher price (thereby avoiding risk). This action locks in a risk-free profit for the arbitrageur (the person engaging in the arbitrage). Funds that engage in arbitrage are truly hedge funds—as opposed to active mutual fund managers in disguise.

Given the potentially huge rewards for discovering arbitrage opportunities, and the amount of brain and computer power available, it would be foolish to think that there would never be arbitrage opportunities that could be exploited, at least *temporarily*. The key word here is *temporarily*. The efficient market hypothesis (EMH) does not preclude that anomalies can be found, or even exploited. It does preclude that they can be exploited on a *consistent* basis. Let's look at how the markets work in the real world, and how they work to eliminate inefficiencies.

The Power of the EMH

An example of how hedge funds could theoretically prosper comes from the world of convertible-bond arbitrage. A hedge fund operating in the asset class of convertible bonds might, for example, be able to buy a convertible bond, simultaneously short the equity of the issuer, and lock in a profit. Or, the fund manager might simultaneously go long the equity and short the convertible bond.

In either case, it is possible that a profit could be locked in without accepting any *net* exposure to the risk of the stock. Searching for these anomalies seems like an attractive proposition. Unfortunately for hedge funds and their investors, the process of arbitrage rapidly brings prices back into equilibrium. Purchasing the undervalued security raises its price, and shorting the overvalued one lowers its price. This is the power of the EMH, as expressed by economics professors Dwight Lee and James Verbrugge:

> The efficient market theory is practically alone among theories in that it becomes more powerful when people discover serious inconsistencies between it and the real world. If a clear efficient market anomaly is discovered, the behavior (or lack of behavior) that gives rise to it will tend to be eliminated by competition among investors for higher returns . . . (For example) if stock prices are found to follow predictable seasonal patterns . . . this knowledge will elicit responses that have the effect of eliminating the very patterns that they were designed to exploit . . . The implication is striking. The more empirical flaws that are discovered in the efficient markets theory the more robust the theory becomes. (In effect) those who do the most to ensure that the efficient market theory remains fundamental to our understanding of financial economics are not its intellectual defenders, but those mounting the most serious empirical assault against it.[41]

The arena of convertible-bond arbitrage provides the perfect real-world example of Lee and Verbrugge's insight. The amount of money flowing into convertible-bond arbitrage has been so great that, according to a June 2004 article in the *Wall Street Journal*, about 95 percent of all trading in convertible bonds was being done by hedge funds.[42] Given that high percentage, it is hard to imagine that there are enough victims to exploit! By the time investors are able to identify a hedge fund with the skills needed to exploit a market anomaly, it is probably too late.

Long-Term Capital Management

In 1912 the Titanic was launched to great fanfare. At the time, it was the heaviest object ever moved by man and surely the finest ocean liner in existence. It was thought unsinkable. In 1994, LTCM was launched to similar fanfare. Its team included not only some of the top trading stars on Wall Street, but also two Nobel Prize–winning economists.

The Death of Genius

By studying the example of LTCM, probably the most famous—or infamous—hedge fund of all, we can learn a lot not only about why there has been no persistence of hedge fund performance, but also about the risks hedge funds and their investors take. LTCM identified several market anomalies (inefficiencies). For example, it noted that the newest 30-year Treasury bond traded much richer (at a higher price) than the previous 30-year issue (until recently, the Treasury had held biannual auctions). This didn't seem to make sense. The newly issued 30-year Treasury bond was an instrument that was not only very similar to the earlier 30-year issue, it was also theoretically marginally riskier given its slightly longer maturity (by six months).

The reason the market placed a premium on the new issue, driving its price up relative to the previous 30-year bond, is that the most recent issue is always the most liquid (most highly traded), and investors are willing to pay a premium for liquidity. Whenever the spread between the two issues widened a bit beyond its historical range, the firm would go long the bond with the higher yield (the older, less-expensive bond) and sell short the more-expensive, lower-yielding new issue.

Note that the firm took no bet on interest rates, as their positions were both long and short instruments of the same credit quality (both U.S. Treasury bonds) and had almost identical maturities. Eventually, the spreads would narrow (due to market efficiency), and the firm would unwind the trade at a profit. Given that the spreads never widened that much, the firm had to both take huge positions and use substantial leverage to achieve great returns for its investors.

LTCM's DOWNFALL: THE TYRANNY OF MARKET EFFICIENCY

The problem for LTCM was that the very market efficiency it counted on to restore prices to "normal" levels came back to haunt everyone involved. For one, competitors quickly copied its success. Billions of dollars from competing firms began to chase the same spread opportunities, and the size of the spreads that it had been exploiting began to narrow. Lured by the prospect of huge profits, almost every investment banking firm had developed its own version of LTCM by the late 1990s. And, of course, that means the profit opportunities diminished. To continue to earn the same returns for its investors, LTCM had to take on ever-larger positions and use more and more leverage.

Leverage is a double-edged sword, magnifying both gains and losses. Experienced investors know that the danger of using leverage is that they may have to be right all the time to be successful, not just in the long term. The reason is that short-term losses may force investors to meet margin calls as the value of their collateral (on which the margin loan is based) shrinks. If they cannot meet the margin call, their collateral will be liquidated, and they never make it to the long term. So even if these investors *would have* been right in the long term, they did not survive to earn the profits. The following insightful quote has often been attributed to John Maynard Keynes, perhaps the most famous economist of modern times: "The market can stay irrational longer than you can stay solvent."

This lesson was one that LTCM either forgot or ignored (making the mistake of treating the highly unlikely as impossible). As profit opportunities began to shrink, the firm needed to take on more and more leverage to achieve the same returns. At the beginning of 1998, the firm had equity of $4.72 billion and had borrowed over $124.5 billion, with assets of around $129 billion. It also had off-balance sheet derivative positions amounting to $1.25 trillion. Eventually, the markets went against LTCM.

Previously, when its positions were smaller, the firm could wait out the period by coming up with more collateral to meet the margin call. In this case, both the size of the market's move and the amount of leverage deployed made meeting margin calls impossible. The firm was eventually forced to liquidate positions at the worst possible time, further driving prices against itself as it unwound these positions. Unfortunately, LTCM had to buy back securities it had previously shorted, thus driving the prices of those securities even higher. Eventually, the losses overwhelmed its ability to raise collateral, and the banks called in their loans.

Another important piece of information that LTCM seemed to have forgotten is that the financial markets are probably the most competitive of all markets. When competitors smell blood, they rush in to profit from the kill. Wall Street is a relatively small community with a highly efficient grapevine. The other investment banking firms all knew LTCM was in a desperate situation, and traders armed with this knowledge began to drive the market against LTCM's positions. They did so based on the almost-certain knowledge that LTCM would then be forced to turn back to the market and buy its positions out at a profit.

In the end, the positions that LTCM initially took turned out to be correct, as spreads eventually narrowed. Unfortunately for LTCM, by that time, it was basically dead, and the "profits" went to the group that bailed the firm out. In other words, LTCM was right in the long term, but dead in the short term.

Another risk that some hedge funds take on is that they treat historical patterns as if they were certain to be repeated. Thus, they take positions whenever prices reach historically "abnormal" levels. They take the risk of treating what looks like the highly unlikely as impossible. At LTCM, the firm relied heavily on financial models that were based on the assumption that returns were normally distributed (like a bell curve). That assumption turned out to be false; a possibility that LTCM should have considered.

For one, the distribution of returns in the financial markets is not bell-shaped. In fact, the distribution of returns has what are called *fat tails*. The best and most recent example was the crash of 1987.

Eugene Fama served as the thesis adviser to Myron Scholes at the University of Chicago, before Scholes worked at LTCM. Fama had done a study on the distribution of stock returns and found, "If the population of price changes is strictly normal, on the average for any stock . . . an observation more than five standard deviations from the mean should be observed about once every 7,000 years. In fact such observations seem to occur about once every three or four years."[43]

Despite this knowledge, hedge funds (and the otherwise smart people that run them) continue to make the same mistakes today. Consider the following statement by Matthew Rothman, global head of quantitative equity strategies for Lehman Brothers Holdings: When interviewed in early August 2007, after three days of huge losses for equities all around the globe, Rothman noted, "Wednesday is the type of day people will remember in quant-land for a very long time. Events that models only predicted would happen once in 10,000 years happened every day for three days."[44] Did the hedge fund managers even stop to think that their models were wrong, because they were built on false assumptions?

Financial death becomes a distinct possibility for investors who get a fat tail in the wrong direction *and* are highly leveraged, so they cannot wait for the markets to recover. LTCM not only didn't anticipate the once-every-hundred-years flood, it employed so much leverage that the firm couldn't survive if it occurred even once.

RISK VERSUS UNCERTAINTY

A similar mistake made by quantitative hedge funds is that they confuse risk with uncertainty. With risk, people can calculate the odds. For example, using actuarial tables, people can calculate the odds of a sixty-five-year-old living beyond age eighty-five. Uncertainty occurs when no one can calculate the odds. An example would be the uncertainty of a nuclear war occurring.

The following is an example of confusing risk with uncertainty. An insurance company might be willing to take on a certain amount of hurricane risk in Dade and Broward counties in Florida. They would price this *risk* based on approximately one hundred years of data, the likelihood of hurricanes occurring, and the damage that they did. But only a foolish insurer would place such a large bet (take on so much risk) that the result of more or worse hurricanes occurring than had previously ever been experienced would be bankruptcy of the company. That would be ignoring *uncertainty*— that the future might not look like the past.

The mistake LTCM made is that it treated the output of proprietary financial models (which had databases with very short lives) as if there was no uncertainty, just risk. In other words, it assumed that these models anticipated "all" the potential trading environments. LTCM could then determine the *exact* likelihood of possible outcomes. The problem was that the firm didn't anticipate that there might be environments outside of the model's database. It was, therefore, wholly unprepared for them.

The mistake LTCM made is worth restating: The firm modeled risk based on its own databases priced for that risk and ignored the possibility that the world might look worse going forward than it ever had previously. In other words, LTCM's models would work until it came across an environment it had not modeled (uncertainty), and then these models would no longer work. LTCM also ignored the most basic of all risk-management principles: *Never make the bet that if you are wrong, you don't get to play again because you are completely out of the game.* In other words, investors shouldn't place bets they cannot afford to lose.

Yet another mistake made by some quantitative hedge funds is that they assume markets will always be liquid. This assumption is key, because if their positions start to go against them, they might have to be unwound in order to meet margin calls. But what if the markets were to become illiquid, which is what happened to LTCM? The firm was forced to unwind huge positions (in order to meet margin calls) at a time when the markets were highly illiquid. That meant trading costs were huge, which contributed to its financial ruin.

LTCM should have known better, especially since a similar episode of illiquidity had occurred less than 10 years earlier as part of the crash of 1987 when believers in what was known as "portfolio insurance" learned that markets are not always liquid, and investors cannot always get out of positions, especially at "market prices."

The same risks surfaced once again in the crisis of the summer of 2007, leading to the demise of many hedge funds, including Sowood Capital Management. Sowood was formed in 2004 by Jeffrey Larson of Harvard Management Company, the investment arm in charge of Harvard University's endowment.

FOOLED BY RANDOMNESS

One of the more common mistakes investors make is that they are fooled by randomness, confusing skill and luck. Hedge fund managers can make the same mistake, committing the deadly sin of hubris. Again, LTCM was a victim of its own success. LTCM delivered such great returns (with seemingly great ease and consistency) that the firm began to believe it could do no wrong. This encouraged taking much greater risks (bigger bets with more leverage), but taking risks that the firm had never engaged in previously. Instead of just making bets on spreads narrowing or tightening, LTCM began to take outright positions on securities. The firm even had short positions on stocks such as General Electric, Dell, and Microsoft.[45] This was a much riskier proposition, especially when adding huge amounts of leverage. It was also not what the firm had told either its investors or its bankers (the providers of leverage) that it would do.

LTCM's actions also had nothing to do with modern financial theory. In fact, it went against everything that modern financial theory represents. LTCM's short positions in these stocks were not bets that would have been indicated by its proprietary quantitative models. Instead, these were bets that the market was inefficient and had somehow mispriced the securities. As one example, the firm took a huge position of almost $500 million in the junk-bond issue of Starwood Hotels & Resorts Worldwide.[46] Clearly, this was well beyond what LTCM had positioned as its mandate. Yet, the traders began to believe that they were infallible.

Keep in mind that all of the mistakes made by LTCM were made by very smart people, including two Nobel laureates, with great long-term track records. And don't think for a minute that this cannot happen to any other hedge fund or actively managed mutual fund. They are all run by smart, well-trained professionals, equipped with reams of research and high-powered computers.

SUMMARY

The body of historical evidence demonstrates that once viewed on a risk-adjusted basis, the average hedge fund has a hard time keeping pace with Treasury bill returns. But just as there are always actively managed mutual funds that outperform their benchmark for a period of time, there will likely be a few hedge funds that also deliver these results, followed by the inevitable financial media hype.

As Gary Weiss, author of *Wall Street Versus America*, noted, "Usually the financial press . . . forgets to mention that the superstar investors tended to make their biggest bucks when they were managing small sums of money. Some of the biggest names in the business liquidated or wound down their funds when their assets swelled beyond reasonable size, the odds caught up with them, and their performance turned lousy."[47] Another problem is that no one has yet found a way to identify the few winners *ahead* of time.

Weiss went on to caution investors about some of the things hedge funds lead to (note that these are his comments):

- "They cause people to pay fees that would be considered highway robbery in even the most wack-a-doo mutual fund."
- "They cause people to buy into 'black box' (give me the money, and I do what I want with it, without telling you what I am doing) investment strategies."
- "They cause people to give their money to creeps they haven't bothered to check out, the kind of people they wouldn't trust to run out and buy them a sandwich, much less manage their investments."
- "They cause people to sign contracts that are so one-sided they would make a credit-card lawyer blush, including 'lock-up' clauses that keep their money confined to their funds for as many years as some fund managers should be confined to prison."
- "They cause people to agree, sometimes eagerly, to be treated like . . . schoolchildren and not be given any information about what is being done with their money."
- "They cause people to buy investments products that are functionally equivalent to mutual funds, except they overcharge you and give you the ability to tell your golf buddies that you've invested in a hedge fund."

And what do investors get in return for all of the above? Weiss concluded, "In return, they provide performance that is subpar, inconsistent, not worth all the risk, or all of the above."[48]

While Weiss's comments might seem excessively harsh, experience dictates that investors looking into hedge funds should be extremely cautious. Carefully consider this advice from Professor Eugene Fama: "If you want to invest in something (hedge funds) where they steal your money and don't tell you what they're doing, be my guest."[49]

The bottom line on hedge funds is this: They are "sinkholes" for investors, and in 2006 alone, nine of these funds—each with assets in excess of $1 billion—closed their doors.[50] Many more followed suit in 2007 and 2008.

Unfortunately, this trend is becoming increasingly commonplace.

As David Swensen, of the Yale Endowment, noted, "In the hedge fund world, as in the whole of the money management industry, consistent, superior, active management constitutes a rare commodity. Assuming that active managers of hedge funds achieve success levels similar to active managers of traditional marketable securities, investors in hedge funds face dramatically higher levels of prospective failure, due to the materially higher levels of fees."[51]

It is important to note that perhaps wealthy investors are finally seeing through the smoke screen surrounding these investment vehicles. The April 21, 2007, *New York Times* article "Getting Out of Hedge Funds" noted, "Americans with a net worth of at least $25 million, excluding the value of their primary homes, reduced their exposure to hedge funds in 2006."

The article cited a survey by the Spectrum Group that found that the percentage of wealthy individuals that invested in hedge funds had fallen from 38 percent in 2005 to just 27 percent in 2006. In addition, the average investment in hedge funds took an even steeper dive, falling 43 percent, from $2.8 million to $1.6 million.[52]

Perhaps those who cannot resist the siren call of the world of hedge funds would be best served by tying themselves to the mast as Ulysses did, or, alternatively, by employing a financial adviser who can keep them from undermining their personal investment plan.

Leveraged Buyouts *16*

L EVERAGED BUYOUTS (LBOs) involve a private equity firm pur-chasing a public company, after which it generally takes it private. When making its acquisitions, the private equity fund typically employs minimal amounts of its own equity, while using unusually large levels of debt. Hence, the term *leveraged buyout*. The high leverage creates the opportunity for incremental returns (when the acquired company is sold again) on the limited amount of equity.

Investment consultants Cambridge Associates studied the performance of more than 300 buyout funds, for the twenty-year period ending June 2003, and found that the average fund produced a mean return of 11.5 percent per year, while S&P 500 Index returned 12.2 percent per year. However, although investors in LBOs were, on average, receiving below-market returns, they were also taking far greater risk. This greater balance-sheet risk was created by a combination of the leverage and the loss of liquidity (the lack of daily access to their assets that investors enjoy in mutual funds).[1]

A study by the Yale University Investments Office provides additional insight into how the use of a similar amount of leverage outside of an LBO would have boosted the 12.2 percent return of the S&P 500. The study examined 542 buyout deals concluded between 1987 and 1998 and found that the *net* returns were 36 percent per year—well above the 17 percent return produced by a comparably timed and sized investment in the S&P 500. However, a comparably timed and sized investment in the S&P 500 that *also* applied the same amount of leverage would have returned 86 percent per year, or 50 percent per year greater than the return of the

LBOs.[2] Perhaps it was these results that led David Swensen, of the Yale Endowment, to draw the following conclusion:

> Investors in buyout partnerships received miserable risk-adjusted returns over the past two decades. Since the only material differences between privately owned buyouts and publicly traded companies lie in the nature of the ownership (private vs. public) and character of capital structure (highly leveraged vs. less highly leveraged), comparing buyout returns to public market returns makes sense as a starting point. But, because the riskier, more leveraged buyout positions ought to generate higher returns, sensible investors recoil at the buyout industry's deficit relative to public market alternatives. On a risk-adjusted basis, market equities win in a landslide.[3]

Swensen also concluded:

> Fees create a hurdle that proves extremely difficult for buyout investors to clear. Aside from substantial year-to-year management fees, buyout funds command a significant share of deal profits, usually equal to one-fifth of the total. On top of the management fee and incentive compensation, buyout managers typically charge deal fees. The cornucopia of compensation ensures a feast for the buyout manager, while the buyout investor hopes, at best, for a hearty serving of leftovers.[4]

SUMMARY

As Benjamin Franklin famously said, "Content makes poor men rich. Discontent makes rich men poor." While buyout funds offer the potential of "supersized" returns, the historical evidence suggests that the high returns are far more likely to be earned by the fund managers and sponsors. This is especially true once the returns are adjusted for the incremental risks.

Clearly, in order to experience a good investment outcome, one does not need to purchase exotic instruments. Investors' objectives are best accomplished without being sidetracked by a leveraged buyout.

Variable Annuities **17**

O N THE SURFACE, investors' appetite for variable annuities (VAs) appears to be increasing. In 2004, sales exceeded $50 billion, and the total dollar amount of VAs outstanding exceeded $1 trillion.[1] Just two years later, by the end of 2006, that amount had swelled to $1.4 trillion.[2]

One possible explanation is that the word *annuity* conveys safety and steady streams of income. However, that halo effect should apply only to fixed annuities. Another plausible explanation is that the sales of VAs are not due to actual demand for the product. Instead, they reflect the successful efforts of commission-based salesmen and investment advisers. In other words, they are products that are sold, not bought.

A VA is a mutual fund–like account wrapped inside an insurance contract that can be purchased by making either a single outlay or a series of payments. VAs differ from fixed annuities in that fixed annuities guarantee that a *specific* sum of money will be paid each period, generally on a monthly basis, regardless of fluctuations in the value of the annuity issuer's underlying investments. However, the value of a VA (and thus the amount that can ultimately be withdrawn) will *fluctuate* over time. In addition, unlike with a fixed annuity, the typical VA offers many different investment options (typically mutual funds called *subaccounts* that can be managed by firms other than the issuer).

There are two types of VAs. One is called a *deferred* (or *accumulating*) *VA*, and the other type is called an *immediate VA*.

Deferred Variable Annuities

There are three investment-related motivations for considering the purchase of a deferred variable annuity. First, its structure (as an insurance contract) allows the investment earnings to grow on a tax-deferred basis. Second, it includes a life-insurance component, which varies from product to product. And third, its investment contract can be converted at a future date into a lifetime annuity.

Let's examine these "benefits" and see if they provide real value for the buyer, as well as consider other related issues.

Tax-Deferred Growth of Earnings

While annuities allow for the tax-deferred growth of earnings, that benefit usually comes at a high price. The first problem is that annuities convert what would otherwise be long-term capital gains into ordinary income. To demonstrate how large a drawback this creates, Jeffrey Brown and James Poterba performed a comparative analysis.

Brown and Poterba assumed a federal tax rate on capital gains and dividends of 15 percent and a federal tax on ordinary income of 33 percent. (The ordinary income tax can run even higher, depending on investors' tax brackets.) They also assumed a total return on stocks of 8 percent, 2 percent of which comes from dividends. The result was that even if we assume that VAs cost only 0.25 percent per year more than an equivalent investment in a mutual or exchange-traded fund (ETF)—the average VA has total expenses of about 1.65 percent—the investment horizon would have to be at least forty years.[3] This forty-year break-even point becomes even more important when considering that the average age of a nonqualified VA buyer is sixty (making the break-even point age one hundred), and that only 4 percent of nonqualified annuities are sold to investors under age thirty-five.[4]

The case against VAs is even more compelling than this analysis showed because it did not consider that holding equities inside of a VA causes the loss of other tax benefits. These include the loss of the potential for a step-up in basis for the estate of the investor, the inability to harvest losses, the inability to donate appreciated shares to charity, and the loss of the foreign tax credit (see the Glossary) if the investor holds international securities in his or her portfolio.

Each of these benefits, especially the ability to harvest losses and the potential for a stepped-up basis, offers significant value. Thus, it seems unlikely that anyone would live long enough to gain the key benefit (the deferral of taxes) that probably most drives the sales of VAs.

There is another important negative that comes with VAs—the penalty for early withdrawal. Should the buyer need unanticipated liquidity prior to age fifty-nine and a half, distributions are subject to an additional 10 percent tax penalty, unless the distribution takes the form of a life annuity. Hopefully, investors are convinced that the benefit of tax deferral is exceeded by the other negative characteristics.

THE LIFE INSURANCE COMPONENT

The second benefit that VAs provide is life insurance. There are many different versions of insurance. One of the most common forms stipulates that if the policyholder dies before annuitization begins, the heirs will receive at least the nominal value of the premiums paid.

A 2001 study on the value of this benefit, "The Titanic Option: Valuation of the Guaranteed Minimum Death Benefit in Variable Annuities and Mutual Funds," by Moshe Milevsky and Steven Posner found that a simple, return-of-premium death benefit was worth between 0.01 percent and 0.10 percent, depending on the investor's gender, purchase age, and the volatility of the underlying asset. In contrast, the authors found that the median mortality and expense-risk charge for a return-of-premium VA was 1.15 percent.[5] In addition, only 5 percent of variable annuity contracts have insurance charges of less than even 0.75 percent, and 12 percent of contracts charge more than 1.40 percent.[6] Clearly, the insurance benefit is far exceeded by its cost. As further evidence of these excessive costs, consider that in any given year only 0.4 percent of VA contracts are surrendered on account of death or disability.[7] And only a small fraction of those reflect losses that trigger a death benefit.

Investors should also understand that the longer they stay in a VA, the less likely it is that the death benefit will pay off. The reason is that the longer the horizon, the less likely it is that the investments will be "under water" (the present value being less than the cost basis). And, finally, with investments in high-quality (low-risk) bonds, there is little chance that the death benefit will have any value. For mixed equity and bond portfolios, the higher the percentage of high-quality bonds, the lower the value of the death benefit.

ABILITY TO ANNUITIZE

This is the third supposed benefit of VAs. While there is no reliable publicly available data on withdrawals, the limited evidence suggests that funds accumulated in VAs are rarely annuitized at retirement. A 2001 study, "Longevity-Insured Retirement Distributions from Pension Plans: Market and Regulatory Issues," by Jeffrey Brown and Mark J. Warshawsky, reported that only about 1 percent of individuals covered by VA products were receiving payments from these accounts.[8] While we cannot know what percent will eventually be annuitized, given the available data, it is difficult to imagine that this benefit is actually driving sales.

It is also important to note that the ability to eventually annuitize is not unique to VAs. As an alternative, an individual could invest in either a taxable account or an individual retirement account (IRA) and, at any point in the future, buy an immediate fixed annuity, which is completely different from a VA.

OTHER NEGATIVE FEATURES

In addition to the aforementioned problems with VAs, the investment is also imbued with other negative characteristics. First, the typical investment choices inside the VA are actively managed, and, therefore, tend to have high expenses. Given the historical evidence on actively managed funds, the likelihood is that investors will also be paying high fees for below-benchmark performance—adding to the negative profile.

Second, each fund usually levies an account charge of $10 to $25 per year, and, thus, the total charges can easily exceed 3 percent.

Compare that to the 0.1 percent to 0.2 percent total cost for some passive equity investments, such as index funds.

Third, most VAs are sold with "back-end loads," otherwise known as *surrender charges*. (These cover the cost of the commissions paid to the sales force.) Depending on the contract, these charges can reach up to 10 percent and can last for as long as fifteen years—although the charges typically decline over time. For example, a penalty of 7 percent would be applied if the annuity were canceled after the first year, 6 percent after two years, and 5 percent after three years. Clearly, there is nothing good about surrender charges.

Fourth, buyers of annuities accept the credit risk and overall financial strength of the insurance company issuing the contract—their guarantee is only as good as their credit. However, it is important to note that the credit risk applies only to the insurance component of the VA, not the underlying investments. This is an important consideration given the long time frame involved, as credit risk increases with time. On the other hand, the financial strength of the issuer can affect its ability to meet its obligations in terms of death benefits or guaranteed benefits (when a contract is annuitized).

While we don't recommend VAs, those who have decided to purchase one should only consider an annuity from a company that has the highest credit rating (that is, AAA).

ARE VAS REALLY THAT BAD?

Consider the following true story related by financial writer Carolyn Geer regarding the experience no-load fund giant T. Rowe Price's variable annuities division had when it sent potential customers software to help them determine whether VAs were right for them. The program factored in the investors' age, income, tax bracket, and investment horizon. The program regularly concluded that potential buyers would be better off in a plain vanilla mutual fund—presumably one from T. Rowe Price. An educated consumer, it turned out, was not a good prospect for annuities.[9] Keep in mind these were results prior to the tax reform act of 2003, which significantly lowered the tax on capital gains and dividends, reducing the tax-deferral benefit of the VA.

SOLD OR BOUGHT?

With all of the negative features inherent in VAs, why are so many sold? It is simply a question of whose interests are at stake. Sales are often in the best interest of the person making the recommendation to buy them—although they may not be in the best interests of the buyer. The typical VA earns a high commission for the seller, often as high as 6 percent or more, and, as noted earlier, this high commission is the reason why commission-based VAs also come with an early surrender charge.

THE ART OF DECEPTION

The sales abuses related to VAs were taken to new heights with the creation of what the industry euphemistically calls "bonus" annuities. The sale of bonus annuities is a particularly aggressive tactic for keeping investors "imprisoned" in a high-cost VA product, and for generating new and even larger commissions for the sales force. VA holders with a few years left in their surrender charge period are generally approached with the following sales pitch:

> I understand that you are unhappy with your current VA because of poor performance of the investment choices. I also understand that you have a 3 percent surrender charge left. We are going to help you out by giving you an up-front bonus of 3 percent to cover the surrender charge. So it will not cost you anything to switch.

Unfortunately, the only "bonus" generated is to the salesperson. The new sale starts the surrender period all over again, and the surrender period is often even longer and more expensive with these new products than it was with the original VA. The surrender charge period may now be extended to as much as ten years, and the prepayment penalty increased from 7 percent to as much as 9 percent (to pay for the sales commission). Given that the VA holder will now be locked into another high-cost (or even higher-cost) product for a much longer time, investors might ask, "What about the bonus they mentioned?" However, as previously mentioned, the only real bonus that occurs is in the form of higher commissions to the sales force. After all, whether they sell investments, cars, or widgets, salespeople earn more from repeat buyers than they do from one-time buyers.

VARIABLE IMMEDIATE ANNUITIES

While most of the general principles we discussed regarding deferred VAs also apply to variable immediate annuities, the latter represent more complex investment vehicles. One of the major differences is that premium amounts are invested in an under-lying portfolio of investments (that is, stock funds, bond funds, or both), although the menu of available investment options will vary from company to company. The insurance company sets the *initial* payment amount. However, the next payment (and all other payments) will fluctuate with the investment experience of the underlying investment portfolio (hence the term *variable* immediate annuity). The payment amount will go up when the investment experience is "good" and down when the investment experience is "bad." To be more precise, the payment will go up when the return on investment exceeds the assumed interest rate (AIR), and the payment will go down when the return is less than the AIR. It may be best to think of the AIR as a "hurdle rate" or benchmark.

Typically, the insurance company offers two or three AIRs from which to choose (for example, 3.5 percent and 5 percent). The higher the AIR, the higher the initial payment and vice versa. That's because a low AIR increases the chance that payments will increase consistently through time.

How Payments Are Determined

To understand how variable immediate annuity payments are deter-mined, let's look at an example. Assume that an annuitant commits $100,000 to this type of investment and then chooses a 3 percent AIR with annual payments. Further, she allocates $100,000 of pre-mium, so that 60 percent of the premium is invested in a diversi-fied stock fund portfolio and 40 percent is allocated to a diversified bond portfolio. The insurance company then sets the initial payment

Table 17.1   Impact of Investment Returns on Annuity Payments

Time	Return	Growth Factor	Payment
0	N/A	N/A	$7,000
1	10%	1.10/1.03 = 1.07	$7,476
2	−15%	0.85/1.03 = 0.83	$6,169
3	5%	1.05/1.03 = 1.02	$6,289
4	3%	1.03/1.03 = 1.00	$6,289
5	25%	1.25/1.03 = 1.21	$7,632

amount at $7,000. **TABLE 17.1** illustrates a hypothetical example of how payments might fluctuate over a five-year period.

The payment effectively grows (or shrinks) by the total return of the investment accounts divided by 1 + AIR. As a result, the payment can fluctuate significantly from one year to the next. In fact, the only way the payment would be the same from one year to the next is if the total return on the portfolio of investments exactly equaled the AIR.

Since most portfolios should exceed the AIR over the long term, the payment is *likely* (but not certain) to grow over time. Again, we want to emphasize that all the other features of fixed immediate annuities (for example, mortality credits or payments ending when the annuitant dies) also apply to variable immediate annuities.

The "advantage" (and at the same time the disadvantage) of variable immediate annuities is also evident: Investors participate (both up and down) in the returns of the underlying investments. As noted previously, this means their payments should, on average, grow. Of course, in any one year or period of years, payments could easily decrease, particularly if the underlying investments are risky. Also, payments will decrease more frequently with a higher hurdle rate (a higher chosen AIR).

THE PURPOSE OF IMMEDIATE ANNUITIES

As discussed in Chapter 5, the reason one should consider an immediate annuity is that it reduces the risk of outliving one's assets. All immediate annuities do that because of the built-in mortality credits. However, by investing in equities inside of an annuity, investors will also be penalized by all of the negative features that are inherent in VAs. These include the typical high costs of commission-based products and the high operating expenses of the typical investment accounts inside the annuity. In addition, for equity investments held inside of variable immediate annuities:

- Long-term capital gains on equity holdings are converted into ordinary income.
- The ability to harvest tax losses is lost.
- The ability to donate appreciated shares to charity is lost.
- The potential for a step-up in basis for the heirs of the estate is lost.
- On international assets, the foreign tax credit is lost.

Investors have to weigh the benefits of the mortality credits in an immediate variable annuity against the negatives that also include the loss of liquidity and the loss of the asset for the estate. If the product is the typical high-cost version, it is likely that the mortality credits will not be sufficient to overcome the negatives. Therefore, retirees who do decide to purchase variable immediate annuities should search out low-cost providers for such products.

Possible Reasons to Buy a Variable Annuity

Despite all the negatives discussed, there are actually some situations in which the purchase of a VA makes sense. Keep in mind that individuals should always maximize their contributions to tax-advantaged accounts, such as a 401(k) or an IRA, before considering a VA. The reason is that while the tax deferral is by far the chief reason for considering a VA, the tax advantages of a VA don't match those offered by a qualified plan. Also, note that it is rarely appropriate to invest in VAs offered through qualified retirement plans because the VA offers no additional tax advantages, but adds to the cost. With that caveat, VAs should be considered *only* when *both* of the following criteria exist:

- The investor has maximized contributions to tax-advantaged accounts, such as IRAs and profit-sharing plans.
- The annuity itself is low-cost, has no surrender charge, and offers low-cost and preferably passive investment options. Vanguard and other mutual fund firms offer such VAs.

These low-cost annuities are also good choices for investors who currently own the other kind of VA—the kind that was sold to investors who did not fully understand all of the product's features, especially the negative ones. These investors have the option of entering into what is called a *1035 exchange*.

1035 EXCHANGES

The 1035 exchange is a provision in the U.S. tax code that allows investors to transfer accumulated funds in one life insurance policy or annuity policy to another, without incurring a tax liability. Using this method, investors who were *sold* the typical high-cost product they should not have bought in the first place can transfer their assets to a lower-cost VA without incurring any tax penalty. When contemplating an exchange, investors should consider not only the cost of the surrender charge, but also the internal costs of the investment choices and the insurance value of their existing policy. These costs should be weighed against the relative benefits of reducing costs and improving investment options.

When investors are evaluating the cost of the surrender charge, they need to know that many VAs allow them to withdraw up to 10 percent a year without incurring any penalty. If this is the case, they can consider a gradual transfer (1035 exchange) from a high-cost to a lower-cost annuity. However, it is our experience that in the majority of cases it makes sense to "bite the bullet" and transfer to a low-cost VA in a more rapid fashion. The cost savings in terms of both fees and lower investment expenses will typically more than offset the surrender charge.

OTHER CONSIDERATIONS

Another reason that an investor might use a VA is his or her tax bracket in retirement. For those anticipating a lower tax bracket in retirement, converting capital gains into ordinary income may not have as great an impact. However, the other negatives of annuities all still apply.

The only other legitimate use of a VA is for creditor protection. Many states—including New York, Florida, and Texas—protect assets in VAs from creditors. However, state laws are complex. Therefore, before purchasing (or getting talked into) a VA for this specific purpose, consult an attorney. For example, doctors worried about malpractice suits might want to consider VAs, but, if this is the case, they should make sure to purchase the right kind of annuity. Also, note that at one time VAs offered potentially more creditor protection than IRAs. However, recent rulings by the Supreme Court and a 2005 law enacted by Congress have enhanced IRA credit protection.

SUMMARY

High-powered, professional salespeople often tempt investors to buy products that offer seemingly attractive benefits. Unfortunately, the benefits are often either illusory or are accompanied by costs that far exceed these benefits. The negatives can include:

- High cost of the insurance "wrapper"
- High operating (investment account) expenses
- Lack of passive, low-cost investment choices inside the annuity
- Lack of liquidity, early surrender charges, and a tax penalty for withdrawal before age fifty-nine and a half
- Loss of the potential for a step-up in basis for the estate of the investor, the inability to harvest losses for tax purposes, the inability to donate appreciated shares to charity, and the loss of the foreign tax credit
- Conversion of low-taxed capital gains into more highly taxed ordinary income

The typical VA has costs that are so high that William Reichenstein concluded this in a 2002 study: Average or high-cost VAs are unfavorable savings vehicles. He also concluded that for equity investors "a passive, low-cost stock fund always provides a larger ending wealth than [even] a low-cost annuity."[10] And the case against using VAs for equity investing becomes more compelling—if that is possible—when one considers the increasing availability of passively managed, highly tax-efficient (that is, tax-managed), low-cost mutual funds and ETFs.

Education—or a good fee-only adviser who is not influenced by commission-based compensation—can be the armor that protects investors. The overwhelming evidence from academic studies on VAs is clear: In general, these investments fall into the category of products that are meant to be sold, not bought.

High-cost VAs are among the worst of traps. And for equity investors, even low-cost VAs will rarely make sense. There are, as we discussed, exceptions to the rule. In those limited cases, consider only those VAs that are inexpensive, carry no surrender charge, and have low-cost—preferably passively managed—funds as investment choices. Before making any decisions, however, remember these words of caution from Gary Weiss, author of the book *Wall Street Versus America*: "Fortunes are made on Wall Street by catering to your greed. Not a penny is to be made protecting you from Wall Street's greed. That's your job."[11]

PART 4

The Ugly

Equity-Indexed Annuities   *18*

T HERE IS AN old adage about something being too good to be true, but the wisdom of the adage is really a matter of perspective. Certainly, if something appears to be too good to be true, it will be from the buyer's perspective. Only after learning all the realities does the investor experience buyer's remorse.

However, this is not the case for the seller, for whom the transaction was highly rewarding. Such is the case for a product known as an equity-indexed annuity (EIA), a form of a variable annuity. Therefore, much of what is true about variable annuities applies to the EIA world.

An EIA is another one of those products described by the people selling them as providing "the best of both worlds"—the potential rewards of equity investing without the downside risks (because of the guaranteed minimum return). The typical EIA offering has the following characteristics:

- A link to a *portion* of the positive changes in an index (typically the S&P 500 Index). This percentage of the index's gain is called the *participation rate*. Participation rates vary, but are typically between 50 and 100 percent.
- Principal protection.
- A minimum rate-of-return guarantee, regardless of the performance of the index.
- Tax-deferred growth potential.
- Income options to meet investors' specific needs.
- A death benefit guaranteeing beneficiaries 100 percent of the annuity's indexed value.

Investors seem to find these characteristics irresistible, purchasing an estimated $25.1 billion worth of EIAs in 2007.[1] Sales have increased almost 80 percent from the $14 billion purchased in 2003 and have more than tripled the $7 billion purchased in 2001.[2]

Another explanation for the explosion in sales is that commissions on EIAs *average* 8.5 percent, but they can run as high as 10 percent. These fees are "hidden" in the form of high internal expenses and surrender charges. Note that 95 percent of EIAs are sold by insurance agents, and that since these are insurance products, the SEC currently does not regulate their sale. The SEC has argued that EIAs qualify as securities and that they should fall under their regulatory supervision and control.[3] Not surprisingly, the insurance industry is fighting this recommendation.

CAVEAT EMPTOR

Another time-honored adage states that the "devil is in the details." In the case of EIAs, this particular devil can be found in the fine print. The typical EIA provides far less than 100 percent of the index's return. This "objective" (from the perspective of the product provider) is achieved in several ways. First, as already mentioned, most EIAs have participation rates below 100 percent; probably between 70 and 90 percent. But this is not the only way these products deliver less than meets the eye.

Another means of reducing investor returns is through the use of an annual cap—the maximum rate at which the annuity can be credited. For example, the S&P 500 rose almost 29 percent in 2003. However, an EIA might have limited the gain that would be credited to perhaps 12 percent, less the fund expenses.

A third method of keeping the payouts down is to credit the investor not with the total return of the index, but with the price-only change of the index. Because the S&P 500 is a price-only index, investor returns in an S&P 500 fund will be greater than the index's change by the amount of the dividends received. As of December 2007 the dividend yield on the S&P 500 was about 2 percent.

A fourth way of reducing payouts is through the use of a margin fee (otherwise called a *spread* or *administrative fee*). If this feature is present, the return is determined by subtracting this percentage from any gain in the index. For example, in the case of an annuity with a spread of 3 percent, if the S&P 500 gained 9 percent, the return credited to the annuity would be 6 (9 minus 3) percent.

A fifth way of reducing returns is to credit investors with their return based on simple interest, instead of compound interest.

Yet another way to reduce investor returns is by altering the way the return of the index is calculated. Instead of basing the return on the actual change in the index, the calculation of return is based on the change in the average daily closing price of the index throughout the year.

Consider this example. Let's say that the S&P 500 begins the year at 10,000 and ends the year at 12,000 (a gain of 20 percent), increasing in a perfectly straight line. The average price during the year would then be 11,000, and investors would be credited with a gain of just 10 percent.

Investors should also be aware that there are several different ways by which the amount of change in the relevant index is determined.

Annual Reset (or Ratchet)

This is the amount of index-linked interest credited to the account based on any *increase* in index value from the beginning to the end of the year, with any declines ignored. This method has the advantage of "locking in" any gain each year.

Point-to-Point

This is the amount of index-linked interest credited to the account based on any increase in index value from the beginning to the end of the contract term. This method has the disadvantage of relying on a single point in time to calculate interest. Therefore, even if the index increases throughout the investment term, if it declines dramatically at the end of the term, earlier gains are lost. Because interest is not credited until the end of the term, investors may not receive any index-linked gain if they surrender their EIA early.

High Watermark

This is the amount of index-linked interest credited to the account based on any increase in the value of the index starting with its value at the beginning of the contract term to the highest index value at various predetermined points throughout that period, often the annual anniversary. The advantages of this method are that investors may be credited with more interest than they might be with other indexing methods, and they are protected against declines in the index. Again, the disadvantage is that, because interest is not credited until the end of the term, investors may not receive any index-link gain if they surrender their EIA early. Also note that for EIAs that use this method, other costs may be higher.

MINIMUMS THAT AREN'T MINIMUMS

Most EIAs come with a guaranteed minimum return of at least 3 percent. However, that guarantee does not always apply to the entire investment. More often, the company guarantees that investors will receive at least 3 percent on just 90 percent of their investment. The result is that they can still lose principal when investing in an EIA, especially if they need to cancel their annuity early.

If there is a bear market, it may take more than a few years for the EIA's minimum guarantee to allow investors to break even on their original investment. And finally, remember that the guarantee is only as good as the credit of the company providing one. If the EIA is offered by an insurance company with a low credit rating, a supposedly "safe" investment takes on the risk of the less financially stable insurance company. Investors should not make the mistake of believing that insurance companies can't go out of business; many have.

Another important point relates to the guaranteed 3 percent minimum-return benefit. Because the guarantee is based on nominal (not real, or inflation-adjusted) returns, the insurance has little value. Since 1931, there has been no ten-year period when the S&P 500 did not produce positive nominal returns. And since 1932 there has been only one ten-year period when the S&P 500 did not produce a return in excess of 3 percent per year. The single exception was 1965 to 1974, when the S&P 500 returned 1.2 percent per year. One can only wonder how many investors were made aware of the data before they paid a steep price for the insurance.

PENALTIES FOR EARLY WITHDRAWAL

In addition to the problem of how the guarantees are calculated, most EIAs have significant early surrender charges, and these can run as high as 22 percent.[4]

On top of that, insurance companies may not credit investors with index-linked interest in some cases if they do not hold their contract to maturity. The reason for the high penalties for early withdrawal is that the provider offers large commissions to the sellers of its products. In the case of early withdrawal, the provider would have already paid out the large commission, which it needs to recoup through its high ongoing costs.

While there may not be a perfect correlation, the following is a good rule of thumb to remember about all financial products: The larger the commission, the worse the investment. The reason is that the worse the investment, the higher the commission that must be offered to entice the salesperson to devote time and energy to selling the product.

The bottom line is that large commissions explain both why the products are heavily sold, and why these are products meant to be sold, but never bought. The obvious conflict of interest created by the large commissions is why prudent investors should work with advisers who are paid on a fee-only basis, thereby minimizing the potential for biased advice.

It is also important to note that EIAs, as annuities, are subject to a 10 percent tax penalty on any withdrawals made before the investor reaches age fifty-nine and a half.

TAX INEFFICIENCY

While annuities do provide tax deferral, all withdrawals are taxed at ordinary income-tax rates. Therefore, when investing in an EIA, investors are converting what would otherwise be capital gains into income that will be taxed at ordinary income-tax rates. Given the wide disparity in rates between ordinary income and capital gains taxes, this represents a distinct disadvantage except for those who expect to be in the lowest tax bracket at the time of withdrawal.

Another disadvantage is that if the same equity investment was located in a taxable account instead of in an EIA, and the investment experienced a loss, the investor would be able to sell the investment and harvest the loss for tax purposes. In addition, if there is a gain, the investor can use the appreciated shares to make charitable contributions, totally avoiding any taxes. Of course, if the EIA is inside a tax-advantaged account—such as a 401(k), or a Roth or traditional individual retirement account (IRA)—there is no additional benefit to the deferral.

There is yet another potential tax inefficiency. Beneficiaries who inherit a mutual fund get a step-up in cost basis that reduces or eliminates the capital gains tax. However, beneficiaries who inherit an EIA pay the tax at their own ordinary income tax bracket.

SUMMARY

In 2006, Dengpan Luo and Craig McCann coauthored a paper on EIAs. They found that an astounding 15 to 20 percent of the premium paid by investors purchasing EIAs represented a transfer of wealth from unsophisticated investors to insurance companies and their sales forces. They concluded, "Insurance companies add trivial insurance benefits, disadvantageous tax treatment and exorbitant costs to mutual funds and sell them as equity-indexed annuities."[5]

Our conclusion is that EIAs are the "poster children" for products that are too good to be true. In most cases, EIAs are sold because they provide the seller with far greater commissions than they receive through the sale of mutual funds. It appears that the National Association of Securities Dealers—now known as the Financial Industry Regulatory Authority—agrees. In June 2005, it issued a detailed investor alert, describing the complexities of EIAs and their potential pitfalls.[6]

The bottom line is that an EIA represents a good reason why investors should avoid products that are inherently complex. Additionally, it is an example of why investors should generally avoid buying products that are sold on a commission basis—it may be difficult to know whose interests the seller is really serving. As William Bernstein, author of *The Four Pillars of Investing*, concluded: "The stock broker services his clients in the same way that Bonnie and Clyde serviced banks."[7]

Structured Investment Products 19

W ALL STREET'S SALES and marketing machine is continuously pumping out fairy tales: fanciful fables filled with legendary deeds and winning exploits. The only differences between many of the Street's product "innovations" and other types of fairy tales are that these stories are designed for adults, and they rarely have happy endings.

Like the apple given to Snow White by the Evil Queen, these products offer enticing features designed to lure investors, but almost all have one thing in common: Despite their seeming appeal, they have attributes that make them more attractive to the seller than the buyer. These products typically fall into the category called *structured products*.

Structured products are packages of synthetic investment instruments specifically designed to appeal to needs that investors *perceive* are not being met by available securities. As a result, they are often packaged as asset-allocation tools that can be used to reduce portfolio risk.

Structured products usually consist of an actual note plus a derivative or spinoff product. This second product *derives* its economic value by linking to the price of another asset, typically a bond, commodity, currency, or equity. A derivative often takes the form of an option (a put or a call). The note pays the interest at a set rate and schedule, and then the derivative pays off at maturity.

Because of their derivative component, structured products are often promoted to investors as "debt securities." Depending on the specific structured product, full protection of the invested principal is sometimes offered. In other cases, only limited protection may be offered, or there may be no protection available at all.

Over the years, we have been asked to review many of these product offerings for our clients. And we have not yet seen one with features making it worth consideration as an investment.

Although the array of structured offerings is virtually infinite, by analyzing two hypothetical products, we can gain a better understanding of "the rules of engagement." While the examples we have created are very realistic, we offer the following disclaimer: "Any similarity to any product, living or dead, is purely coincidental." By examining how these cleverly engineered, complex products work, we can also expose their underlying myths and learn why they are sold. Along the way, investors will also learn why, although the marketers of the products highlight certain features, their complexity often serves to obscure negative features.

Some version of a "principal protection note" is probably the most common structured product offered. Principal protection notes are just another version of the equity-indexed annuities that we discussed in the last chapter. Thus, the first example we will analyze is a hypothetical principal protection note offered by Mondo National Bank at the end of the first quarter of 2006.

MONDO NATIONAL BANK PRINCIPAL PROTECTION NOTES: PRODUCT FEATURES

- The notes were debt instruments—unsecured obligations of the bank that were linked to the change in the Dow Jones Euro Stoxx 50 and the Nikkei 225 indexes, both indexes of large-cap stocks.
- The payment was guaranteed to be no less than the return of the original principal, and the return was linked to the changes in the two indexes. This aspect was the shiny apple: the bait and the trap.
- The return was based on the *lesser* of the change in *either* index, subject to a maximum return of principal, plus 11.7 percent.
- The term was one year with a maturity of March 2007.

The following were the negative features (the poison hidden in the shiny apple):

■ The return was based on changes in the indexes, not the total return of an investment in the index. (Thus, investors wouldn't earn the dividends.)

■ An investor would lose the upside potential beyond the cap of 11.7 percent.

■ There was no secondary market for the investment, and, therefore, no liquidity.

Clearly, the attraction of the principal protection note was the guaranteed return of principal. The problem was that investors gave up too much of the upside to obtain the downside protection.

To demonstrate this point, consider an alternative portfolio that was 50 percent MSCI EAFE ex-Japan (a large-cap index) and 50 percent Japanese large-cap stocks (similar to the Nikkei 225). The data cover the period from 1970 through 2006, when the notes were offered.

■ With annual rebalancing, this portfolio would have provided an annualized return of 12.3 percent—greater than the *maximum* return one could earn on the note.

■ The gains would have been taxed at advantageous capital gains rates.

■ There were eleven years (30 percent of the time) when the principal protection provided by the note would have been required. In two of those years, however, the loss was less than 1 percent. If we eliminate those years (assuming investors were not concerned about such a small loss), the "insurance" was only needed in nine of the years, or 24 percent of the time.

■ The average loss during the eleven negative years was about 13 percent, and the worst loss was just over 24 percent. However, there were twelve years when the portfolio would have gained more than the *worst* single loss:
—Nine years with gains over 30 percent
—Four years with gains over 40 percent

—Three years with gains over 50 percent
—Two years with gains over 60 percent
—One year with a gain in excess of 70 percent
—Twenty-six years (72 percent of the time) when the
portfolio return exceeded the cap.

Hopefully, it is clear that one gives up much more upside potential than gained in downside protection, which is why a bank wants
investors to bite the apple by purchasing such notes. This happens
because stock returns are not normally distributed—they exhibit fat
tails, both large gains and losses. However, the large gains not only
occur more frequently than the large losses, they tend to be greater
in size as well.

MORE EFFICIENT ALTERNATIVES

While an investor who is highly risk-averse might have found the
protection offered by these notes an attractive tradeoff, there is a
better way to achieve the same type of result. Instead of buying the
Mondo National Bank note, the highly risk-averse investor could
have created a portfolio that was mostly fixed income, but then
added in a small amount of equity risk. **TABLE 19.1** demonstrates this
point.

The allocation for Portfolio A is 90 percent 1-year Treasury
notes, 5 percent MSCI EAFE ex-Japan, and 5 percent Japanese
large-cap stocks. The allocation for Portfolio B is 80 percent 1-year
Treasuries and 10 percent each for the two equity allocations. The
allocation for Portfolio C is 70 percent 1-year Treasuries and 15 percent for each of the equity allocations.

Table 19.1 More Effective Alternative Portfolios, 1970–2006

	Portfolio A	Portfolio B	Portfolio C
Annualized return	7.0%	8.4%	9.1%
Percent of cap	59.8%	72.0%	77.5%
Number of years with negative returns	0	1	4
Worst loss	N/A	−0.03%	−2.15%

A highly risk-averse investor investing in Portfolio A would have earned 7 percent, without ever experiencing a loss. With the exception of a single year when the loss rounded to zero, an investor in Portfolio B would have earned 8.4 percent, without experiencing a loss. And an investor willing to take a bit more risk with Portfolio C would have earned 9.1 percent (78 percent of the maximum rate payable under the terms of the note), while experiencing just four years of losses (11 percent of the period), with no loss greater than 2.15 percent.

We can create similar portfolios using domestic equities and 1-year Treasuries. In **TABLE 19.2**, Portfolio A is 10 percent S&P 500 Index, Portfolio B is 20 percent, and Portfolio C is 30 percent. Portfolio D is 10 percent Fama-French U.S. Small Value Index, Portfolio E is 20 percent, and Portfolio F is 30 percent. (Note that Fama-French benchmark indexes represent distinct asset classes, which are based on academic definitions, within the U.S. equity universe.) The remainder of each portfolio contains 1-year Treasuries.

The results for the three portfolios (A, B, and C) with allocations to the S&P 500 are similar to those of the prior example (Table 19.1) for which we used the two international large-cap indexes—the MSCI EAFE ex-Japan and Japanese large-cap stocks. However, investors willing to assume a bit more risk using an allocation to small-cap value stocks saw even better results. Neither portfolio (D nor E), with an allocation of 10 or 20 percent to U.S. small-cap value stocks, experienced a single year of loss. And Portfolio F, with a 30 percent allocation, experienced just three years of losses, with not a single loss of even 4 percent. And its annualized return of 10.7 percent is just 1 percent less than the *maximum* return that

Table 19.2 More Effective Alternative Portfolios, 1970–2006

	Portfolio A	Portfolio B	Portfolio C	Portfolio D	Portfolio E	Portfolio F
Annualized return	7.5%	8.0%	8.5%	8.3%	9.5%	10.7%
Percent of cap	64%	68%	73%	71%	81%	91%
Years with losses	0	1	2	0	0	3
Worst loss	N/A	−1.71%	−4.26%	N/A	N/A	−3.39%

could be earned with the note. Again, we can see why Mondo National Bank wanted to sell these notes. We just cannot understand why an investor would want to buy them.

The next hypothetical structured product to consider we will call *FRATS*, or Floating Rate Assets-Backed Trust Securities. They were issued in March 2006 by Colossal Investment Bank. Colossal is a highly regarded investment bank with a long-term credit rating of AA and a commercial paper credit rating of A1/P1 (almost the highest rating).

A Closer Look at Hypothetical FRATS

Colossal Investment Bank's debt instruments acted as the underlying security for making payments. An interest swap was also involved. Thus, the buyer also accepted the credit risk of the provider of the swap—which we will call National Bank.

The following are the highlights of one of the securities in the series that were marketed by the hypothetical Colossal's army of investment bankers and brokers:

- The first year rate was set at 7.5 percent.
- After the first year, the rate would be set at 0.9 percent above the benchmark 3-month Treasury rate.
- A lifetime cap of 7.5 percent was set as the maximum rate that could be paid on the note.
- The security had a term of 30 years.
- Colossal had an option to call (redeem) the security at any time after the first year.
- The notes would be listed on a major exchange.

At first blush, this looked like an enticing product, particularly because the yield curve was almost perfectly flat when the security was offered—an atypical situation. In March 2006 the yield on the various maturities of Treasury bills was between 4.5 and 4.7 percent. In addition, Colossal's commercial paper was yielding about 4.8 percent, only about 0.2 percent more than the three-month Treasury bill rate. Certainly, 7.5 percent looked like a great deal to an investor.

WHY SUCH "ATTRACTIVE" TERMS?

Whenever presented with the opportunity to *buy* a security, it is helpful to ask why the issuer would raise capital (*sell*) under the proposed terms. So let's examine why Colossal wanted to issue these securities and then also see how owning them would have fit into an investor's portfolio.

While the FRATS cost Colossal more than similar alternative short-term funding sources, two features made this offering attractive to the bank. These included a rate cap of 7.5 percent—capping the benchmark rate at 6.6 percent (6.6 + 0.9 = 7.5). By issuing the security, Colossal ensured that it would never pay more than 7.5 percent for its funding, whatever the level of interest rates and, equally important, regardless of the firm's future credit rating. And remember that the maturity was thirty years.

It is worth noting that data from Federal Reserve Statistical Release H15 show that, from 1966 through 2006, the rate on one-month FDIC-insured bank certificates of deposits was 6.8 percent, which is 0.2 percent higher than the benchmark cap rate set on these notes.

Now let's analyze whether an investor should have considered purchasing Colossal's FRATS. The starting point for prudent investors is to decide what role fixed income should play in their portfolio. As we discussed in prior chapters, for most investors the main roles of fixed income in the portfolio are as follows:

■ To serve as a source of emergency cash
■ To provide stable cash flow in real (inflation-adjusted) terms
■ To reduce portfolio risk to an acceptable level

Let's examine whether FRATS met these investment objectives.

The first problem was that by purchasing FRATS the investor sacrificed important liquidity. While the securities were listed on a public exchange, they were not likely to trade actively, if at all. And thus it was likely that even if an investor needing liquidity were able to find a potential buyer, the sale would have involved significant transaction costs.

The second problem was that because the then current yield curve was virtually flat (all maturities of the notes had similar yields), a 0.9 percent premium above 3-month Treasuries looked unusually attractive relative to other alternatives (more on this later). Colossal was taking advantage of this unusual scenario to market this particular security.

The third problem was that if rates rose to the cap, the stability of *real* (inflation-adjusted) cash flow would have been lost. In fact, because the investor should have been receiving a risk premium (relative to comparable-maturity Treasuries) for investing in a Colossal security, there was an effective loss of that credit-risk premium once the rate on 3-month Treasury bills exceeded 6.6 percent.

The fourth problem was that this security had a final maturity of 2036. Thus, the investor was actually buying a security with a term of 30 years, not three months, and was assuming Colossal's credit risk for the full period. Therefore, the credit spread the investor received should be viewed as what the spread would have been for Colossal's long-term debt; not its short-term debt.

At the time, the spread above Treasuries on Colossal's long-term debt was 1.25 percent. Thus, with this transaction, Colossal was effectively borrowing money at a credit spread above Treasuries of 0.90 percent (after the first year) instead of 1.25 percent, and the security provided a cap on the benchmark of 6.6 percent.

Keep in mind that Colossal was not only obtaining a long-term cap on the benchmark, but it was also locking in its credit spread for the long term. The cap on the benchmark effectively put a cap on the credit spread. On the other hand, if credit spreads on its debt were to narrow in the future, Colossal had the right to redeem the security at no penalty.

We can see why this was such a good deal for Colossal. The company obtained caps on both the benchmark rate and its credit spread. Because the investor gave away the cap on both, it became a "lose-lose" situation. Should Colossal's credit have deteriorated, investors would have lost. On the other hand, if Colossal's credit rating had improved, and it could have raised funds at better terms, it could have redeemed the security at any time, and investors would not have benefitted.

The fifth problem was that if interest rates rose to the cap level, the market value of the security would begin to fall, and possibly fall sharply (depending on how high above the cap rates went and the remaining term to maturity). Once the cap was breached, the security would cease to trade as a short-duration instrument and would begin to trade like a fixed-rate bond with a maturity of 2036. This created the potential for considerable price risk.

In addition, once the cap was breached, because the security would begin to trade like a longer-term bond, the correlation of the security with the equity portion of the investor's portfolio would rise, increasing the risk of the overall portfolio. This runs counter to the role of fixed income being used to help stabilize a portfolio's value. Of course, if Colossal's credit rating were to deteriorate, the market value of the security would also have been negatively affected.

Another good test of the worthiness of such a transaction is the answer to the question "Would sophisticated institutional investors purchase such a security?" Based on the above observations, it is easy to see why they would not. But to be sure, we asked an institutional bond firm to analyze a similar real-life security when it was issued. While the explanation we received was too complicated to be related here (which is the way an issuer wants and needs it to be), the response from the traders on the bond desk was that institutional investors with access to the swap market could replicate the transaction on their own on more favorable terms. As a result, there should have been no institutional demand for the product.

MORE EFFICIENT ALTERNATIVES

As we saw in the case of the Mondo National Bank principal protection notes, better alternatives existed for investors seeking a bit more yield than was offered by 3-month Treasury bills.

The first was to extend the maturity from three months (the benchmark for our FRATS) to one year. In this case, investors would have assumed no credit risk, no liquidity risk, and almost no price risk. Also, they would have gained inflation protection, and there would have been no correlation to the equities in their portfolio.

Extending the maturity to two years would have enhanced returns a bit more with very little increase in risk. Additionally, this alternative did not undertake the cap risk that our FRATS entailed.

The second alternative was to buy AAA-rated short-term securities, such as those issued by the Federal Home Loan Bank as well as other publicly traded companies. Because of their high credit quality and short duration, these securities entail little risk. At the time our FRATS were issued, a 1-year AAA-rated security yielded about 0.3 percent above the 1-year Treasury rate. And they entailed minimal price risk or inflation risk, involved significantly less credit risk, and were not burdened by a yield cap.

A third alternative was to buy a high-quality short-term fixed-income fund, such as those offered by Vanguard or an equivalent exchange-traded fund (ETF). These investments typically provide similar premiums over the 3-month Treasury bill to what was being offered by our FRATS, but they entail less risk.

Being Careful Out There

On the critically acclaimed 1980s television show *Hill Street Blues*, Desk Sergeant Phil Esterhaus warned his officers daily, "Let's be careful out there." Those words should also serve as a warning to investors that they need to be cautious, or else they can end up buying an investment product that benefits the issuers or marketing organizations far more than it benefits the investors.

One would also be wise to heed the following words of wisdom from Charles Ellis, author of *Investment Policy*: "Don't invest in new or 'interesting' investments. They are all too often designed to be sold to investors, not to be owned by investors."[1]

Another prudent rule is to avoid complex instruments because the complexity is almost certainly designed in favor of the seller. A good way to test this hypothesis is to ask the seller how much he or she has personally invested in the product, and how much the senior managers of the firm he represents have invested. If they are not "eating their own cooking," there is a good chance that something may be wrong with the dish!

SUMMARY

Through the detailed examination of two hypothetical structured products, we hope to have provided convincing evidence of why investors should avoid "structured-product land." And while the fact that a security or investment is a "structured product" doesn't automatically make it a poorly structured one, that is the overwhelming likelihood.

Furthermore, the complexity of these investments will almost certainly make it difficult to differentiate poisoned apples from untainted ones. And, finally, the number of participants in the transaction (the underwriter, the trustee, and so forth), each of whom must be compensated (increasing costs and thereby decreasing returns), makes it unlikely that the transaction can be an efficient one.

The bottom line is that many structured products torture investors with their fees in ways that would make the Inquisition proud.

Leveraged Funds **20**

THROUGHOUT HISTORY, CAPITAL markets around the globe have rewarded investors for the risk that they take when they provide capital. Thus, all investors have the potential for a good investment experience—assuming they are willing to accept market returns. The most effective way to do this is to build a globally diversified portfolio of passively managed funds.

Not surprisingly, however, the overwhelming majority of individual investors aren't content to settle for market returns. Instead, they try to outperform the market through various methods such as stock picking, market timing, and fund selection. The unfortunate result for most investors has been below-benchmark returns.

Leveraged funds are one of the products that Wall Street's sales and marketing machine has created to entice investors with the tantalizing "promise" of outperformance. *Leverage* refers to the concept of increasing, multiplying, or magnifying the return of an investment through the use of funds that an investor or investment firm borrows. Salespeople hawk these investments with pitches like this one: "If the market returns 10 percent, why settle for that rate when you can earn 15 percent using the power of leverage?"

An example of a mutual fund that uses leverage to deliver the prospect of additional returns is the Rydex Nova Fund (RYNVX). A member of the Rydex family of mutual funds, this leveraged product is a no-load fund designed to provide investment returns corresponding to 150 percent of the performance of the S&P 500 Index. The fund achieves its target beta (exposure to the change in the S&P 500) of 1.5 through the purchase of shares of individual securities, stock index futures contracts, and options on securities and stock indexes. The key question for investors is whether the fund actually delivers this attractive return of 50 percent above the S&P 500.

THE PROOF IS IN THE PUDDING

Rydex Nova Fund's first full year of operation was 1994. For the period from the fund's launch in 1994 through 2007, the S&P 500 provided an annualized return of 10.52 percent. If the Nova Fund delivered 150 percent of the returns of the benchmark, it would have realized an annualized return of 15.78 percent. However, fund investors actually earned just 9.41 percent, or only 60 percent of the goal and significantly below the return of the S&P 500.

In addition, the increase in exposure to the market caused the standard deviation of the fund to be 26.3 percent versus 18.1 percent for the S&P 500. As a result, Rydex Nova investors earned only 90 percent of the returns of the S&P 500, yet experienced 45 percent greater volatility.

TABLE 20.1 shows the results of Rydex Nova performance for the period from 2003 through 2007. The "alpha" listed in the last row of the table compares the returns realized by fund investors against the targeted benchmark of 150 percent of S&P 500 performance. A negative alpha indicates a shortfall.

Clearly, the fund failed to achieve its objective. In fact, it did not even meet its target for a single year. This illustrates one of the basic tenets of finance: It is often a long way from a strategy's theoretical results to actual, desired outcomes. That's because while strategies have no costs, implementing them *does*. Let's look

Table 20.1   It's a Long Way from Strategy to Outcome!

	2003 (%)	2004 (%)	2005 (%)	2006 (%)	2007 (%)	2003–2007 (%)
Rydex Nova (A)	40.5	15.4	4.6	19.7	1.8	15.6
S&P 500 (B)	28.7	10.9	4.9	15.8	5.5	12.8
150% of the S&P 500 (C)	43.0	16.4	7.4	23.7	8.3	19.2
Alpha (A–C)	−2.5	−1.0	−2.8	−4.0	−6.5	−3.6

Table 20.2 Volatility Matters

Fund	X	Y	Z
Beginning Investment	$100	$100	$100
Year 1 Return	10%	20%	50%
Year 2 Return	10%	0%	−30%
Average Annual Return	10%	10%	10%
Investment After 2 Years	$121	$120	$105

at the various factors that contributed to the Nova fund's dramatic shortfall:

- The first consideration is that the fund charges a high expense ratio of 1.25 percent, more than 1 percent above the cost of low-cost alternatives such as exchange-traded funds (ETFs) or index funds. Greater expenses lead to lower net returns.
- The second factor is that the use of options to increase exposure to the S&P 500 involves costs in the form of option premiums. These additional costs also have a negative impact on returns.
- The third factor is that volatility creates a phenomenon that might be called *decompounding*. Essentially, it means that the greater the volatility, the larger the difference between the average *annual* return of an investment and its compound, or *annualized*, rate of return.

A three-fund comparison illustrates this point (see **TABLE 20.2**). While all three funds produced the same *annual* return, Fund X, which had the lowest volatility, provided the greatest ending value. Also note that Fund Z, with the greatest volatility, provided the lowest ending value.

SUMMARY

Without question, investment firms excel at creating product, and they are even better at stimulating demand—even when the products are defective.

If the Rydex Nova Fund were an automobile, a factory recall would have been issued many years ago. This fund is just another example of why the use of margin for investing represents an inefficient use of capital. The supposed rewards are simply not commensurate with the risk. The bottom line is that leveraged funds are just another pitfall that wise investors should avoid.

If you decide to make any alternative investments, you should do three things:

- First, before making a commitment, have your financial adviser (preferably your accountant or a fee-only adviser who will not be receiving any commission based on product sales) review the product's prospectus.

- Next, have your adviser explain all of the nuances of the product, so that you can be sure you fully understand all of the risks and drawbacks.

- And, finally, make the appropriate changes to your investment policy statement. This financial plan outlines your goals and objectives and includes both your specific asset-allocation targets and your rebalancing table (the minimum and maximum percentages you will allow your allocations to reach).

In closing, we offer the following surprising advice: *Investing was never meant to be exciting.* Instead, investing is meant to be about giving yourself the best chance to achieve your financial goals, without taking more risk than you have the ability, willingness, or need to take. If you require a higher level of excitement, consider other ways to achieve that objective so that your financial life will not be put at risk.

Be careful out there!

Final Thoughts

Hopefully, you have enjoyed our tour of the world of alternative investments. Now that you are a more informed investor, you should be better able to separate the good from the bad and the ugly. You will also be able to determine if an offering has flaws and whether the flaws outweigh any positive attributes. At the very least, you will be more skeptical of the sales pitches and claims made by Wall Street's product-selling machines and its purveyors.

If this book has met its objectives, you will have learned:

- To remember that the more complex the product, the more likely it is that the complexity is designed in favor of the seller or issuer, not the investor.
- To not think of risk and expected return of assets in isolation, but in terms of how the addition of an asset affects the *overall* risk and expected portfolio return. Some assets (for example, Treasury inflation-protected securities, commodities, and fixed annuities) mix well with others in a portfolio, while others (for example, hedge funds and venture capital) mix poorly.
- To consider that standard deviation is not the only measure of risk. Skewness and kurtosis should also be factored into your evaluation.
- Not to be blinded by enticing features, such as the potential for high returns or guaranteed minimum returns. They are likely to be accompanied by negative features—including the potential for huge losses, high costs, and tax inefficiency—that outweigh the potential benefits.
- To keep in mind that the location of the asset is important. You want to hold as much equity risk in your taxable accounts as possible and as much fixed-income risk in your tax-advantaged accounts as possible.

Notes

Introduction

1. Gregory Baer and Gary Gensler, *The Great Mutual Fund Trap* (New York: Broadway Books, 2004).

Chapter 1

1. Susan Hudson-Wilson, Frank J. Fabozzi, Jacques N. Gordon, Mark J. P. Anson, and Michael Giliberto, "Why Real Estate," *Journal of Portfolio Management*, Special Issue: Real Estate (2005).
2. Joseph Gyourko, "Real Estate Returns in the Public and Private Markets: A Reexamination Following the Rise of Equity REITs," Working Paper (January 7, 2004).
3. Karen Damato, "Ghosts of Dead Funds May Haunt Results," *Wall Street Journal*, April 4, 1997.
4. Dimensional Fund Advisors, *Quarterly Institutional Review* (Second Quarter 2007).
5. Standard and Poor's.

Chapter 2

1. Robert J. Shiller, "The Invention of Inflation-Indexed Bonds in Early America," Yale ICF Working Paper No. 04-09, Cowles Foundation Discussion Paper No. 1442 (October 2003): 2.
2. Ibid.; *Handbook of Inflation Indexed Bonds*, edited by John Brynjolfsson and Frank Fabozzi (Hoboken, N. J.: Wiley, 1999).
3. Brynjolfsson and Fabozzi, 15.
4. S. P. Kothari and Jay Shanken, "Asset Allocation with Inflation-Protected Bonds," *Financial Analysts Journal* 60 (January/February 2004): 61.
5. Brynjolfsson and Fabozzi, 13.
6. Ibid., 43.
7. Ibid., 158.
8. Ibid., 31.
9. Kothari and Shanken, 63.
10. Abdullah Mamun and Nuttawat Visaltanachoti, "Diversification Benefits of Treasury Inflation Protected Securities: An Empirical Puzzle," Working Paper (February 15, 2006): 17.
11. Philipp Karl Illeditsch, "Idiosyncratic Inflation Risk and Inflation-Protected Bonds," Working Paper (August 24, 2007): 1.
12. Brynjolfsson and Fabozzi, 43.

Chapter 3

1. Paul D. Kaplan and Scott L. Lummer, "An Update: GSCI Collateralized Futures As a Hedging and Diversification Tool for Institutional Portfolios," *Journal of Investing* (Winter 1998): 13.
2. Gary Gorton and K. Geert Rouwenhorst, "Facts and Fantasies About Commodity Futures," *Financial Analysts Journal* (March/April 2006): 47–68.
3. Mark J. P. Anson, *The Handbook of Alternative Assets* (Hoboken, N. J.: Wiley, 2002): 202–203.
4. Anson, 203.
5. Gorton and Rouwenhorst.
6. Thomas Idzorek, "Strategic Asset Allocation and Commodities," Ibbotson Associates (March 2006): iii, 45, 48.
7. Claude B. Erb and Campbell R. Harvey, "The Tactical and Strategic Value of Commodities," Working Paper (January 2006): 5.
8. William Fung and David A. Hsieh, "Survivorship Bias and Investment Style in the Returns of CTAs," *Journal of Portfolio Management* (Fall 1997): 32.
9. Ibid., 33.
10. William Fung and David A. Hsieh, "Performance Characteristics of Hedge Funds and CTAs: Natural vs. Spurious Biases," *Journal of Financial and Quantitative Analysis* (September 2000): 295.
11. Stephen J. Brown, William N. Goetzmann, and James Park, "Career and Survival: Competition and Risk in the Hedge Fund and CTA Industry," (October 2000): 1869.
12. Gorton and Rouwenhorst.
13. Yanbo Jin and Philippe Jorion, "Firm Value and Hedging: Evidence from the U.S. Oil and Gas Producers," *Journal of Finance* (April 2006): 903, 907, 915.
14. Anson, 180.
15. Gorton and Rouwenhorst.

Chapter 4

1. Raghuram G. Rajan and Luigi Zingales, *Saving Capitalism from the Capitalists* (Princeton, N. J.: Princeton University Press, 2004), 160.
2. Ibid., 161.
3. Richard Oppel, "INVESTING; Untangling Emerging Markets," *New York Times*, January 24, 1999.
4. Peter Bernstein (ed.), *The Portable MBA in Investment* (Hoboken, N. J.: Wiley, 1995), 5.

Chapter 5

1. David F. Babbel and Craig B. Merrill, "Investing Your Lump Sum at Retirement," Wharton Financial Institutions Center Policy Brief (August 2007): 4.

2. John Ameriks, Robert Veres, and Mark J. Warshawsky, "Making Retirement Income Last a Lifetime," *Journal of Financial Planning* (December 2001): 76.

3. William Reichenstein, "Allocations During Retirement: Adding Annuities to the Mix," *AAII Journal* 36 (November 2003).

4. Moshe Arye Milevsky, "Optimal Annuitization Policies: Analysis of the Options," *North American Actuarial Journal* 5 (January 2001): 66.

5. David F. Babbel and Craig B. Merrill, "Rational Decumulation," Wharton Financial Institutions Center Working Paper No. 06-14 (July 2006).

Chapter 6

1. Stable Value Investment Association, "Why Investors Want Stable-Value Funds," (February 2004): 3.

2. "Questions About Stable Value," www.stablevalue.org (accessed July 23, 2007).

3. Ibid.

4. "Why Investors Want Stable-Value Funds."

Chapter 7

1. Martin S. Fridson, "Do High-Yield Bonds Have an Equity Component?" *Financial Management* (Summer 1994): 83.

2. Bradford Cornell and Kevin Green, "The Investment Performance of Low-Grade Bond Funds," *Journal of Finance* 46 (March 1991): 32, 47.

3. Edwin J. Elton, Martin J. Gruber, Deepak Agrawal, and Christopher Mann, "Explaining the Rate Spread on Corporate Bonds," *Journal of Finance* 56 (February 2001): 247–277.

4. Howard Qi, Sheen Liu, and Chunchi Wu, "Personal Taxes, Endogenous Default, and Corporate Bond Yield Spreads," *Management Science* 52 (June 2006): 951.

5. Fridson, 83.

6. Ibid.

7. Ulf Herold and Raimond Maurer, "How Much Credit?" *The Journal of Fixed Income* (March 2003): 4.

8. Mark J. P. Anson, *Handbook of Alternative Assets* (Hoboken, N. J.: Wiley, 2002), 99.

9. Ibid., 100.

10. Ibid., 200.

11. Antti Ilmanen, Rory Byrne, Heinz Gunasekera, and Robert Minikin, "Which Risks Have Been Best Rewarded?" *The Journal of Portfolio Management* (Winter 2004): 54.

12. Edward I. Altman and Brent Pasternack, "Defaults and Returns in the High Yield Bond Market: The Year 2005 in Review and Market Outlook," *Journal of Applied Research in Accounting and Finance* 1, No. 1 (2006).

13. Martin Fridson, "Original Issue High-Yield Bonds," *The Journal of Portfolio Management* (Fall 2007).
14. Cornell and Green, 29.
15. David Swensen, *Unconventional Success* (New York: Free Press, 2005), 109.

Chapter 8

1. Ludovic Phalippou and Oliver Gottschalg, "The Performance of Private Equity Funds," Working Paper (April 2007): 2.
2. National Venture Capital Association, www.nvca.org, April 14, 2008.
3. David H. Hsu and Martin Kenney, "Organizing Venture Capital: The Rise and Demise of American Research & Development Corporation, 1946–1973," Working Paper (December 1, 2004): 13, 16–17.
4. Venture Economics, October 31, 2005.
5. Data from CRSP and Fama-French series.
6. Venture Economics.
7. Steven N. Kaplan and Antoinette Schoar, "Private Equity Performance: Returns, Persistence, and Capital Flows," *Journal of Finance* 60 (August 2005): 1791.
8. John H. Cochrane, "The Risk and Return of Venture Capital," *Journal of Financial Economics* 25 (January 2005): 4.
9. Tobias J. Moskowitz and Annette Vissing-Jorgensen, "The Returns to Entrepreneurial Investment: A Private Equity Premium Puzzle?" *The American Economic Review* 92 (September 2002): 746.
10. Phalippou and Gottschalg.
11. Cochrane, 20.
12. Peng Chen, Gary T. Baierl, and Paul D. Kaplan, "Venture Capital and Its Role in Strategic Asset Allocation," *The Journal of Portfolio Management* (Winter 2002): 2, 4.
13. Cochrane, 3, 10, 30, 32.
14. Erin Arvedlund, "Private-Equity Funds Lower the Bar," *Wall Street Journal*, August 2, 2005.
15. Phalippou and Gottschalg.
16. Alexander Ljungqvist and Matthew Richardson, "The Cash Flow, Return and Risk Characteristics of Private Equity," NYU Finance Working Paper No. 03-001 (January 2003).
17. Chen, Baierl, and Kaplan, 5.
18. Moskowitz and Vissing-Jorgensen, 771–773.
19. David Swensen, *Unconventional Success* (New York: Free Press, 2005), 92–93.
20. Kaplan and Schoar, 1791–1823.

Chapter 9

1. Karyl B. Leggio and Donald Lien, "Covered Calls: A Lose/Lose Investment?" *Journal of Financial Planning* (May 2005): 72–77.
2. Data from Fama-French series.

Chapter 10

1. "2007 Report on Socially Responsible Investing Trends in the United States," *Social Investment Forum* (March 5, 2008): 3, 5.
2. Christopher C. Geczy, Robert F. Stambaugh, and David Levin, "Investing in Socially Responsible Mutual Funds," Wharton School Working Paper (May 2003): 49.

Chapter 11

1. William Bernstein, "What Is the Expected Return of Precious Metals Equity? Part II," *Efficient Frontier* (October 1997): 1.
2. Gary Baierl, Robert Cummisford, and Mark W. Riepe; updated by James St. Aubin, "Investing in Global Hard Assets: A Diversification Tool for Portfolios," Ibbotson Associates (March 2005): 4, 11.
3. William Bernstein, "The Longest Discipline," *Efficient Frontier* (December 2005).
4. William Bernstein, "The Expected Return of Precious Metals Equity," *Efficient Frontier* (January 1997).

Chapter 13

1. Henny Sender, "Hedge Funds Skid on Convertible Bonds," *Wall Street Journal*, June 30, 2004.
2. Josh Fineman and Jonathan Keehner, "Citigroup Said to Close Remaining Tribeca Global Fund," Bloomberg News, August 4, 2008.

Chapter 14

1. Claude B. Erb, Campbell R. Harvey, and Tadas E. Viskanta, "Understanding Emerging Markets Bonds," *Emerging Markets Quarterly* (Spring 2000): 3–4.
2. Ibid., 5.
3. Mark J. P. Anson, *Handbook of Alternative Assets* (Hoboken, N. J.: Wiley, 2002), 99.
4. Erb, Harvey, and Viskanta, 1.
5. William Goetzmann and Philippe Jorion, "Re-Emerging Markets," Yale School of Management Working Paper (August 2000).
6. Erb, Harvey, and Viskanta, 15.

7. Ibid., 9.
8. Ibid., 7.
9. Jonathan M. Kelly, Luis F. Martins, and John H. Carlson, "The Relationship Between Bonds and Stocks in Emerging Countries," *The Journal of Portfolio Management* 24 (Spring 1998): 9.
10. Ibid., 8.

Chapter 15

1. Raymond Fazzi, "Going Their Own Way," *Financial Advisor*, March 2001.
2. Gaurav S. Amin and Harry M. Kat, "Hedge Fund Performance 1990–2000: Do the 'Money Machines' Really Add Value?" *Journal of Financial and Quantitative Analysis* 38 (June 2003).
3. Roger G. Ibbotson and Peng Chen, "The A, B, Cs of Hedge Funds: Alphas, Betas, and Costs," Yale ICF Working Paper No. 06-10 (September 2006): 3.
4. Gregory Zuckerman, "Hedge Funds Weather Stormy Year," *Wall Street Journal*, January 2, 2008.
5. hedgefundresearch.com (accessed August 1, 2007).
6. Stephen J. Brown, William N. Goetzmann, and Roger G. Ibbotson, "Offshore Hedge Funds: Survival and Performance, 1989–95," *Journal of Business* 72, No. 1 (1999): 98.
7. David Dreman, "Las Vegas on Wall Street," *Forbes*, January 11, 1999.
8. Ibbotson and Chen, 5, 13.
9. Burton G. Malkiel and Atanu Saha, "Hedge Funds: Risk and Return," *Financial Analysts Journal* (November/December 2005): 82–83.
10. Greg Gregoriou, "Hedge Fund Survival Lifetimes," *Journal of Asset Management* 3, No. 3 (December 2002): 249.
11. Ken Brown, "New Study Snips Away at Hedge Funds," *Wall Street Journal*, February 22, 2001.
12. Gaurav S. Amin and Harry M. Kat, "Hedge Fund Performance 1990–2000: Do the 'Money Machines' Really Add Value?" *Journal of Financial and Quantitative Analysis* 38 (June 2003).
13. Harry M. Kat, "10 Things That Investors Should Know About Hedge Funds," *Journal of Wealth Management* (Spring 2003): 8–9.
14. Stephen J. Brown, William N. Goetzmann, and Roger G. Ibbotson, "Offshore Hedge Funds: Survival and Performance, 1989–95," *Journal of Business* (January 1999): 108.
15. Kat, 7.
16. Gretchen Morgenson, "Connecticut Investigates Hedge Fund for Solvency," *New York Times*, August 25, 2005.
17. Malkiel and Saha, 81.
18. Ibbotson and Chen, 14.

19. Nolke Posthuma and Pieter Jelle van der Sluis, "A Reality Check on Hedge Fund Returns," Working Paper (July 2003): 20, 25.
20. Gretchen Morgenson, "Connect the Dots. Find the Fees," *New York Times*, September 4, 2005.
21. Ianthe Jeanne Dugan and Ian McDonald, "Several Prominent Firms Invested in Bayou Hedge Funds," *Wall Street Journal*, August 30, 2005.
22. Gretchen Morgenson, "A Hedge Fund Falls Off the Face of the Earth," *New York Times*, August 28, 2005.
23. Vince Calio, "Active Managers Make Their Case to Stay with Troubled Ohio Fund," *Pensions & Investments* (October 3, 2005).
24. Lothar Komp and Nancy Spannaus, "G-8 Meet to 'Manage' Hedge-Fund Crisis," *Executive Intelligence Review* (July 8, 2005).
25. David Reilly, "How to Make $600 Million? Get $1.3 Billion," *Wall Street Journal*, May 23, 2005.
26. Henny Sender, "Marin Capital Closes Up Shop Amid Losses," *Wall Street Journal*, June 16, 2005.
27. Ibid.
28. Henny Sender, "Gloom Over Hedge Funds, Convertible Bonds May Lift," *Wall Street Journal*, July 19, 2005.
29. Komp and Spannaus.
30. "Report of Losses Hits Fund," *The Standard: China's Business Newspaper*, May 6, 2005.
31. Komp and Spannaus.
32. Edward Taylor, Kate Kelly, and Dana Cimilluca, "UBS Shutters Hedge Fund in Another Setback," *Wall Street Journal*, May 4–6, 2007.
33. Anita Raghavan, Ianthe Jeanne Dugan, and Gregory Zuckerman, "Despite Blue-Chip Gains, Hedge Funds Increasingly Are Faltering and Closing," *Wall Street Journal*, October 4, 2006.
34. David Reilly, "Vega Trips Into a Steep Decline," *Wall Street Journal*, July 13, 2005.
35. Jeremy Siegel, "Amaranth and Hedge Funds' Hidden Risks," *Yahoo! Finance*, September 27, 2006.
36. Jason Zweig, *Your Money or Your Brain* (New York: Simon and Schuster, 2007), 85–86.
37. Richard Bookstaber, *A Demon of Our Own Design* (Hoboken, N. J.: Wiley, 2007), 179–180.
38. Anne Tergesen, "A Fee Frenzy at Hedge Funds," *BusinessWeek*, June 6, 2005.
39. Christine Williamson, "Alpha Called Finite Resource," *Pensions & Investments* (March 6, 2006).
40. Ibid.
41. Dwight Lee and James Verbrugge, "The Efficient Market Theory Thrives on Criticism," *Journal of Applied Corporate Finance* (Spring 1996): 36.

42. Henny Sender, "Hedge Funds Skid on Convertible Bonds," *Wall Street Journal*, June 30, 2004.
43. Roger Lowenstein, *When Genius Failed* (New York: Random House, September 2000), 71.
44. Kaja Whitehouse, "One 'Quant' Sees Shakeout For the Ages—'10,000 Years,' " *Wall Street Journal*, August 11–12, 2007.
45. Lowenstein, 128.
46. Ibid., 129.
47. Gary Weiss, *Wall Street Versus America* (New York: Portfolio, April 2006), 111.
48. Ibid., 112–113.
49. Lynn O'Shaughnessy, "Brain Trust," *Bloomberg Wealth Manager*, November 2002.
50. Robert Whitelaw and Sujeet Banerjee, "Hedge Funds for the Rest of Us," *Journal of Indexes* (July/August 2007).
51. David Swensen, *Unconventional Success* (New York: Free Press, 2005), 126.
52. Paul B. Brown, "Getting Out of Hedge Funds," *New York Times*, April 21, 2007.

Chapter 16

1. David Swensen, *Unconventional Success* (New York: Free Press, 2005), 134–135.
2. Ibid.
3. Ibid., 134.
4. Ibid., 138.

Chapter 17

1. Jeffrey Brown and James Poterba, "The Household Ownership of Variable Annuities," NBER Working Paper No. 11964 (October 2005).
2. "NAVA Reports Fourth Quarter Variable Annuity Industry Data," National Association for Variable Annuities (NAVA) (March 28, 2007).
3. Brown and Poterba, 14, 29.
4. William Reichenstein, "Claim that Variable Annuities Usually Beat Mutual Funds Proves Lame: Critique of Huggard's Analysis in March 1999 Issue of *Financial Planning*," Baylor University (July 24, 2002): 5.
5. Moshe A. Milevsky and Steven E. Posner, "The Titanic Option: Valuation of the Guaranteed Minimum Death Benefit in Variable Annuities and Mutual Funds," *The Journal of Risk and Insurance* 68 (March 2001): 93.
6. Brown and Poterba, 7.
7. Carolyn T. Geer, "The Great Annuity Rip-Off," *Forbes*, February 1998.

8. Jeffrey R. Brown and Mark J. Warshawsky, "Longevity-Insured Retirement Distributions from Pension Plans: Market and Regulatory Issues," NBER Working Paper No. 8064 (January 2001): 28.

9. Geer.

10. William Reichenstein, "Who Should Buy a Nonqualified Tax-Deferred Annuity?" *Financial Services Review* (Spring 2002): 14.

11. Gary Weiss, *Wall Street Versus America* (New York: Portfolio, April 2006), 13.

Chapter 18

1. Fran Matso Lysiak, "Fourth-Quarter U.S. Sales of Equity-Indexed Annuities up 7.6% From Prior Year," *BestWire*, March 4, 2008.

2. Joan Warner, "EIAs: Behind the Hype," *Financial Planning* (October 2005).

3. Ibid.

4. Ibid.

5. Craig McCann and Dengpan Luo, "An Overview of Equity-Indexed Annuities," for the Securities Litigation & Consulting Group (February 2006).

6. Warner.

7. William Bernstein, *The Four Pillars of Investing* (New York: McGraw-Hill, 2002), 297.

Chapter 19

1. Charles Ellis, *Winning the Loser's Game* (New York: McGraw-Hill, 1998), 106.

Glossary

401(k). A defined contribution plan offered by a corporation to its employees that allows employees to set aside tax-deferred income for retirement purposes.

403(b). A retirement plan offered by nonprofit organizations, such as universities and charitable organizations, rather than corporations. It is similar to a 401(k) plan.

active management. The attempt to uncover securities the market has either undervalued or overvalued. Also, the attempt to time investment decisions in order to be more heavily invested when the market is rising and less so when the market is falling.

agency risk. A risk that only applies to investors in funds, or separate accounts. There is always the risk (the agency risk) that the manager will act in his or her own best interest and not in the best interest of investors. There is also the risk of fraud.

alpha. A measure of performance against a predetermined benchmark. *Positive alpha* represents outperformance; *negative alpha* represents underperformance.

annuitization. The conversion of part or all of the assets in a qualified retirement plan or nonqualified annuity contract into a stream of regular income payments.

arbitrage. The process by which investors exploit the price difference between two securities that are exactly alike by simultaneously buying one at a lower price and selling the other at a higher price (thereby avoiding risk). This action locks in a risk-free profit for the arbitrageur (person engaging in the arbitrage) and, in an efficient market, eventually brings the prices back into equilibrium.

asset allocation. The process of determining what percentage of a portfolio's assets should be dedicated to which specific asset classes; also, the outcome of that process.

asset class. A group of assets with similar risk and reward characteristics. Cash, debt instruments, real estate, and equities are examples of asset classes. Within a general asset class, such as equities, there are more specific classes such as large-cap stocks and small-cap stocks, and domestic and international stocks.

basis point. One one-hundredth of 1 percent (1/100 percent or 0.01 percent). Thus, 25 basis points equal one-quarter of 1 percent. One hundred basis points equal 1 percent.

benchmark. An appropriate standard against which investments can be judged. Actively managed large-cap funds should be judged against a large-cap index, such as the S&P 500 Index, while small-cap actively managed funds should be judged against a small-cap index, such as the Russell 2000 Index.

bid. An offer to buy at a specified price or yield; also, the price at which a dealer is willing to buy a security.

bid-offer spread. See *spread*.

bond. A negotiable instrument (as distinguished from a loan) evidencing a legal agreement to compensate the lender through periodic interest payments and the repayment of principal in full on a stipulated date.

bond premium. The amount above the par (or face) value of a bond or note at which it is bought or sold, not counting accrued interest, if any.

book-to-market value (BtM). The ratio of the book value per share of stock to the market price per share, or book value divided by market capitalization.

book value. An accounting term for the equity of a company. Equity is equal to assets less liabilities. It is often expressed in per share terms. Book value per share is equal to equity divided by the number of shares.

broker-dealer. Any individual or firm in the business of buying and selling securities for itself and others (for example, Merrill Lynch or Goldman Sachs). Broker-dealers must register with the Securities and Exchange Commission (SEC). When acting as a broker, a broker-dealer executes orders on behalf of his or her client. When acting as a dealer, a broker-dealer executes trades for his or her firm's own account. Securities bought for the firm's own account may be sold to clients or other firms, or become a part of the firm's holdings.

call. An option contract that gives the holder the right, but not the obligation, to buy a security at a predetermined price on a specific date (*European call*) or during a specific period (*American call*).

callable bond. A bond or note that is subject to redemption at the option of the issuer prior to its stated maturity. The call date and call premium, if any, are stated in the offering statement or broker's confirmation.

call premium. The percentage above the principal amount of a bond that is paid by the issuer when it calls the bond.

collateralized commodities futures (CCFs). Fully collateralized futures position in a broad-based commodity futures index (for example, the S&P GSCI or the Dow Jones-AIG Commodity Index [DJ-AIGCI]). The collateral, representing the full value of the futures position, is generally invested in very-high-quality instruments such as Treasury bills.

commercial paper. Short-term, unsecured promissory notes issued primarily by corporations.

compensated risk. Risk that cannot be diversified away (for example, the risk of owning stocks). The market rewards investors for accepting compensated risk with a risk premium (greater *expected* return) commensurate with the amount of risk accepted.

convertible security. A security that can be exchanged for a specified amount of another, related security, at the option of the issuer or the holder.

correlation. In statistics, the measure of the strength of the linear relationship between two variables. Values can range from +1.00 (perfect correlation) to −1.00 (perfect negative correlation). See *negative correlation*.

CPI. Consumer price index. A measure of price inflation.

CRSP. Center for Research in Security Prices at the University of Chicago, a financial research center at the University of Chicago Graduate School of Business. CRSP creates and maintains premier historical U.S. databases for stocks (Nasdaq, AMEX, NYSE), indexes, bonds, and mutual funds. These databases are used by leaders in academic and corporate communities for financial, economic, and accounting research.

currency risk. The risk that an investment's value will be affected by changes in exchange rates.

current yield. The ratio of the coupon rate on a bond to the current price expressed as a percentage. Thus, if paying par, or one hundred cents on the dollar, for the bond with a coupon rate of 6 percent, the current yield is 6 percent; however, if paying 97 for a 6 percent discount bond, the current yield is 6.186 percent (6 divided by 0.97). If paying 102 for a 6 percent bond, the current yield is 5.88 percent (6 divided by 1.02).

debenture. An unsecured bond that is backed by the issuer's legally binding promise to pay.

default. Failure to pay principal or interest in a timely manner.

denomination. The face value of a security.

derivative. A financial instrument whose characteristics and value depend upon the characteristics and value of an underlying investment, typically a bond, a commodity, a currency, or an equity.

discount. The percent by which the market value of a bond is less than its par, or face, value.

distressed stocks. Stocks with high book-to-market value or low price to earnings ratios, or both. Distressed stocks are generally considered to be value stocks.

DJIA. Dow Jones Industrial Average, an index of thirty of the largest U.S. stocks.

duration. The percentage change in the price of a bond that can be expected given a percentage change in the yield on that bond. A higher duration number indicates a greater sensitivity of that bond's price to changes in interest rates.

EAFE Index. The Europe, Australasia, and Far East Index, similar to the S&P 500 Index in that it consists of the stocks of the large companies from the EAFE countries. The stocks within the index are weighted by market capitalization. Maintained by Morgan Stanley Capital International, it is also known as the MSCI EAFE Index.

efficient frontier model. A model based on the assumption that investors care about the volatility of their portfolio, in addition to its expected return. The model computes portfolios (mixes of risky investments) that have the highest expected return for every attainable level of volatility.

efficient market. A state in which investors can't use trading systems to increase their expected return without at the same time increasing the risks to which they are exposed.

efficient market hypothesis (EMH). A hypothesis that markets are "informationally efficient." In other words, prices on traded assets, such as stocks and bonds, already reflect all known information and are unbiased. They reflect the collective beliefs of all investors about future prospects. The EMH states that it is not possible to consistently outperform the market by using any information that the market already knows—except through luck.

emerging markets. The capital markets of less-developed countries that are beginning to develop characteristics of developed countries, such as higher per capita income. Countries typically included in this category are Brazil, Mexico, and Thailand.

event risk. The risk that something unexpected will occur, such as a war, political crisis, flood, or hurricane, that will negatively affect the value of a security.

exchange-traded fund (ETF). For practical purposes these act like open-ended, no-load mutual funds. Like mutual funds, they can be created to represent virtually any index or asset class. Like stocks (but unlike mutual funds) they trade throughout the day.

expense ratio. The operating expenses of a fund expressed as a percentage of total assets. These expenses are subtracted from the investment performance of a fund in order to determine the net return to shareholders.

face value. For a debt security, the amount paid to the investor at maturity.

foreign tax credit. A credit against U.S. tax for tax due in a foreign country on foreign-source income.

forward currency contract. An agreement to buy or sell a country's currency at a specific price, usually 30, 60, or 90 days in the future. This guarantees an exchange rate on a given date. It is typically used to hedge risk (that is, currency risk).

full faith and credit. The pledge that all taxing powers and resources, without limitation, will, if necessary, be used to repay a debt obligation.

fundamental security analysis. The attempt to discover mispriced securities by focusing on predicting future earnings.

futures contract. An agreement to purchase or sell a specific collection of securities or a physical commodity at a specified price and time in the future. For example, a futures contract for the S&P 500 Index represents ownership interest in the S&P 500 Index at a specified price for delivery on a specific date on a particular exchange.

growth stock. A stock trading, relative to the overall market, at a high price-to-earnings ratio (or at a relatively low book-to-market value ratio) because the market anticipates rapid earnings growth relative to the overall market.

hedge fund. A fund that generally has the ability to invest in a wide variety of asset classes. These funds often use leverage in an attempt to increase returns.

high-yield bond. See *junk bond*.

hybrid security. A security that has both equity and fixed-income characteristics. Examples of hybrids are convertible bonds, preferred stocks, and junk bonds.

I bond. A U.S. government bond that provides both a fixed rate of return and an inflation-protection component. The principal value of the bond increases by the total of the fixed-rate component and the inflation component. The income is deferred for federal tax purposes until funds are withdrawn from the account holding the bond. Income from the bond is exempt from state and local income tax.

index fund. A passively managed fund that seeks to replicate the performance of a particular index by buying and holding all, or a representative sample, of the securities in that index in direct proportion to their weight by market capitalization within that index.

initial public offering (IPO). The first offering of a company's stock to the public.

investment grade. The rating of a bond whose credit qualities are at least adequate to maintain debt service, but which may also have some speculative qualities. Moody's Investors Service investment grade ratings are Baa and higher. Standard & Poor's are BBB and higher. Ratings below investment grade suggest a primarily speculative credit quality.

IPS. Investment policy statement. This statement establishes the investor's financial goals and the strategies that will be employed to achieve them.

Specific information on matters such as asset allocation, risk tolerance, and liquidity requirements should be included in the IPS.

IRA. A tax-deferred individual retirement account.

junk bond. A bond rated below investment grade; also referred to as a *high-yield bond*.

kurtosis. The degree to which exceptional values, either much larger or smaller than the average, occur more frequently (high kurtosis) or less frequently (low kurtosis) than they would in a normal (bell-shaped) distribution. High kurtosis results in exceptional values that are called *fat tails*. Low kurtosis results in *thin tails*.

leverage. The use of debt to increase the amount of assets that can be acquired (for example, to buy stock). Leverage increases the riskiness of a portfolio.

leveraged buyout (LBO). An acquisition of a business using mostly debt and a small amount of equity. The debt is secured by the assets of the business.

liquidity. A measure of the ease of trading a security in the market.

loser's game. A game in which, while it is not impossible to win, the odds of winning are so low that it does not pay to play.

markdown. The amount by which the price received by a retail investor selling a bond is *less than* the wholesale price (the price in the interdealer market).

market capitalization. The market price per share times the number of shares outstanding.

market impact. The extent to which the buying or selling moves the price against the buyer or seller (upward when buying and downward when selling).

maturity. The date upon which the issuer promises to repay the principal of a bond.

mean-variance analysis. The process of identifying optimal mean-variance portfolios. These are portfolios with the highest expected return among all portfolios with the same variance (or standard deviation), or portfolios with the lowest variance (or standard deviation) among all portfolios with the same expected return.

mezzanine financing. A late-stage venture capital investment, usually the final round of financing prior to an IPO; typically used by companies expecting to go public within six to twelve months. The financing is usually structured to be repaid from the proceeds of a public offering.

microcap. The smallest stocks by market capitalization: Those that fall within the ninth and tenth CRSP (Center for Research in Security Prices at the University of Chicago) deciles. Other definitions used are the smallest 5 percent of stocks by market capitalization and stocks with a market capitalization of less than about $200 million.

modern portfolio theory (MPT). A body of academic work founded on the following concepts: First, markets are too efficient to allow returns in excess of the market's overall rate of return to be achieved consistently through trading systems. Active management is therefore counterproductive. Second, asset classes can be expected to achieve, over sustained periods, returns that are commensurate with their level of risk. Riskier asset classes, such as small companies and value companies, are expected to produce higher returns as compensation for their higher risk. Third, diversification across asset classes can increase returns and/or reduce risk. For any given level of risk, a portfolio can be constructed that will produce the highest expected return. Finally, there is no one right portfolio for every investor. Each investor must choose an asset allocation that results in a portfolio with an acceptable level of risk.

MPT. Modern portfolio theory.

MSCI EAFE Index. See *EAFE Index.*

NASD. The National Association of Securities Dealers.

Nasdaq. The National Association of Securities Dealers automated quotation system. A computerized marketplace in which securities are traded, frequently called the *over-the-counter market.*

NAV. Net asset value. For a mutual fund, the NAV is the total value of portfolio holdings minus the total value of all liabilities. The NAV is usually calculated on a daily basis and is quoted per share (for example, NAV is $14.68 per share).

negative correlation. The relationship between two assets whereby when one asset experiences above-average returns the other tends to experience below-average returns, and vice versa.

no-load fund. A mutual fund that does not impose any charge for purchases or sales.

nominal returns. Returns that have not been adjusted for the effect of inflation.

NYSE. New York Stock Exchange.

offer. The price or yield at which a security is offered for sale.

par. The nominal dollar amount assigned to a security by the issuer. Most bonds have a face value of $1,000. They are also traded in blocks of a minimum of $1,000. Par, or 100 percent of the face value, is considered $1,000.

passive asset-class funds. Funds that buy and hold all (or a large sample of) securities within a particular asset class. The weighting of each security within the fund is typically equal to its weighting by market capitalization within the asset class. Each security is typically held until it no longer fits the definition of the asset class to which the fund is seeking exposure. For example, a small company might grow into a large company and no longer fit within the small company asset class. Fund managers may also use common sense and research to implement screens to eliminate certain securities from consideration (in an attempt to improve risk-adjusted returns). To be considered a passive fund, however, those screens cannot be based on any fundamental security analysis. Examples of passive screens would be minimum market capitalization, a minimum number of years of operating history, and a minimum number of market makers in the company stock.

passive management. A buy-and-hold investment strategy, specifically contrary to active management. Characteristics of the passive-management approach include lower portfolio turnover, lower operating expenses and transactions costs, greater tax efficiency, full investment at all times, no style drift, and a long-term perspective.

P/E ratio. The ratio of stock price to earnings. Stocks with high P/E ratios (relative to the overall market) are considered growth stocks. Stocks with low P/E ratios (relative to the overall market) are considered value stocks. For example, if the weighted average P/E ratio of the overall market is 15, then a stock with a P/E ratio of 12 or lower would be considered a value stock, and a stock with a P/E ratio of 18 or higher would be considered a growth stock.

premium. The amount, if any, by which the price exceeds the principal amount (par value) of a bond.

principal. The face value of a bond, exclusive of interest.

put. An option contract that gives the holder the right, but not the obligation, to sell a security at a predetermined price on a specific date (*European put*) or during a specific period (*American put*).

ratings. Various alphabetical and numerical designations used by institutional investors, Wall Street underwriters, and commercial rating companies to give relative indications of bond and note creditworthiness. Standard & Poor's and Fitch Investors Service Inc. use the same system, starting with their highest rating of AAA and then going down through AA, A, BBB, BB, B, CCC, CC, C, and D for default. Moody's Investors Services uses Aaa, Aa, A, Baa, Ba, B, Caa, Ca, C, and D with the top four grades considered investment-grade ratings.

real estate investment trust (REIT). A corporation or trust that uses the pooled capital of many investors to purchase and manage income property (*equity REIT*) and mortgage loans (*mortgage REIT*). These securities sell like stocks on the major exchanges and invest in real estate directly, either through properties or mortgages. Equity REITs invest in and own properties. Mortgage REITs loan money for mortgages to owners of real estate, or purchase existing mortgages or mortgage-backed securities. The revenues for these types of REITs are generated primarily by the interest that they earn on the mortgage loans.

real returns. Returns that reflect purchasing power because they are adjusted for the effect of inflation.

rebalancing. The process of restoring a portfolio to its original asset allocation. Rebalancing can be accomplished either through adding newly investable funds or by selling portions of the best-performing asset classes and using the proceeds to purchase additional amounts of the underperforming asset classes.

redemption. The process of retiring existing bonds at or prior to maturity. It also refers to redeeming shares in a mutual fund by selling the shares back to the sponsor.

registered investment adviser (RIA). A designation signifying that a financial consultant's firm is registered with the appropriate national (SEC) or state regulators and that the financial consultant has passed the required exams. RIA is not an accredited professional designation.

reinvestment risk. The risk that future interest and principal payments when received will earn lower than current rates.

REIT. Real estate investment trust.

risk premium. The higher *expected*, but not guaranteed, return for accepting the possibility of a negative outcome.

S&P (Standard & Poor's) 500 Index. A market-cap-weighted index of 500 of the largest U.S. stocks that is designed to cover a broad and representative sampling of industries.

SEC. Securities and Exchange Commission. It is the agency responsible for administering federal securities laws in the United States.

secondary market. The trading market for outstanding bonds and notes. This is an over-the-counter market, a free-form, negotiated method of buying and selling, usually conducted by telephone or a trading system such as Bloomberg's.

serial correlation. The correlation of a variable with itself over successive time intervals; also known as *autocorrelation*.

Sharpe ratio. A measure of the return earned on an asset that is above the rate of return on riskless 1-month U.S. Treasury bills relative to the risk taken, with risk measured by the standard deviation of returns of the asset. For example: The average return earned on an asset is 10 percent. The average rate of 1-month Treasury bills is 4 percent. The standard deviation is 20 percent. The Sharpe ratio equals 10 percent minus 4 percent (6 percent) divided by 20 percent, or 0.3.

short selling. Borrowing a security for the purpose of immediately selling it, with the expectation that the investor will be able to buy the security back at a later date at a lower price.

skewness. A measure of the asymmetry of a distribution. Negative skewness occurs when the values to the left of (less than) the mean are fewer but *farther* from the mean than are values to the right of the mean. For example: the return series of –30 percent, 5 percent, 10 percent, and 15 percent has a mean of zero percent. There is only one return less than zero percent, and three higher, but the one that is negative is much farther from zero than the positive ones. Positive skewness occurs when the values to the right of (more than) the mean are fewer but *farther* from the mean than are values to the left of the mean.

spread. The difference between the price a dealer is willing to pay for a bond (the bid) and the price for which a dealer is willing to sell a bond (the offer).

stable-value fund. A fixed-income investment vehicle offered through defined-contribution savings plans and individual retirement accounts. The assets in stable-value funds are generally high-quality bonds and insurance contracts, purchased directly from banks and insurance companies, that guarantee to maintain the value of the principal and all accumulated interest.

standard deviation. A measure of volatility or risk. For example, given a portfolio with an approximately normal (bell-shaped) distribution of returns with a 12 percent annualized return and an 11 percent standard deviation, an investor can expect that in 13 out of 20 annual periods (about two-thirds of the time) the return on that portfolio will fall within one standard deviation, or between 1 percent (12 percent − 11 percent) and 23 percent (12 percent + 11 percent). The remaining one-third of the time an investor should expect that the annual return will fall outside the range of 1 percent to 23 percent. Two standard deviations (11 percent × 2) would account for 95 percent (19 out of 20) of the periods. The range of expected returns would be between − 10 percent (12 percent − 22 percent) and 34 percent (12 percent + 22 percent). The greater the standard deviation, the greater the volatility of a portfolio. Standard deviation can be measured for varying time periods (such as monthly, quarterly, or annual).

style drift. The moving away from the original asset allocation of a portfolio, either by the purchase of securities outside the particular asset class a fund represents or by not rebalancing to adjust for significant differences in performance of the various asset classes within a portfolio.

subordinated debt. A debt that ranks below another liability in order of priority for payment of interest or principal.

survivorship bias. A bias in performance data that can appear when funds that perform poorly close because of redemptions by investors, or are merged out of existence by their sponsor. If care is not taken to include the performance data of all funds that existed during an analysis period (even the funds that disappeared), results can be skewed to appear better than the reality.

systematic risk. Risk that cannot be diversified away. The market must reward investors for taking systematic risk or they would not take it. That reward is in the form of a risk premium, a return that is *expected* to be higher than that earned by investing in a less risky instrument.

term to maturity. The number of years left until the maturity date of a bond.

three-factor model. A model that proposes that the differences in the performance among diversified equity portfolios are best explained by the amount of exposure to the risk of the overall stock market, company size (market capitalization) and price (book-to-market [BtM] ratio) characteristics. Research has shown that, taken together, the three factors on average explain more than 96 percent of the variation in performance of diversified U.S. stock portfolios.

TIPS. Treasury inflation-protected security. A bond that receives a fixed stated real rate of return, but also increases its principal according to the changes in the Consumer Price Index (CPI). Its fixed-interest payment is calculated on the inflated principal, which is eventually repaid at maturity.

tracking error. The amount by which the performance of a fund differs from the appropriate index or benchmark. More generally, when referring to a whole portfolio, the amount by which the performance of the portfolio differs from a widely accepted benchmark, such as the S&P 500 Index or the Dow Jones Wilshire 5000 Total Market Index.

transparency. The extent to which pricing information for a security is readily available to the general public.

Treasuries. Obligations that carry the full faith and credit of the U.S. government.

Treasury bills. Treasury instruments with a maturity of up to one year. Bills are issued at a discount to par. The interest is paid in the form of the price rising toward par until maturity.

Treasury bonds. Treasury instruments whose maturity is beyond ten years.

Treasury notes. Treasury instruments whose maturity is beyond one year, but not greater than ten.

turnover. The trading activity of a fund as it sells securities from a portfolio and replaces them with new ones. Assume that a fund began the year with a portfolio of $100 million in various securities. If the fund sold $50 million of the original securities and replaced them with $50 million of new securities, it would have a turnover rate of 50 percent.

uncompensated risk. Risk—that is, the risk of owning a single stock or sector of the market—that can be diversified away. Since the risk can be diversified away, investors are not rewarded with a risk premium (higher expected return) for accepting this type of risk. It is also called *unsystematic risk.*

unsecured bond. A bond that is backed solely by a good faith promise of the issuer.

unsystematic risk. See *uncompensated risk.*

value stocks. The stock of companies that have relatively low P/E ratios or relatively high BtM ratios. These are considered the opposite of growth stocks.

variable annuity. An investment product with an insurance component. Taxes are deferred until funds are withdrawn.

venture capital. An investment in a start-up firm or small business, prior to its initial public offering. It typically entails a high degree of risk.

volatility. The standard deviation of the change in value of a financial instrument within a specific time horizon. It is often used to quantify the risk of the instrument over that time period. Volatility is typically expressed in annualized terms.

yield curve. A graph showing the relationship between the yields on bonds of the same credit quality with different maturities.

zero-coupon bond. A discount bond on which no current interest is paid. Instead, at maturity, the investor receives compounded interest at a specified rate. The difference between the discount price at purchase and the accreted value at maturity is not taxed as a capital gain but is considered interest.

Recommended Reading

The following represent recommendations for serious investors, although we believe there should be no other kind:

Belsky, Gary, and Thomas Gilovich. *Why Smart People Make Big Money Mistakes—and How to Correct Them: Lessons from the New Science of Behavioral Economics.* New York: Simon & Schuster, 1999.

Bernstein, Peter. *Capital Ideas: The Improbable Origins of Modern Wall Street.* New York: Wiley, 2005; and *Against the Gods: The Remarkable Story of Risk.* New York: Wiley, 1998.

Bernstein, William. *The Intelligent Asset Allocator: How to Build Your Portfolio to Maximize Returns and Minimize Risk.* New York: McGraw-Hill, 2001; and *The Four Pillars of Investing: Lessons for Building a Winning Portfolio.* New York: McGraw-Hill, 2002.

Ellis, Charles. *Winning the Loser's Game: Timeless Strategies for Successful Investing.* New York: McGraw-Hill, 2002.

Fridson, Martin. *Investment Illusions: A Savvy Wall Street Pro Explodes Popular Misconceptions About the Markets.* New York: Wiley, 1993.

Kurtz, Howard. *The Fortune Tellers: Inside Wall Street's Game of Money, Media, and Manipulation.* New York: Free Press, 2000.

Malkiel, Burton G. *A Random Walk Down Wall Street: The Time-Tested Strategy for Successful Investing.* New York: W. W. Norton, 2007.

Ross, Ron. *The Unbeatable Market: Taking the Indexing Path to Financial Peace of Mind.* Eureka, CA: Optimum Press, 2002.

Shefrin, Hersh. *Beyond Greed and Fear: Understanding Behavioral Finance and the Psychology of Investing.* Boston: Harvard Business School Press, 2000.

Sherden, William. *The Fortune Sellers: The Big Business of Buying and Selling Predictions.* New York: Wiley, 1998.

Simon, W. Scott. *The Prudent Investor Act: A Guide to Understanding.* Camarillo, Calif.: Namborn, 2002.

Swensen, David. *Unconventional Success: A Fundamental Approach to Personal Investment.* New York: Free Press, 2005.

Taleb, Nassim Nicholas. *Fooled by Randomness: The Hidden Role of Chance in Life and in the Markets.* New York: Random House Trade Paperbacks, 2005.

Temkin, Bruce J. *The Terrible Truth About Investing: How to Be a Savvy Investor.* St. Petersburg, Fla.: Fairfield Press, 2000.

Warwick, Ben. *Searching for Alpha: The Quest for Exceptional Investment Performance.* New York: Wiley, 2000.

For those interested in learning about the history of various financial follies, we recommend three excellent books. The first is Charles Mackay's *Extraordinary Popular Delusions and the Madness of Crowds* (1841). His book is as relevant today as it was when it was first published more than 160 years ago. The others are *Devil Take the Hindmost: A History of Financial Speculation* (2000), by Edward Chancellor; and *Irrational Exuberance* (2005), by Robert Shiller.

Sources of Data

The following are the sources for the data contained in the text:

Standard and Poor's for data on the S&P 500, S&P GSCI, and the S&P/Citigroup REIT indexes. Used with permission.

The Center for Research in Security Prices at the University of Chicago for data on the CRSP 1–10 and CRSP 6–10 indexes. Used with permission.

Lehman Brothers for data on the Lehman Brothers U.S. Treasury Bond Index, the Lehman Brothers U.S. Treasury Inflation Notes 1–30 Year Index, the Lehman Brothers Intermediate Credit Bond Index, and the Lehman Brothers Intermediate Treasury Bond Index (1–10 years). Used with permission.

Style Research Limited for the data on the Dimensional Fund Advisors International Small Cap Index. Used with permission.

Nomura Securities for data on Japanese small stocks prior to July 1981 that are part of the Dimensional Fund Advisors International Small Cap Index.

ABN AMRO Hoare Govett for data on UK small stocks prior to July 1981 that are part of the Dimensional Fund Advisors International Small Cap Index.

Merrill Lynch for data on the Merrill Lynch One-Year Treasury Index. Used with permission. Prior to June 1991, the index complied by Dimensional Fund Advisors based on data from CRSP US Treasury Database, © 2008 Center for Research in Security Prices (CRSP®), Graduate School of Business, The University of Chicago. Used with permission.

Professor Kenneth R. French for the data on the various Fama-French series. Used with permission.

Dow Jones for data on the DJ-AIGCI and the Dow Jones Wilshire REIT Index.

Federal Reserve Statistical Release H15 for data on one-month bank certificates of deposit.

JP Morgan Chase for data on the JP Morgan Chase Emerging Markets Bond Index. Used with permission.

Professor Donald B. Keim for data on the Don Keim Equity REIT Index. Used with permission.

Morgan Stanley for data on the MSCI indexes.

Index

About the Authors

Larry E. Swedroe is a principal and the director of research for Buckingham Asset Management, LLC (www.bamservices.com). He is the author of *Wise Investing Made Simple, The Only Guide to a Winning Investment Strategy You'll Ever Need, What Wall Street Doesn't Want You to Know, Rational Investing in Irrational Times,* and *The Successful Investor Today.* He also coauthored *The Only Guide to a Winning Bond Strategy You'll Ever Need.* Swedroe has an MBA in finance from New York University. He lives in St. Louis with his wife Mona and their dog Molly.

Jared Kizer, CFA, previously worked as an investment adviser for Buckingham Asset Management, LLC, and authored this book with Larry while he worked there. He has published articles on investing in the *Journal of Portfolio Management, Journal of Indexes,* and for indexuniverse.com. Kizer has a master's degree in finance from Washington University in St. Louis. He lives in St. Louis with his wife Lezlie and two sons, Carson and Owen.

Bloomberg L.P., founded in 1981, is a global information services, news, and media company. Headquartered in New York, the company has sales and news operations worldwide.

Serving customers on six continents, Bloomberg, through its wholly-owned subsidiary Bloomberg Finance L.P., holds a unique position within the financial services industry by providing an unparalleled range of features in a single package known as the Bloomberg Professional® service. By addressing the demand for investment performance and efficiency through an exceptional combination of information, analytic, electronic trading, and straight-through-processing tools, Bloomberg has built a worldwide customer base of corporations, issuers, financial intermediaries, and institutional investors.

Bloomberg News®, founded in 1990, provides stories and columns on business, general news, politics, and sports to leading newspapers and magazines throughout the world. Bloomberg Television®, a 24-hour business and financial news network, is produced and distributed globally in seven languages. Bloomberg Radio^{SM} is an international radio network anchored by flagship station Bloomberg® 1130 (WBBR-AM) in New York.

In addition to the Bloomberg Press® line of books, Bloomberg publishes *Bloomberg Markets*® magazine. To learn more about Bloomberg, call a sales representative at:

London:	+44-20-7330-7500
New York:	+1-212-318-2000
Tokyo:	+81-3-3201-8900